Foreign Investment
and Industrialisation
in Singapore

Foreign Investment and Industrialisation in Singapore

Edited by
Helen Hughes and You Poh Seng

The University of Wisconsin Press
Madison   1969

Published in the United States of America by
The University of Wisconsin Press
Box 1379, Madison, Wisconsin 53701

Published in Australia by
Australian National University Press

Printed in Hong Kong

SBN 299–05420–9
LC 69–14301; AUS 68–2591

Preface

Foreign investment has become widely accepted as an 'engine of growth' for the industrialisation of developing countries. Sought and welcomed not so much for the capital itself as for the advanced technology it injects into an economy, it has the added merit of supplying foreign exchange for the industrialisation process to the extent to which it supplements domestic savings. In developed countries among which the bulk of foreign investment in industry takes place, the opinion that the benefits of foreign investment greatly exceed its costs prevails, and this has stilled much of the fear and criticism common in developing countries even a decade ago. Developing countries wishing to industrialise rapidly in a free enterprise and politically democratic environment have not, moreover, been able to find satisfactory alternatives.

Yet in spite of the attention it has received in development planning and economic analysis, many questions about the course and effects of foreign investment remain unanswered, and on some of these this study of foreign investment in Singapore manufacturing attempts to throw light. The study is confined to direct foreign investment, that is investment which involves an equity interest and some degree of control in the sense that the lender wishes to, and is able to, influence the borrowing company's policy. Direct foreign investment can be in a branch or wholly-owned subsidiary or in a public or private company in which the foreign investors hold equal, majority, or minority, shares. It includes investment through licensing, technical, or managerial agreements. It does not include portfolio investment.

With its success in attracting foreign investors from a number of countries in the 1960s, Singapore was well suited for such an investigation, particularly as the Economic Development Board, the principal government agency concerned with foreign investment and industrial growth, was sympathetic to the aims of the study and very co-operative throughout its progress. We would like to thank its staff members for their help. To overcome the difficulties of gaining the confidence of foreign businessmen of various nationalities, a team of economists, one from each of the principal investing countries, interviewed the firms with foreign investment.

Manufacturing firms with Japanese and Australian investment were interviewed during 1966 and surveys of United States, United Kingdom,

Hong Kong, and Taiwan investment followed in 1967. Questionnaires were standardised as far as possible, and all the participants in the study were able to meet at a seminar in Singapore in July 1967 to co-ordinate their work and discuss it with economists from the Economic Development Board and the University of Singapore, and with representatives of Singapore business organisations.

The study and its publication were organised jointly by the Economic Research Centre of the University of Singapore and the Department of Economics of the Research School of Pacific Studies, the Australian National University, and these two departments have borne much of the incidental work and some of the expense. We are particularly indebted to Ruth Daroesman who helped with the organisation of the surveys and seminar, Ung Gim Sei who compiled the appendix tables, and Patricia Brown who assisted with the editorial work. The Ford Foundation made the study possible by generously financing the field work and the seminar.

H. H.
Y. P. S.

Editors and Contributors

GETHYN DAVIES — Professor of Economics, Institute of Science and Technology, University of Wales

RYOKICHI HIRONO — Associate Professor of Economics, Seikei University

HELEN HUGHES — Senior Fellow in Economics, Australian National University

PETER H. LINDERT — Assistant Professor of Economics, University of Wisconsin

PAUL LUEY — Lecturer in Economics, University of Hong Kong

UNG GIM SEI — Research Assistant, Economic Research Centre, University of Singapore

YOU POH SENG — Director, Economic Research Centre, University of Singapore

Exchange Values

All values are in Malayan dollars unless otherwise stated. Average exchange rates for Malayan dollars in 1966 were as follows:

$ Malayan 100 = $ Aust. 29·56
= $ HK 189·35
= Yen 11,904·00
= $ New Taiwan 1,306
= £ Stg 11·72 (£11.14s. 5d.)
= $ US 32·94

Percentages are expressed in round figures and therefore totals do not always add up to 100.

Contents

Tables

Tables

MAP

FIGURE

From Entrepôt Trade to Manufacturing

Singapore owes its existence as an independent city state to its situation at the southern tip of the Indo-Pacific peninsula, not only at the centre of the Malay archipelago, but at the crossroads between eastern and western Asia. For at least two thousand years the river mouths of the peninsula and archipelago have served as harbours to tranship spices, silk, and tea from the east for a trade which eventually found its way as far west as Europe and for a time even to North America. In return came gold dust and opium, and later, more prosaically, cotton cloth and enamelware of European manufacture. Chinese, Indian, and Arab traders had mingled here, and some remained to settle and mix with older inhabitants, creating settlements and civilisations wherever land or trade gave a livelihood.

In the thirteenth and fourteenth centuries when the pace of trade was quickening, *Singapura*, the City of the Lion, became one of the three great cities of the Sumatran Srivijaya empire which thrived on the tolls of the archipelago's trade. By the time the Portuguese came to trade, conquer, and preach in the fifteenth century, Malacca had replaced the island of Singapore as the principal harbour of the straits between Sumatra and the mainland. It was retained, fortified, by the Portuguese who beat across the Indian Ocean from Goa to sail down the coast of the Malay peninsula. The Spanish came from the east to Luzon and the Visayas, but scarcely penetrated the southernmost islands of the Philippine group before their wide-ranging days were ended. The Dutch, being better sailors than the Portuguese, were able to take the Cape route east to the Australian continent, and then sailed north along its inhospitable shores to Java and other islands south of the Indo-Pacific peninsula. The East India Company's merchantmen sailed south-east

1

from Ceylon to the British base at Bencoolen on the west coast of Sumatra and then passed through the Sunda Strait between Java and Sumatra to the China seas.

To secure their journeys the East India Company in 1786 acquired from the Sultan of Kedah the island of Penang which commanded the Straits of Malacca. Britain's stewardship of the Dutch possessions in the archipelago during the Napoleonic Wars gave Stamford Raffles a better insight into the trade and trading routes of the area than the East India Company, comfortable in its monopoly of the China trade, had sought to learn. He was supported by mercantile interests hostile to the Company's privileged position. Raffles was convinced that Dutch traders would threaten British interests in the archipelago unless new ports were acquired within reach of both the Sunda and Malacca Straits.

On Britain's return of the Dutch colonies in 1815 both governments had agreed that territorial claims in the area should be negotiated by the home governments, but Raffles obtained permission from the Governor of India, Lord Hastings, to search for a suitable new base for trade at the centre of the archipelago. Setting out in 1819 with Colonel Farquhar who had been the wartime Resident at Malacca, Raffles examined several islands only to find them unsuitable. The Dutch had beaten him to Riau. Then in January 1819 Raffles and Farquhar landed on Singapore where about 120 Malays and 30 Chinese were eking out a living on the shores of the Singapore River. Otherwise the 224 square-mile, jungle-covered, island was uninhabited. Recognising the value of the river and harbour as well as the island's central position, Raffles made a preliminary agreement with the Dato Temenggong, the senior administrative chief of the Johore Sultanate which claimed possession of Singapore, to establish a trading factory on the island. To assure the legality of the transaction Raffles claimed that the recently installed pro-Dutch Sultan of Johore was not the proper heir to the Sultanate because he was a younger brother, and called the older brother, Tunku Husein, to Singapore from Riau to make a treaty granting the British government the right to settle on the island. He recognised him as Sultan of Johore in return. A formal treaty was signed between Raffles on the one hand and Sultan Husein and the Temenggong on the other granting the British government the right to settle on the island of Singapore on the payment of annual pensions of 3,000 Spanish dollars to the Temenggong and 5,000 Spanish dollars to Sultan Husein.[1]

---

[1] This account of the early history of Singapore is based on a number of sources, the principal ones being: C. B. Buckley, *An Anecdotal History of Old*

Not unexpectedly the Dutch complained to the British government and Lord Hastings denied that he had given Raffles authority to obtain Singapore. The British Resident at Penang, fearing for its trade, also grumbled to the East India Company. Anglo-Dutch discussions attempted to settle this and similar problems in 1820, but without avail. Singapore remained British and its trade grew.

> In little more than a twelve-month . . . its harbour presented a pleasing promise of future prosperity; besides ships, brigs, prows, etc. we are informed by Colonel Farquhar, the then resident, that upwards of twenty junks, three from China, two from Cochin-China, and the rest from Siam and other quarters, were lying at anchor. Merchants of all descriptions were congregating so fast, that nothing was heard of in the shape of complaint, but the want of more ground to build upon.[2]

In 1824 Great Britain gave up Bencoolen to the Dutch and agreed to seek no further bases in the islands; in return the Netherlands gave Malacca back again to Britain, agreed that Britain could retain Singapore, and promised not to establish bases on the mainland. The East India Company gradually brought these dependencies together with Penang to form the Straits Settlements, transferring the capital from Penang to Singapore in 1832.

When Raffles paid his last visit to Singapore in 1823 the population had grown to over 10,000 (Table 1.1). Chinese and European merchants had become established, and the total value of exports and imports was more than 13 million Spanish dollars.[3] There was no doubt in Raffles's mind that Singapore's success was due to its establishment as a free port. To the merchants of Singapore who farewelled him with a statement of their gratitude for his role in founding the settlement, he somewhat disingenuously replied:

> It has happily been consistent with the policy of Great Britain, and accordant with the principles of the East India Company, that Singapore should be established as a free port; that no sinister, no sordid view, no considerations

---

Times in Singapore, 2 vols. (Singapore, 1902), W. Makepeace, G. E. Brooke, and R. St J. Braddell (eds.), *One Hundred Years of Singapore*, 2 vols. (London, 1921), L. A. Mills, *British Malaya 1824–67* (Kuala Lumpur, 1966), T. J. Newbold, *Political and Statistical Account of the British Settlements in the Straits of Malacca*, 2 vols. (London, 1839), Sophia Raffles, *Memoir of the Life and Public Services of Sir Thomas Stamford Raffles*, 2 vols. (London, 1835), Sir Frank Swettenham, *British Malaya* (London, rev. ed. 1948), K. C. Tregonning, *The British in Malaya* (Tucson, 1965), and R. O. Winstedt, *A History of Malaya* (Singapore, 1935).

[2] Newbold, op. cit., Vol. I, p. 290.

[3] Ibid., p. 291.

either of political importance or pecuniary advantage, should interfere with the broad and liberal principles on which the British interests have been established. Monopoly and exclusive privileges, against which public opinion has long raised its voice, are here unknown, and while the Free Port of Singapore is allowed to continue and prosper, as it hitherto has done, the policy and liberality of the East India Company, by whom the Settlement

Table 1.1   Population of Singapore by ethnic group, 1819–1966, in thousand persons[a]

Year	Malay[b]	Chinese	Indian and Pakistani	Others	Total
1819	0·12	0·03			0·15
1824	6·4	3·3	0·8	0·18	10·7
	(60·2)	(31·0)	(7·1)	(1·7)	
1836	12·5	13·7	2·9	0·80	30·0
	(41·7)	(45·9)	(9·8)	(2·7)	
1860	16·2	50·0	13·0	2·5	81·7
	(19·8)	(61·2)	(15·9)	(3·1)	
1871 Census	26·1	54·6	11·5	4·9	97·1
	(26·9)	(56·2)	(11·8)	(5·0)	
1881 ,,	33·0	86·8	12·1	5·9	137·8
	(23·0)	(63·0)	(8·8)	(4·3)	
1891 ,,	36·0	121·9	16·0	7·7	181·6
	(19·8)	(67·1)	(8·8)	(4·2)	
1901 ,,	36·0	164·0	17·8	9·8	227·6
	(15·8)	(72·1)	(7·8)	(4·3)	
1911 ,,	41·8	219·5	27·8	14·2	303·3
	(13·8)	(72·4)	(9·2)	(4·7)	
1921 ,,	53·6	315·1	32·3	17·3	418·3
	(12·8)	(75·3)	(7·7)	(4·1)	
1931 ,,	65·0	418·6	50·8	23·3	557·7
	(11·7)	(75·1)	(9·1)	(4·2)	
1947 ,,	113·8	729·5	69·0	25·9	938·2
	(12·1)	(77·8)	(7·4)	(2·8)	
1957 ,,	197·0	1,090·6	124·1	34·2	1,445·9
	(13·6)	(75·4)	(8·6)	(2·4)	
1966[c]	276·1	1,427·0	156·6	53·8	1,913·5
	(14·4)	(74·6)	(8·2)	(2·8)	

Figures in parentheses are percentage of total population.

[a] Figures exclude the populations of Christmas Island and Cocos-Keeling Islands, transients afloat, and non-locally domiciled services personnel and their families.

[b] Malay figures include Indonesians.

[c] 1966 figure is a mid-year estimate.

Sources: 1819 to 1836, T. J. Newbold, *Political and Statistical Account of the British Settlements in the Straits of Malacca* (London, 1839).

  1860, T. Braddell, *Statistics of the British Possessions in the Straits of Malacca* (Pinang [*sic*], 1861).

  1871 to 1966, Singapore, *Monthly Digest of Statistics*, Vol. 6, December 1967, p. 11.

was founded, and under whose protection and control it is still administered, can never be disputed.

That Singapore will long and always remain a free port, and that no taxes on trade or industry will be established to check its future rise and prosperity, I can have no doubt. I am justified in saying thus much, on the authority of the Supreme Government of India, and on the authority of those who are most likely to have weight in the Councils of our nation at home.[4]

Singapore's free port status owed a great deal to the East India Company's lack of concern with it. It became a convenient repository for Indian convicts, but until 1834 when it lost its tea monopoly the Company was content merely to keep the tea trade moving, and after that its interest waned even further. Much of the initiative of government came from the local merchants who wished to see improvement in the stability of the Malay peninsula firstly for trade and later for tin production. This was the background to the suppression of piracy which consumed much of the energy of the Straits Residents and other officials and such naval vessels as came to the area for the next thirty years.[5] In the absence of taxes on trade, Singapore's revenue was raised by a farm of taxes on opium consumed on the island. The farm was not abolished until 1910 when a more profitable government monopoly of opium manufacture was recommended by a Commission of Inquiry which found that the purely physical effects were, so far as moderate smoking was concerned, relatively harmless.[6]

By 1836 there were twenty mercantile houses in Singapore: seventeen were British-owned, two were European, and one was American. There were also a number of Chinese merchants and a few Arab and American ones, and these were included when the Chamber of Commerce was formed in 1837.[7] China was the largest single source of trade, India came next, then Java and the Malay peninsula. Siam, Cochin-China, Cambodia and the islands of the archipelago sent their junks and praus. Trading ships came from Europe, and after 1835 when Singapore was opened to them, from the United States of America. A large range of articles was traded, with manufactured goods from Europe beginning to compete with Asian handicraft products (Table 1.2).

Raffles's contemporaries and the administrators who followed them endorsed the view that the freedom of its trade was the principal source

---

[4] Quoted in Swettenham, op. cit., p. 74.

[5] N. Tarling, *Piracy and Politics in the Malay World* (Melbourne, 1963).

[6] 'The Opium Commission', in Makepeace, Brooke, and Braddell, op. cit., Vol. II, p. 61.

[7] Newbold, op. cit., Vol. I, pp. 391–4, and Buckley, op. cit., Vol. I, pp. 313–14.

of Singapore's rapid growth, and this certainly gave it a great advantage over the toll-exacting Dutch and Malay Sultans' ports. But Singapore also had the prime geographic situation, and it had a good sheltered roadstead which was able to take bigger ships than Penang or Malacca. This became more important as ships grew in size and as steam replaced sail from the 1850s. Singapore became the major coaling centre of the area, enjoying the external economies which its growing size fostered in provisioning and other services to shipping.

Singapore, moreover, had become an entrepôt not only for goods, but also for people. By 1836 the population was 30,000, and of these nearly 14,000 were Chinese and 12,500 Malays. The Malays collected agar-agar seaweed off the rocks in season, selling it to merchants for the China trade; they fished and there was a smattering of agriculture. The city served as a distributing point for Chinese going to the tin mines of the peninsula and Netherlands East Indies and to other trades

Table 1.2 Principal commodity imports and exports to and from Singapore, by principal country of origin and destination, year ending 30 April 1836[a]

Imports into Singapore	Principal place of origin	Value in Spanish dollars '000
Bêche-de-mer	Java, Celebes, and a neighbouring island	60
Birds' nests	Borneo and Java	148
Chinaware	China	96
Cigars	Manilla	90
Coffee	Sumatra and Celebes	62
Cotton	Sumatra, Calcutta, and Java	52
Cotton twist	Britain	68
Gold dust	East side of Malay Peninsula and Borneo	320
Iron	Britain	53
Opium	Calcutta and Bombay	1,083
Pepper	Rhio, Java, and Borneo	136
Piece goods:		
European	Britain and Java	954
Indian	Calcutta and Madras	288
Rattans	Java and Borneo	77
Raw silk	China	117
Rice	Java, Siam, and Bali	226
Spirits	Britain and other European countries and Java	51
Sugar	Siam and Cochin China	189
Tea	China	63
Tin	Java, Malay Peninsula, neighbouring islands	313
Tobacco	China and Java	104
Tortoiseshell	Java and Celebes	92
Woollens	Britain and Java	62

Table 1.2 *(continued)*

Exports from Singapore	Principal place of destination	Value in Spanish dollars '000
Bêche-de-mer	China	75
Birds' nests	China	163
Betel nut	China and Calcutta	52
Cigars	Calcutta, Java, and New South Wales	85
Coffee	Britain, Europe, and North America	136
Cotton twist	Celebes, Malay Peninsula, China, and Siam	135
Gambier	Britain, Celebes, and Calcutta	55
Gold dust	Calcutta and Bombay	524
Iron and steel	Manilla, China, and Celebes	55
Opium	China, Malay Peninsula, and Java	795
Pepper	Britain, China, and Calcutta	237
Piece goods:		
European	Manilla, Siam, and Celebes	476
Indian	Java, Borneo, Celebes, and Sumatra	435
Malay	Malay Peninsula, Sumatra, and Borneo	57
Rattans	China, Calcutta, Siam, and Britain	79
Raw silk	Britain, Java, and Celebes	158
Rice	China, Rhio, and neighbouring islands	108
Sago	Britain	50
Spices	Britain and Bombay	73
Sugar	Britain, North America, and Bombay	162
Tea	Britain and Java	71
Tin	China, Britain, and Calcutta	411
Tobacco	Malay Peninsula, Celebes, and Java	51
Tortoiseshell	Britain	145
Woollens	Cochin China, China, and Manilla	88

ᵃ Valued at 50,000 Spanish dollars or over.

Source: Compiled from T. J. Newbold, *Political and Statistical Account of the British Settlements in the Straits of Malacca* (London, 1839), Vol. 1, pp. 291–342 (Newbold's spelling of place names).

and occupations throughout the archipelago. Some remained in Singapore to trade or engage in other services, and some became farmers on the island, although the difficulty of obtaining land and poor soils eventually drove them to Johore. There they supplied Singapore's domestic needs and exported pepper and gambier. From the 1840s Singapore became the distribution centre for Indian labourers brought by planters from Ceylon. By 1860 13,000 Indians had been added to the 16,200 Malays, 50,000 Chinese, and 2,500 Europeans who now shared the island (Table 1.1).

The European merchants, becoming dissatisfied with the East India Company's rule, began to agitate for separate colonial status directly under Great Britain which would give them some local political representation. They also wanted to see a more stable mainland Malaya brought under British influence. Suggestions that British advisers should be appointed to assist the Sultans in ruling the mainland states had been made for some time, and this policy was adopted in 1874, shortly after the Straits Settlements had become a Crown Colony with an executive and Legislative Council under the Colonial Office in 1867. After the assassination of the Resident of Perak in 1875 the British government put sufficient teeth into the Residency policy to ensure the pacification of the mainland. The expansion of tin mining and the growth of plantations followed.

Netherlands East Indies exports were expanding rapidly in response to Europe's growing demand for tropical products, and the second half of the nineteenth century saw a great increase in rice growing, tin mining, and plantation crops in mainland Southeast Asia. The opening of the Suez Canal in 1870 gave a fillip to the Singapore route. Communications were further improved when the overland telegraph line passed through Singapore on the way to Australia and China. There was no dearth of labour for mines, plantations, and trade. The aftermath of the Taiping rebellion accelerated migration from China, there was an ample supply of Indian labour, and Malays continued to move from the archipelago to the peninsula.

In the last decade of the century came rubber, introduced to the peninsula through Singapore in 1887. By the 1900s rubber exports were substantial but Singapore contributed little except shipping because sales were made at London auctions. In 1908 Singapore firms began to sell rubber locally, but sales were small and mostly confined to unsmoked sheet which required further processing. Singapore's opportunity to bypass the English auctions, particularly for the American market, came when London auctions were suspended during the war. Whereas only 2,666 tons of rubber were sold in Singapore in 1914, by 1917 24,316 tons were sold, and in the following year sales were up to 31,663 tons, establishing Singapore as a rubber auction centre with concomitant grading, packing, and processing functions.[8]

At the end of World War I it was clear that the pattern of Singapore's entrepôt trade had taken a new shape. The traditional trade between China and India, and among the countries of Southeast Asia, had largely been replaced by specialisation between raw material producers

[8] H. Price, 'Growth of the Rubber Trade', in Makepeace, Brooke, and Braddell, op. cit., Vol. II, pp. 84–8.

and manufactured goods importers, and Singapore's trans-shipment functions reflected the change in the composition of goods traded (Table 1.3). It now collected the raw materials, principally tin and rubber, from the Malay mainland and the archipelago for shipping to the rest of the world, and in the course of this activity undertook some of the preliminary sorting and processing. The service and maintenance needs of the growing port, building and construction activity, and consumers' demands were beginning to stimulate other manufacturing activities, but trade dominated the economy.

The commercial and financial services for Singapore's new entrepôt trade were provided by commercial houses and banks which were predominantly British-owned, with some European and American participation in the former. The trading agency houses mostly grew out of small nineteenth-century merchant partnerships to handle the export trade in raw materials and to import manufactured products for distribution in the Malay peninsula and further afield throughout Southeast Asia. Their interests had expanded to direct and indirect control of plantations and tin mines, while in the distribution of manufactured goods they had ventured into wholesale and retail trade.[9] Control over raw materials gave an advantage in exports, and as most of the manufactured goods came from Europe they had an edge over their Chinese competitors in imports as well. A few Chinese merchants managed to establish direct contact with manufacturers in Europe, but they were exceptional. The division between European and Chinese traders was reflected in the establishment of a separate Chinese Chamber of Commerce in 1906, and Chinese merchants and bankers were by and large merely able to fill the interstices of Singapore's entrepôt activities.

There were premonitions of the weakening demand for tropical products in the early 1920s, and trade deteriorated from 1927 when the stagnating Netherlands East Indies began to suffer from the collapse of world prices. The depression grew deeper until the trough of rubber prices in 1933. The agency houses were affected through their tin and plantation interests as well as through falling commercial turnover which was exacerbated by the Chinese merchants' ability to exploit the shift in demand towards cheap manufactured products of Japan and China. But with resources built up over many years most of the agency houses were able to carry on through the depression period, and it was the small

---

[9] G. C. Allen and A. G. Donnithorne, in *Western Enterprise in Indonesia and Malaya* (New York, 1957), give an account of commercial and banking enterprises in Singapore.

Table 1.3   Singapore's principal commodity imports and exports for 1936[a]

Imports	Value in Malay dollars '000
Rice	22,323
Wheat flour	2,573
Sago, flour	2,726
Swine	1,785
Coffee, raw	1,580
Fish, dried, and salted	6,637
Fruits: fresh, dried, and preserved	3,411
Milk, condensed (sweetened)	4,503
Areca nuts	1,697
Pepper	3,618
Sugar, coarse and refined	4,186
Vegetables	2,480
Cigarettes	9,790
Tin ore and concentrates	7,281
Saw-logs	1,178
Copra	9,805
Ground nuts	1,098
Damar	1,048
Ground-nut oil	1,401
Jelutong	1,238
Rubber	78,176
Rattans	1,146
Cement	1,879
Bars, rods, angles, shapes, and sections (steel)	1,551
Tin plates	5,500
Other manufactures of iron and steel unenumerated	3,008
Parts for machines and machinery	1,385
Cotton piece goods	10,553
Cotton sarongs	2,161
Silk piece goods	1,632
Artificial silk piece goods	2,058
Jute piece goods	1,085
Cotton underwear	1,975
Medicines, proprietary	1,556
Other raw drugs and medicines	1,181
Kerosene	11,962
Liquid fuel	14,967
Lubricating petroleum	1,013
Motor spirit	30,859
Turpentine	1,827
Motor cars: passenger	4,502
commercial	1,429
Tyres (outer covers), motor car and truck	1,115
Unspecified miscellaneous manufactures	1,062

10

Table 1.3   *(continued)*

Exports	Value in Malay dollars '000
Rice	8,646
Sago, flour	3,682
Fish, dried and salted	6,750
Pineapples, canned	7,099
Areca nuts	3,796
Pepper, white	2,011
Cigarettes	1,963
Copra	11,541
Damar	1,401
Coconut oil	4,634
Palm oil	3,006
Jelutong	1,573
Rubber	129,356
Rattans	1,747
Tin (blocks, ingots, bars, or slabs)	63,457
Cotton piece goods, dyed in the piece	1,169
Gunnies	1,080
Kerosene	9,720
Liquid fuel	5,316
Motor spirit	27,380
Turpentine	1,516
Motor cars, passenger	1,519

ᵃ Over one million Malay dollars.

Source: Straits Settlements and Federated Malay States, Department of Statistics, *Foreign Imports and Exports during the Year 1936* (Singapore, 1937).

traders, Chinese and Indian, and the unemployed, who bore the brunt and bitterness of the depression.

Recovery was very slow and wages had not been restored to pre-depression levels when World War II came to Singapore. The Japanese occupation, from 12 February 1942 to 5 September 1945, was a period of acute shortages and depressed living standards. Because it was predominantly Chinese and lacked an agricultural base, the population of Singapore suffered more than most parts of Southeast Asia. The Japanese occupation was replaced by British military rule until March 1946 when Singapore became a separate Crown Colony. Penang and Malacca had been incorporated in the new Union of Malaya which became the Federation of Malaya in 1948, but the British government felt that it had to exclude Singapore from the Malay States because of its importance as a military base and because the large proportion of

Chinese in its population would add too much weight to the Chinese population of the Federation.[10]

The rehabilitation of tin mines and plantations in Malaya was followed by the peak primary commodity prices of the Korean war period. Singapore's commerce quickly recovered and the 1950s were prosperous with some diversification of the economy. Primary product processing revived and expanded with new coconut oil factories and an expansion of tin smelting and rubber processing. Indonesia's troubled politics meant that in spite of official policy to the contrary there was little shift in processing from Singapore to Indonesia, so that Singapore continued to be a shipping and processing centre for Indonesian as well as Malayan raw materials. There was also some expansion of manufacture of consumer goods for the rapidly growing local market. This was mainly confined to food and tobacco processing and the building and structural materials needed for the city's housing and public works, but some other producers' goods such as glass containers and cans for the food industries also began to be manufactured. By 1959, the year of the first census of manufacturing, there were 554 establishments employing ten or more workers. Twenty-three of these were engaged in rubber processing, and this accounted for 75 per cent of the value of output, and 9 per cent of the value added in production in manufacturing (Table 1.4).

Politically Singapore was, however, far from stable. It was not only affected by communist-led insurgency—the 'Emergency'—on the mainland, but reflected, as it had always done, the struggles and problems of China. There was a vigorous and at times turbulent movement for independence, and a strong and militant trade union movement was often more concerned with political than with industrial aims. These were the problems inherited by the People's Action Party when it won forty-three of the fifty-one seats of the first independent parliamentary election in 1959. It took office on condition that eight People's Action Party members detained under the Preservation of Public Security Ordinance in Changi prison were released. Ironically these were the men who were to leave the People's Action Party to found the left wing *Barisan Sosialis* in opposition to it only two years later.[11]

[10] In 1947 38 per cent of the 4·9 million people of the Malay states were of Chinese ethnic origin.

[11] This brief account of recent political developments is based on Singapore, *Annual Reports*, 1959–64, T. H. Silcock, 'Communal and Party Structure' and E. Sadka, 'Malaysia: The Political Background', in T. H. Silcock and E. K. Fisk (eds.), *The Political Economy of Independent Malaya* (Canberra, 1963), and M. E. Osborne, *Singapore and Malaysia* (Data Paper No. 53,

Table 1.4   Principal statistics of Singapore manufacturing establishments
with ten or more workers, 1959–66[a, b]

Year	No. of establishments	All workers	Value of output $ million	Value added $ million	Employees' remuneration $ million	Capital expenditure $ million
1959	554	31,222	1,585·7	156·9	69·0	13·8
1960	572	32,900	1,661·5	185·1	78·4	10·4
1961	584	33,109	1,410·1	199·6	84·0	11·1
1962	630	34,699	1,734·5	236·2	90·5	35·6
1963[c]	885	42,131	1,584·4	285·8	109·3	18·2
1964	952	45,178	1,536·0	303·2	118·4	53·1
1965	1,022	50,721	1,677·8	362·0	138·4	59·4
1966	1,146	56,334	1,972·3	431·2	158·3	75·8

[a] Includes rubber processing. This accounts for fluctuations in the value of output. The value of output and value added excluding rubber processing were as follows:

	Value of output $ million	Value added $ million		Value of output $ million	Value added $ million
1959	398·9	142·8	1963	843·8	252·6
1960	465·6	142·1	1964	927·9	282·5
1961	518·4	174·4	1965	1,086·4	348·4
1962	660·3	201·7	1966	1,325·8	415·0

[b] Excludes manufacturing activities of public sector. These were slaughtering, printing and publishing, mechanical engineering, shipbuilding and repairing, manufacture of wood furniture, and pharmaceutical products. In 1965, the first year for which the figures are available, these public sector activities employed 3,959 workers. Their value of output was $32·2 million, their value added $26·1 million, and their employees' remuneration $15·9 million. (Singapore, *Report on the Census of Industrial Production 1965*, p. 13.)

[c] The 1963 Industrial Census improved the coverage of small establishments with 10–39 workers, including an extra 200 manufacturers in this group for the first time. This accounts for some of the increase recorded in 1963.

Sources: Singapore, *Report on the Census of Industrial Production*, 1959–65, and Singapore Department of Statistics data.

Singapore's political and social ties with Malaya were so close that their unification seemed only a matter of time in spite of Malay fears of Chinese preponderance. For economic reasons it seemed clear that Singapore needed Malaya and Malaya needed Singapore. Both needed each other for the creation of a common market to make the development of secondary industry viable. The People's Action Party had campaigned on a platform which included the creation of a 'united Malayan nation'

Southeast Asia Program, Department of Asian Studies, Cornell University, Ithaca, 1964).

and negotiations on these lines proceeded, culminating in agreement in principle in 1961, although effective implementation was delayed until the creation of the Malaysian Federation in 1963 when Singapore became a state of Malaysia. For Singapore, however, this brought the difficulties of 'Confrontation' with Indonesia. In 1962 entrepôt trade with Indonesia represented at least 8·7 per cent of Singapore's Gross Domestic Product,[12] and although some smuggling between Indonesia and Singapore continued almost throughout Confrontation, Singapore's trade fell substantially in 1964 and 1965 (Table 1.5). No sooner was this crisis solved than Singapore and the Federation separated. In August 1965 Singapore had to face the problems of independent statehood and economic development alone.

Table 1.5   External trade of Singapore, 1957–66

Year	Trade with the States of Malaya and West Malaysia		Total trade	
	Imports	Exports	Imports	Exports
	in million dollars			
1957	784·7	705·0	4,062·1	3,478·1
1958	639·5	659·3	3,740·1	3,140·5
1959	802·7	719·8	3,908·2	3,440·5
1960	852·9	843·0	4,077·7	3,477·1
1961	723·6	886·2	3,963·3	3,308·5
1962	727·7	941·1	4,035·9	3,416·7
1963	756·6	1,011·1	4,279·0	3,474·5
1964	791·9	925·5	3,478·7	3,771·9
1965	884·9	938·6	3,807·2	3·004·1
1966	943·5	907·6	4,065·7	3,373·6

Sources: Singapore, *Singapore External Trade (Including Trade with the Federation of Malaya) for the Year 1958*, pp. 20–1, and *Monthly Digest of Statistics*, Vol. 3, June 1964, p. 49, and Vol. 6, December 1967, p. 39.

[12] An estimate made by Dr Goh Keng Swee in his 1964 Budget statement to the Singapore Legislative Assembly, 28 November 1963 (*Legislative Assembly Debates*, State of Singapore, Vol. 22, 1963, p. 76). Gross Domestic Product was estimated at $2,500 million. Estimates made by an International Bank for Reconstruction and Development Mission in *Report on the Economic Aspects of Malaysia by a Mission of the International Bank for Reconstruction and Development, Under the Chairmanship of Mr Jacques Rueff* (1963), Chapter 8, and Tables IX and X, pp. 106–9, and by H. V. Richter, 'Indonesia's Share in the Entrepôt Trade of Malaya and Singapore Prior to Confrontation', *Malayan Economic Review*, Vol. 11, October 1966, pp. 38–41, suggest this was a minimum estimate.

14

POPULATION, WORKFORCE, AND EMPLOYMENT

From its foundation business openings and employment in service industries had given migrants who came to Singapore a better opportunity to become settled than the tin mines and plantations of the archipelago and mainland, but Singapore's population structure nevertheless showed the characteristics of a city of transients well into the 1930s with a high ratio of males to females (Table 1.6).

Table 1.6   Male to female ratios in Singapore by ethnic groups, 1871–1966;[a] number of males to 100 females

Year	Malay[b]	Chinese	Indian and Pakistani	Others	Total
1871	127	628	475	172	326
1881	128	511	404	127	309
1891	138	467	416	120	320
1901	128	388	409	109	295
1911	118	279	497	137	245
1921	123	212	498	144	204
1931	116	167	535	135	171
1947	121	113	299	111	122
1957	110	104	226	110	112
1966	105	102	172	125	107

[a]Figures exclude the populations of Christmas Island and Cocos-Keeling Islands, transients afloat, and non-locally domiciled services personnel and their families. 1871 to 1957 are Census figures, 1966 figures are mid-year estimates.

[b] Malay figures include Indonesians.

Source: Singapore, *Monthly Digest of Statistics*, Vol. 6, December 1967, p. 11.

Natural increase was therefore low, and immigration swamped it until the end of the 1920s. The high proportion of male migrants also meant that Singapore had an unusually high proportion of its population in the workforce. Both English and Chinese schools had been established in the 1820s, Chinese education grew in the 1900s, and Malay and Indian schools followed, so that literacy was high. But education was largely limited to primary schools until the 1950s. A small English-speaking élite sufficed for the clerical openings available to non-Europeans in the public service and in private enterprise, and others entered the workforce at ten or eleven years of age. The Chinese community also showed some concern for the old from the 1820s, and hospitals were built and maintained for the various racial groups, but employment was largely related to the expectation of life, and many of the older workers returned to their homeland. Public and private burdens of dependency were negligible.

The demographic situation began to change in the 1930s. Singapore and the Malay States restricted male immigration from China, but ship owners deprived of a lucrative cargo found another in women migrants.[13] This helped to improve the sex ratio for the Chinese community. The Indian government stopped the emigration of unskilled labourers in 1937, and the 1930s saw some emigration from Singapore as the economic situation showed only slow signs of recovery. By 1947 the population was therefore much better balanced than it had ever been, both in the male to female ratio (Table 1.6), and in age structure,[14] although there were now few children in the very young age groups because the deprivations of the war had lowered marriage rates and fertility and increased infantile mortality rates.

In the decade after the 1947 Census, in a period of very high population growth rates in developing countries, the population of Singapore reached an annual growth rate of 4·3 per cent per annum, perhaps the highest in the world.[15] The causes are now familiar. Birth rates were high

[13] J. C. Caldwell, 'The Demographic Background', in Silcock and Fisk (eds.), op. cit., p. 63.

[14] Age groups

	Percentage of total population	
	1931	1947
0–14 years	26·2	36·0
15–34 years	44·1	34·3
35 years and over	29·7	29·7

Singapore, *Census Reports*, 1931 and 1947.

[15] You Poh Seng, 'The Population Growth of Singapore', *Malayan Economic Review*, Vol. 4, October 1959, pp. 56–7. Professor You Poh Seng calculated the following table to compare Singapore's population growth rate with that of other countries with rapid population growths:

	Average annual percentage growth rate		
Country	Comparison of two latest censuses	Comparing latest mid-year estimate with latest census	Crude rate of natural increase 1956–7
Costa Rica	(1927–50) 2·30	3·60	3·08
Dominican Republic	(1935–50) 2·41	3·38	3·15
El Salvador	(1930–50) 1·29	3·35	3·42
Venezuela	(1941–50) 2·98	3·00	2·70
Mexico	(1940–50) 2·65	2·80	3·45
Iraq	(1947–57) 3·01	n.a.	n.a.
Ceylon	(1946–53) 3·01	2·75	2·66
Hong Kong	n.a.	4·32	3·04
Federation of Malaya	(1947–57) 2·52	3·16	3·42
Singapore	(1947–57) 4·33	4·61	3·52
Mauritius & dep.	(1944–52) 2·22	3·10	3·20

for all racial groups, and fell only slightly between 1947 and 1957 from 45·9 to 42·5 per thousand of population. The death rate in the same period fell dramatically from 13·3 to 7·3 per thousand of population as a result of improved health and sanitation facilities, rising living standards, and the changing composition of the population. The rate of natural increase was therefore about 3·5 per cent per annum.[16] Although immigration to Singapore and Malaya was now restricted, there was no control on movement between Malaya and Singapore, and Singapore attracted some 100,000 people from Malaya between 1947 and 1957. A magnet in itself as the largest city in the area it also had higher living standards and better employment opportunities than the mainland. This accounted for the rest of the population growth.

But 1957 was a turning point in natural growth rates. It was followed by a marked decline in population growth which between 1957 and 1966 had decreased to an annual total growth of about 3·25 per cent. Between 1957 and 1966 there was a continuing, though lessened, flow of population to Singapore from Malaya of some 40,000 to 45,000 people. Natural increase had fallen to about 3 per cent per annum between 1957 and 1966. Rates of natural increase fell from 35·5 per thousand for 1957 to 23·5 per thousand for 1966.[17]

The principal reasons for the decline in natural growth rates are clear. A better sex ratio and a younger population have to some extent been offset by older age at marriage, particularly for Chinese women, but the main cause of change lies in the success of the voluntary family planning program. The government-supported Singapore Family Planning Association began its activities in 1949, but it took time to make an impact on population growth.[18] The reduction in birth rates did not become evident until 1958, but by 1966 the trend was very clear. The Singapore government has increased its participation in the Family Planning Association's work, and birth rates should fall further in the future, while strict control over all immigration practically restricts population growth to natural increase.

[16] Ibid., p. 64.
[17] You Poh Seng, 'The Population of Singapore, 1966: Demographic Structure, Social and Economic Characteristics', *Malayan Economic Review*, Vol. 12, October 1967, pp. 59–60.
[18] Total attendances at family planning clinics rose from 3,841 in 1952 to 103,986 in 1965. Quoted in S. H. K. Yeh, *Some Observations on Fertility Decline in Singapore* (Reprint Monograph Series No. 5, Economic Research Centre, University of Singapore, n.d., mimeographed), p. 2.

But the growth of population, particularly the natural increase which took place from the late 1940s, had already created grave problems for Singapore. They were all the more marked because the wartime drop in the birth rate shielded the government from their full implications until the mid-1950s when children born after the war began to put a strain on the primary school system. The pressure on primary schools continued to grow, and by the end of the decade the bulge began to show in pressure on secondary schools, and to an even more serious extent in the demand for employment by the juvenile school leavers entering the workforce for the first time.

When the People's Action Party came to power it estimated that a workforce increase of 105,000 was needed by 1972 merely to maintain the relatively low work participation levels of 33 per cent of 1957. In that year there were also 24,000 unemployed for whom jobs had to be found (Table 1.7). These figures implied annual workforce increases of 10,000 to 12,000. They were minimum estimates, for the government was aware that net immigration inflow from Malaya would mean that more new jobs would be required.[19] It was considered that the bulk of these jobs would have to be found in manufacturing, related industries, and economic activity arising out of industrial growth. In 1957 33,100 people, or 7 per cent of the workforce, were employed in agriculture, forestry, hunting and fishing (Table 1.7). Employment opportunities in primary production were limited by Singapore island's small size, and improvements in agriculture would to some extent be labour-saving so that total employment in agriculture could not be expected to rise significantly even if development opportunities were pushed to the limit. It was estimated that entrepôt trade accounted for 61,815 people in 1957.[20] But although the new government continually stressed that entrepôt trade could not be neglected, it considered that the opportunities for its expansion were limited, and here too increasing labour efficiency would limit the expansion of employment opportunities. Similar considerations applied to other, private and public, service sectors. The development of manufacturing, although in its infancy, already account-ed for the employment of 73,800 people (Table 1.7). It seemed the only solution to the problem posed by the growing workforce.

[19] *Development Plan, 1961–1964* (Singapore, 1963), pp. 8–10.
[20] Ibid., p. 12. This excludes 9,567 workers employed in raw material pro-cessing included in manufacturing employment in the *Development Plan* statistics.

18

Table 1.7   Singapore workforce by industrial sector, 1957 and 1966[a]

	Employment '000		Percentage of total workforce	
	1957	1966	1957	1966
Agriculture, forestry, hunting, and fishing	33·1	19·2	7·0	3·5
Mining and quarrying	1·6	1·4	0·3	0·3
Manufacturing[b]	73·8	104·4	15·6	19·2
Construction	24·6	34·5	5·2	6·3
Electricity, gas, water, and sanitary services	5·6	7·5	1·2	1·4
Commerce	121·5	128·9	25·8	23·7
Transport, storage, and communications	50·4	52·7	10·7	9·7
Services	161·3	194·4	34·2	35·8
Total in workforce	471·9	543·0	100·0	100·0
Not included in workforce[c]	8·4	33·8		
Total in workforce and wishing to join workforce	480·3	576·8		
Total unemployed	24·2	52·6		
Percentage unemployed as total of workforce and wishing to join workforce	5·0	9·1		

[a] Persons aged ten and over.

[b] Includes rubber processing and packaging.

[c] Persons who had never worked before but were looking for a job and, in 1966, 4,994 persons whose activities were inadequately described.

Sources: Singapore, *Report on the Census of Population 1957* (Singapore, 1964) and *Singapore Sample Household Survey, 1966. Report No. 1. Tables Relating to Population and Housing* (Singapore, 1967). These reports were not compiled on the same basis and figures for the two years have been adjusted to avoid discrepancies as much as possible. See H. T. Oshima, 'Growth and Unemployment in Singapore', *Malayan Economic Review*, Vol. 12, October 1967, Tables 2a, 2b, and 5, pp. 50–1, 54.

THE IMPETUS TO INDUSTRIALISATION

The 1955 International Bank for Reconstruction and Development Mission's report on Singapore and Malaya saw the beginning of a new attitude to industrialisation in both countries. The governments recognised that in addition to providing an adequate infrastructure they had an essential and direct role to play in the encouragement of industrial growth. The Bank Mission recognised the importance of industrialisation and laid down some guide lines for it. It envisaged a national market for Singapore and Malaya in which there would be a movement from naturally sheltered industries to those competing with imports, with a concomitant shift from small- to large-scale enterprise. While this should be a private enterprise process, the government's assistance would be needed in feasibility investigations and the promotion of industrial activities, in helping to provide industrial finance, and, to a carefully limited extent, in introducing tariffs to protect infant industries.[21]

Although 1957 and 1958 were years of great difficulty for Singapore's last colonial government, faced by intense pressure for full independence, it did take some steps to implement the Bank Mission's suggestions. An Industrial Promotion Board was created in 1957 but it lacked power and financial resources. In August 1958 Malaya adopted legislation giving tax relief to pioneer industries—new industries with good economic prospects the existence of which was in the public interest—and similar legislation was planned for Singapore. A Protection Advisory Committee was established, but it was dominated by importers and made no progress. The government also requested a Canadian industrial expert, Mr F. J. Lyle, to advise it on industrialisation policy, and Lyle's report, delivered in November 1958,[22] set the initial direction of Singapore's industrial development.

Lyle concluded that the need for economic union between Singapore and Malaya was so overwhelming for both that it could be assumed that it would be accomplished, and his recommendations were tied to this premise. Secondly, strongly influenced by Canada's success in industrialising behind tariffs, Lyle felt that 'the unrestricted Free Port Era appears to be ended'.[23] The entrepôt trade could be continued by a system of drawbacks, but he placed great emphasis on a Joint Industrial Development Council with the Federation which would plan the promotion of industries on a national basis.[24]

Lyle recommended the creation of a strong Division of Industrial Development, within the Ministry of Commerce and Industry, but divorced as much as possible from the Ministry's other work, and given a great deal of independence and initiative. Impressed by Puerto Rico's success in industrialising he suggested that Singapore should engage a foreign consulting firm to advise and assist the Division in its work, particularly in dealing with foreign investors who would be needed to play an important role in industrialisation.

[21] International Bank for Reconstruction and Development, *The Economic Development of Malaya* (Washington, 1955), Chapter 6, pp. 84–95, and Technical Report 8, pp. 301–16.
[22] 'An Industrial Development Programme', Legislative Assembly, Singapore, *Sessional Paper*, No. Cmd 5 of 1959.
[23] Ibid., p. 31.
[24] Ibid., p. 11.

Finding the manufacturing opportunities identified by a current survey of existing industries very encouraging because several openings for the manufacture of new products were indicated, Lyle suggested that this should be followed by a survey of imports to enable the government to find new industries for which support would be worthwhile. He stressed the importance of foreign investment, recommending that a list of manufacturers exporting to Singapore who might be induced to manufacture there would be the best way to start attracting foreign investors. The Singapore Trade Commissioner in London should seek potential United Kingdom investors to manufacture in Singapore, although investors from the United States, Canada, Japan, Hong Kong, India, West Germany, and Italy might also be found.

Lyle thought that financial assistance would be necessary for indigenous industrialists, and suggested that the Malayan Industrial Development Finance Limited, then being established with the assistance of the International Bank for Reconstruction and Development in Kuala Lumpur, might be persuaded to function in Singapore as well as Malaya. If not, a separate institution for Singapore would have to be established.

Early in 1959 three legislative enactments attempted to stimulate industrialisation. The Pioneer Industries (Relief from Income Tax) Ordinance (No. 1 of 1959) gave pioneer product manufacturers tax exemption from the prevailing 40 per cent company income tax for five years with a proviso that losses might be carried over beyond this period. Accelerated depreciation allowances, enabling firms to treat their assets as new for the purposes of depreciation at the end of the first five years, were granted. Exemptions from import duties on raw material and equipment were to be given if deemed advisable. The Industrial Expansion (Relief from Income Tax) Ordinance (No. 2 of 1959) allowed concessions for existing enterprises whose investment expansion was approved. The tax exemptions were on a sliding scale adjusted to the amount of new capital invested. For a minimum amount of $10,000 the taxation concession was 11 per cent per annum, and the concession rose by 1 per cent for each $10,000 of capital expenditure, reaching a maximum of 15 per cent for amounts of $50,000 or over. Although the second ordinance was principally designed to prevent existing firms from establishing pioneer industries in the Federation rather than expanding in Singapore, it also followed the 1955 Bank Mission's recommendation that tax concessions for new industries should not obscure the contribution which could be made by the expansion of existing industries. A Control of Manufacture Ordinance appointed a

21

Table 1.8   Development Plan capital expenditure estimates and
actual expenditure, 1961–5

	Capital expenditure estimates	Actual expenditure 1961–5[a]	Actual expenditure as percentage of planned expenditure
		$ million	
I Economic Development			
1. Land and agricultural development			
1.1 Land purchases for general development and resettlement	11·31	23·89	211·2
1.2 Swamp reclamation schemes	4·00	0·50	12·5
1.3 Flood alleviation schemes	11·81	10·12	85·7
1.4 Rural development schemes	26·10	2·80	10·7
1.5 Animal Husbandry and Agricultural Station, Sembawang	0·05	—	—
Other expenditure, not originally in the Plan	—	0·82	—
Total land and agricultural development	53·27	38·13	71·6
2. Industry and commerce			
2.1 Economic Development Board	100·00	52·32[b]	52·3
2.2 Kallang project	40·00	3·51	8·8
2.3 Jurong project	45·00	90·89	202·0
2.4 Land acquisition for industrialisation and other development costs for industrialisation	5·60	5·82	103·9
2.5 Electricity	78·50	187·90	239·3
2.6 Water	54·23	46·27	85·3
2.7 Gas	14·03	18·61	132·6
Total industry and commerce	337·36	405·32	120·1
3. Transport and communications			
3.1 East Wharf development	12·70	40·23[c]	316·8
3.2 Improvement of Singapore River	15·70	0·23	1·5
3.3 Marine	0·10	0·09	90·0
3.4 Meteorological services	0·15	0·06	40·0
3.5 Civil aviation	10·90	10·80	99·0
3.6 Telecommunications	12·88	7·65	59·4
3.7 Roads	29·60	37·01	125·0
3.8 Drainage	6·54	—	—
3.9 Bridges	10·43	4·64	44·5
3.10 Posts	0·87	0·58	66·7
3.11 Telephone Board	17·45	32·78	18·8
Other expenditure, not originally in the Plan	—	3·23	—
Total transport and communications	117·32	137·30	117·0

Table 1.8   *(continued)*

		Capital expenditure estimates	Actual expenditure 1961–5[a]	Actual expenditure as percentage of planned expenditure
			$ million	
II	Social Development			
1.	Health	35·80	10·4	29·1
2.	Education	94·48	67·17	71·1
3.	Social welfare	1·77	1·53	86·4
4.	Housing	153·60	199·11	129·6
5.	Sewerage	47·36	35·66	75·3
6.	Community services	6·07	0·75	12·4
7.	Culture	10·80	12·70	117·6
	Other expenditure, not originally in the Plan	—	7·44	—
Total Social Development		349·88	325·40	93·0
III	Public Administration			
1.	Police	7·50	1·94	25·9
2.	Prisons	2·17	2·39	110·1
3.	Judicial	0·03	—	
4.	Customs	0·77	1·89	245·5
5.	Vehicles Department	0·45	—	
6.	General improvement to government buildings and quarters	2·13	3·69	173·2
7.	Defence	0·14	3·65	2,607·1
	Other expenditure, not originally in the Plan	—	1·16	—
Total	Public Administration	13·19	14·72	111·6
	Grand Total	871·02	920·87	105·7

[a] Includes expenditure not in the original Plan.
[b] Loans, industrial financing, and equity participation only.
[c] Includes all Port of Singapore Authority port development.
Sources: Singapore, *Development Plan 1961–1964* (Singapore, 1963), p. 35, and information provided by Ministry of Finance, Economic Planning Unit.

Registrar of Manufacturers to limit the number of persons who engaged in specified manufacturing if desirable.

When the People's Action Party came to office in 1959 it was overwhelmed by political problems. Its very election as a socialist party and the militant trade union activity which followed made the climate for

23

private investment in manufacturing unfavourable in Singapore, and there was some movement of potential industrial investors to Malaya. But the employment situation was so grave that the new government had to apply itself to the problem of stimulating industrial growth immediately. It requested additional advice from the World Bank and asked the United Nations for two surveys of industrial opportunities. The first was to cover a wide range of industrial possibilities in Singapore, the second was to inquire into the feasibility of establishing an integrated iron and steel industry. Industrialisation was the central feature of the Development Plan which set out the structure for the public contribution to economic development from 1961 to 1964.

By the time the Development Plan was published in 1961, it was evident that Singapore's circumstances had forced its socialist government into a mixed economy welfare state rather than a planned economy framework. Private enterprise was expected to play the leading role in agriculture, commerce, and particularly in industry, while the government looked after the infrastructure and social services.

The Plan again drew attention to the critical nature of population growth and the consequent employment problems, stressing that there could be no significant reduction of dependence on entrepôt trade within the Plan period even though industrialisation was to be pursued vigorously.[25] Although union with Malaya was very much in the political air when the Plan was drawn up, the planners refrained from the luxury of believing that national Singapore-Malaya development would solve their problems. The Plan concentrated on the creation of public services, an efficient administrative structure, and on social services, all financed out of public revenues and economically feasible loans. Its main objective was 'to expend the resources at the disposal of the Government and other Public Authorities in such a way that it would contribute to increasing employment opportunities for those who would be entering the labour market each year'.[26]

The largest single item of expenditure, $100 million (Table 1.8), was devoted to the work of the Economic Development Board which was created in August 1961 to replace the Singapore Industrial Promotion Board as an independent government instrumentality to take charge of the industrialisation program. When the Board was established the lack of impetus in industrial growth was critical, and its powers were correspondingly strong:

[25] *Development Plan, 1961–1964*, pp. 10–11.
[26] Ibid., p. 33.

(a) with the written approval of the Minister [of Finance], to underwrite the issue of stocks, shares, bonds or debentures by industrial enterprises;

(b) with the written approval of the Minister, to guarantee on such terms and conditions as may be agreed upon, loans raised by industrial enterprises which—

    i. are repayable within a period not exceeding twenty-five years; or

    ii. are floated in the public market;

(c) to grant loans or advances to, or subscribe to stocks, shares, bonds or debentures of industrial enterprises;

(d) to manage, control or supervise industrial enterprises by nominating directors or advisers or otherwise collaborating with them or entering into partnerships or any other arrangement for jointly working with them;

(e) with the written approval of the Minister, to establish, sell shares of, invest in and manage industrial enterprises;

(f) to act as agent for the Government or, with its approval, for any other person in the transaction of any business with an industrial enterprise in respect of loans or advances granted or debentures subscribed by the Government or such other person;

(g) to acquire, sell or lease land for the purposes of industrial sites, for the housing of employees or for general economic development;

(h) to lay out industrial estates for sale or lease;

(i) to provide technical advice and assistance to industrial enterprises and to build up a corps of engineering and managerial staff to provide such assistance;

(j) to exercise all functions and powers and perform all duties which, under or by virtue of any other written law, are or may be or become vested or delegated to it;

(k) to receive in consideration of the services rendered by it such commission as may be agreed upon; and

(l) generally to do all such matters and things as may be incidental to or consequential upon the exercise of its powers or the discharge of its duties under this Ordinance.[27]

The Economic Development Board became active in the second half of 1961, and by 1962 its promotional work began to be effective.

[27] Quoted from the Economic Development Board Ordinance, 1961 (No. 21 of 1961).

The immediate task was to disseminate publicity and to take care of industrialists, foreign and local, who became interested in manufacturing possibilities in Singapore. Twenty-four pioneer certificates were granted between 1959 and 1962, and ninety-five in 1963 before the formation of Malaysia, when approval by federal authorities in Kuala Lumpur became necessary. Bringing pioneer firms into production was more difficult. In 1962 there were 14, in 1963 29, and in 1966 111 pioneer firms in production. In 1963 they accounted for 6 per cent of employment and 12 per cent of value added in production in manufacturing establishments with ten or more workers. By 1966 they contributed 20 per cent to employment and 28 per cent to value added in production in such establishments (Table 1.9). The pioneer firms had, moreover, expanded the variety of output in manufacturing by producing cement, paints, flour, new metal products, petroleum products, and textiles.

Table 1.9   Value added, value of output, and employment
in pioneer firms, 1963–6

Year	No. of firms	Value added		Value of output		Employment	
		$ m.	% of all mfg	$ m.	% of all mfg	No.	% of all mfg
1963	29[a]	34	12	153	10	2,654	6
1964	56	50	16	220	14	5,416	12
1965	95	80	22	318	19	10,495	21
1966	111[b]	119	28	490	25	11,102	20

[a] One firm ceased production during the year.
[b] One of these firms did not make returns to the Economic Development Board.
Sources: Economic Development Board, *Annual Reports*, 1964–6, and Table 1.4.

To speed the implementation of manufacturers' plans the Economic Development Board undertook liaison between manufacturers and government departments such as Health, Fire, Customs, Taxation, and Labour. The Economic Development Board also assisted manufacturers in dealing with public utility organisations. Electricity and gas supply, telephone services, and the railway linking Singapore with the mainland have traditionally been in the hands of government departments or statutory corporations. Public services and utilities were well developed when the independent government took over in 1959, and one of the main accents of the 1961–4 Development Plan was 'building a solid base of the infrastructure for industrialisation by the development of essential

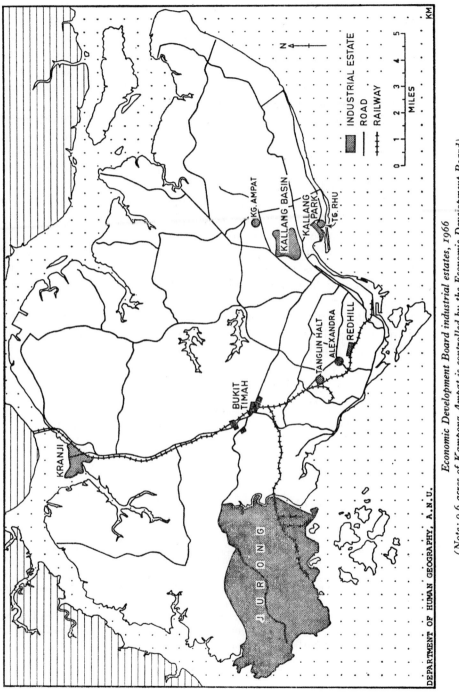

KG. AMPAT

KALLANG BASIN

KALLANG
PARK

TG. RHU

TANGLIN HALT

ALEXANDRA

REDHILL

BUKIT
TIMAH

KRANJI

J U R O N G

INDUSTRIAL ESTATE

ROAD

RAILWAY

N

0   1   2   3   4   5
MILES

KM

DEPARTMENT OF HUMAN GEOGRAPHY, A.N.U.

Economic Development Board industrial estates, 1966

(Note: 0.6 acres of Kampong Ampat is controlled by the Economic Development Board)

services like power, water, gas, port, transport and communications'.[28] Singapore's infrastructure was, in fact, one of its principal advantages for industrial growth, being by and large on a par with that of developed countries, and the People's Action Party government ensured that the availability and quality of services were improved in the early 1960s. The Economic Development Board in turn assisted new entrants into manufacturing to utilise the services available.

Industrial land, on the other hand, was not easily available, particularly for small enterprises. The colonial government had therefore already in the 1950s begun to follow United Kingdom precedents by developing industrial estates. The first was the Alexandra Estate, and this was followed by Bukit Timah and Redhill (see map); these were all completely filled by the end of 1965. Public utilities and roads were brought to the estates by the authorities responsible and land was available for lease or purchase. The Economic Development Board took over the management of industrial estates shortly after its establishment, and in addition it was given charge of Jurong, a large industrial estate and residential 'new town' being developed on a deep harbour site thirteen miles from Singapore, following recommendations of the 1961 United Nations Industrial Survey Team.[29] The industrial estates being managed by the Economic Development Board in 1966 are shown in Table 1.10.

Table 1.10   Locations and acreages of industrial estates, 1966

Location	Acreage
Jurong	7,340
Kranji	237
Kallang Basin	40
Tanglin Halt	39
Kallang Park	21
Redhill	46
Tangjong Rhu	4
Total	7,727

Sources: Economic Development Board, *Annual Report '66*, p. 40; Industrial Facilities Division, Economic Development Board.

[28] *First Development Plan 1961–1964. Review of Progress for the Three Years Ending 31st December, 1963* (Singapore, 1964), p. 37.
[29] 'Singapore', information paper on industrial estate development in United Nations, Department of Economic and Social Affairs, *Industrial Estates in Asia and the Far East* (New York, 1962), pp. 346–8.

The Jurong estate was by far the largest of these, and it is, in many ways, the prestige estate of Singapore. It has a heavy industry sector consisting of shipbreaking, a shipyard, oil refineries, and an iron and steel rolling mill, and a light industry sector closer to the housing development. Housing is being undertaken by the Housing and Development Board, and the physical planning of the entire Jurong new town area has been passed to the Urban Renewal Unit of the Housing Development Board. At the end of 1966 more than 2,000 acres of industrial sites had been prepared at Jurong. Drainage channels and canals had been dug, roads had been built, the principal services connected, and the railway to Bukit Timah, the junction with the main railway line, was completed. The first wharf had come into operation. Sixty factories were in production on the estate and another twenty were to commence production in 1967.[30]

Attracting workers to Jurong proved more difficult than bringing factories out of the city. People were reluctant to move out to Jurong in spite of the shortage of housing in Singapore, and it was not possible to let all the flats available. In 1964 only 101 flats were occupied. The government used some of the empty flats to house army personnel. During 1964 and 1965 the building of a primary school, post office, markets and some shops improved the position. By the end of 1965, 964 flats were occupied by about 2,000 industrial workers,[31] but the 'new town' still lacked social amenities. In 1966 an open-air cinema and a lake recreation area were therefore added.

The Economic Development Board joined with the Commonwealth Development Corporation to form the Singapore Factory Development Limited which assists firms to purchase or build factories on industrial estates and finances some outside the estates. Singapore Factory Development Limited also builds standard factories for rental on industrial estates. Flatted factories of three stories have been introduced to enable small manufacturers to rent small units with possibilities of expansion. These are particularly suitable for labour-intensive industries which require little capital installation, and they have therefore been built close to housing estates.

Both Lyle and the International Bank for Reconstruction and Development's Mission had emphasised the need to assist industry by providing capital funds. The Singapore government was aware that investment capital was available in Singapore, but felt that government

[30] Economic Development Board, *Annual Report '66*, pp. 47–51 and p. 67.
[31] Economic Development Board, *Annual Report '65*, p. 35.

investment encouragement, some of it in the shape of government equity participation, would be needed to bring it into manufacturing ventures. It was therefore envisaged that a considerable proportion of the Economic Development Board's grant of $100 million would go towards such financing. It was also hoped that the International Bank for Reconstruction and Development would assist Singapore to create an industrial finance corporation on the lines of the Malaysian Industrial Development Finance Limited, but this hope was not fulfilled.

The Board's first investment was $1,250,000, representing 20 per cent of the issued capital of the National Iron and Steel Mills Ltd, an enterprise established by the government to set up a plant for melting and re-rolling scrap from shipbreaking. The United Nations Mission had found that the setting up of an integrated iron and steel works was not warranted although shipbreaking and re-rolling opportunities existed, and this was the compromise solution adopted by the government for the establishment of this 'basic' industry.

The Board went on to invest in a number of enterprises, mainly to encourage other entrepreneurs to do so, and by the end of 1966 its equity commitments in industry amounted to $24·4 million, of which $17·3 million had been paid. It made loans available, mainly for the purchase of capital assets such as land, buildings, and machinery, charging fixed interest rates at prevailing commercial bank levels which averaged 6 to 7 per cent per annum. At the end of 1966 the Board's total loan commitments stood at $57·2 million of which $43 million was disbursed. The Board also issued letters of guarantee in favour of suppliers of machinery and credit. By the end of 1966 total equity shares and loan commitments were $81·7 million and of this $60·3 million had actually been paid.[32]

In granting pioneer certificates and loans the Economic Development Board was concerned not only to assist firms which had feasible manufacturing proposals, but also to favour those which were particularly suited to Singapore's needs. It also seemed necessary to investigate and promote the establishment of industries on the Board's initiative, and for this purpose a Projects Division was formed. Its work was helped initially by a United Nations team headed by Dr A. Winsemius which listed a number of industries which should be developed in Singapore. The Division gradually found itself moving from the evaluation of projects

[32] Economic Development Board, *Annual Report '66*, pp. 70–1. These sums exclude loans of $1·5 million and equity interest of $2·0 million in Singapore Factory Development Limited, and $3·8 million in special short-term financial assistance for shipbreaking authorised up to 1966.

to their promotion by bringing together foreign investors with local entrepreneurs, and also by trying to induce the latter to invest in new industries on their own.

The Projects Division also served as the Secretariat for the Singapore government's Committee on Tariff Matters, a supplementary committee to the Tariff Advisory Commission established in 1962.[33] The Committee was set up to investigate the problems of the Malaysian Common Market and the establishment of a Free Trade Zone in Singapore after the formation of Malaysia in 1963. Although the Singapore government was well aware of the necessity of maintaining, and if possible improving, its entrepôt trade, its manufacturing industries were pressing for a protected market. At the time of the formation of Malaysia only paints, enamels and varnishes, soap, tobacco, intoxicating liquors, and petroleum were protected by tariffs, but a number of tariff applications were pending, and quotas on imports were being used to protect struggling pioneers. The International Bank for Reconstruction and Development's Mission on the economic aspects of Malaysia, headed by Mr J. Rueff, reinforced the earlier Bank Mission's report and Lyle's conclusions. The Rueff Mission was 'convinced that the growth of the Malaysian manufacturing sector can best be assured by (i) creating a common Malaysian market in domestically produced goods; and (ii) judiciously using tariffs to protect this market'.[34]

Singapore's manufacturers were already selling a substantial proportion of their products to the Federation of Malaya, although the relatively high standard of living of Singapore's population had meant that in the early 1960s Singapore's own markets were as great as the Federation's for many products. However, the Rueff Mission considered that with the creation of Malaysia a potential $2,000 million market came into view for import replacement of goods currently imported into Malaysia.[35] On balance the advantages of employment which could be created by tariffs designed to shelter an all-Malaysian market seemed to outweigh the likely losses which would come with the diminution of entrepôt trade. In pursuit of the common market promise, but also pressed by manufacturers coming into production, and by the dangers of unemployment, Singapore turned towards protectionism in 1963 and tariff increases

[33] Ordinance No. 23 of 1962.
[34] *Report on the Economic Aspects of Malaysia* . . . , p. 31.
[35] Ibid., p. 28. This is the estimated value of Malaysian retained imports of manufactured goods in 1961. Local production was estimated to account for another $1,100 million.

came in 1964 and 1965 together with more import quotas on goods competing with pioneer industries. These were intended to give the latter breathing space.

With the separation of Singapore from Malaysia the government was faced with an entirely new set of problems. The importance of entrepôt trade again came to the fore in spite of the losses sustained through Confrontation. Industrialising behind a tariff was not viable for a small city state dependent on raw material imports. Balance of payment difficulties loomed on the horizon. The Economic Development Board put a new emphasis on export markets, and while the employment a new firm was likely to create remained an important criterion, the Board began to pay particular attention to firms interested in export markets. Late in 1965 firms were able to deduct twice from their taxable income expenses incurred in exploring new export markets. Tariffs were still felt to be unavoidable in some cases where existing or large potential employment was threatened, and in retaliation against Malaysia which began to introduce high tariffs against Singapore goods, but import quotas were abandoned wherever possible. The necessity of turning from the internal market to manufacturing for export became dominant.

Singapore's small industries are of particular concern to the Economic Development Board both because of the difficult problems they face and because they represent some of the growth points for the future. In 1963 there were 684 very small establishments with five to nine workers each. They employed 4,754 workers, or 10 per cent of all workers in manufacturing establishments with five or more workers, but their value added in production was only $15·4 million, or 5 per cent of all value added in manufacturing establishments with five or more workers. The small to medium size establishments, employing ten to forty-nine workers, were much more important in the development of manufacturing. In 1963 there were 693 such establishments and they employed 15,032 workers, or 41 per cent of all workers in establishments with ten or more workers. However, they contributed only $62·9 million, or 25 per cent of value added in establishments with ten or more workers.[36] To assist these industries, and to provide consulting services not yet commercially available in Singapore, the Board has therefore built up a Technical Service Division. The Division's Industrial Research Unit is the principal industrial research organisation in Singapore, and it is in addition the nucleus of a standards organisation. Services for small industries include market and production investigations, a training and

[36] Singapore, *Report on the Census of Industrial Production 1963*, p. 7.

demonstration service, a site planning service, and a loans service specifically designed to help small industries that wish to modernise and expand but cannot find funds through normal commercial channels. Loans are granted through, and administered by, local commercial banks to reduce the Board's administrative load and at the same time bring small manufacturers into contact with commercial banks.

Small firms also tend to lack managerial skills and the Board's Productivity and Training Unit attempts to stimulate management training in co-operation with the Singapore Institute of Management. The Productivity and Training Unit is also designed to reduce industrial tension which for several years appeared to be a major barrier to successful industrialisation in Singapore.

LABOUR AND INDUSTRIAL RELATIONS

It was inevitable that in a colonial country striving for independence as Singapore was in the late 1940s and in the 1950s, trade union organisation and aims should become entwined in politics. The 'Emergency' in Malaya and the communist victory in mainland China made the relationship particularly tense in Singapore.

Before World War II trade union organisation in Singapore was largely confined to clerical workers, seamen, and wharf labourers, and to skilled metal tradesmen.[37] Union leadership was strongly communist-influenced, and communists also played the leading role in the wartime guerrilla warfare against the Japanese. At the end of the war the old unions were revived and new ones began to form rapidly; by 1948 there were 74,367 trade union members in Singapore (Table 1.11). The unions were very successful in raising wage levels to meet high food prices and at this stage the communist leadership of the unions turned them to political action. During the Emergency, however, the number of trade unions and trade unionists was severely reduced and their means of operation was restricted by government regulation. Yet in spite of restrictions on communist leadership on the one hand, and the opposition of old-fashioned employers on the other, the movement grew to another peak in 1956 when the largest union, the Factory and Shopworkers'

[37] S. S. Awbery and F. W. Dalley, *Labour and Trade Union Organisation in the Federation of Malaya and Singapore* (Kuala Lumpur, 1948), C. Gamba, *The Origins of Trade Unionism in Malaya* (Singapore, 1962), and A. Josey, *Trade Unionism in Malaya* (Singapore, 1958), give accounts of the development of trade unionism in Singapore.

Table 1.11   Membership of employee trade unions in Singapore, 1946–66

Year	Unions registered during year	Unions dissolved or cancelled during year	Unions remaining at end of year	Membership at end of year
1946	8	—	8	18,673
1947	118	—	126	96,060
1948	10	18	118	74,367
1949	9	34	93	47,301
1950	6	8	91	48,595
1951	18	2	107	58,322
1952	19	4	122	63,831
1953	20	9	133	73,566
1954	12	9	136	76,452
1955	61	10	187	139,317
1956	27	9	205	157,216
1957	20	9	216	140,710
1958	18	16	218	129,159
1959	14[a]	56	176	146,579
1960	2	48	130	144,770
1961	3	9	124	164,462
1962	—	2	122	189,032
1963	1	11	112	142,936
1964	4[b]	10	106	157,050
1965	3	1	108	154,052
1966	c	c	108	141,925

[a] Registration of one union cancelled in 1958 was restored in 1959.
[b] Registration of one union cancelled in 1963 was restored in 1964.
[c] Not available.

Sources: Singapore, *Annual Report of the Ministry of Labour 1965*, Table XXXII, p. 180, and *Monthly Digest of Statistics*, Vol. 6, December 1967, p. 26.

Union, was dissolved, again on political grounds, because it had come under communist leadership and had moved from industrial to political agitation. The first years of independence saw a violent conflict between the left-wing *Barisan Sosialis* unions and those supporting the People's Action Party which sought to persuade the unionists that a policy of industrial peace was compatible with industrial justice. The establishment of an Arbitration Court brought disputes out of the arena of direct action, the Commissioner for Labour assisted the settlement of disputes arising out of contracts or government ordinances, but above all the government succeeded in persuading trade union leaders that Singapore's economic situation was dangerous and that only industrialisation could solve the state's problems. The government claimed as a result that for the first time in Singapore, a vigorous non-Communist leadership is emerging from the unions as militant and as active as the Communists, but not using and exploiting the trade union movement for direct political objectives. Employers have also come to realize the wisdom of a fair wage policy to ensure stability. The stage is now set where with an intelligent policy on the part of the employers it is possible to ensure that the non-Communist trade union movement strengthens as the Communists are isolated and prevented from re-establishing influence and control over the workers.[38]

A Pioneer Industries Employees' Union was organised for workers in pioneer firms to free the firms of trade unions with communist and *Barisan Sosialis* influence.

Wages and earnings continued to rise and working conditions to improve, but from 1964 the small number of days lost in industrial disputes reflected the vastly improved industrial climate (Table 1.12).

Table 1.12   Industrial stoppages in Singapore, 1959–66

Year	No. of stoppages beginning in year	Workers involved	Man days lost during year in manufacturing
1959	40	1,939	23,634
1960	45	5,939	129,893
1961	116	43,584	71,579
1962	88	6,647	87,458
1963[a]	47	33,004	302,289
1964	38	2,535	4,390
1965	29	3,374	34,589
1966	14	1,288	30,447

[a] Figures include a two-day general strike in October involving approximately 14,150 manufacturing workers.

Sources: Singapore, *Annual Reports* of the Ministry of Labour, 1964–5, Table XIV. Figures for 1966 from Singapore, *Monthly Digest of Statistics*, Vol. 6, December 1967, p. 28.

Table 1.13 shows the level and trends in average weekly and hourly earnings in Singapore since independence. Hourly earnings are minima because a significant proportion of manufacturing workers are entitled to various additional benefits under contracts negotiated between employers and unions. Employees on monthly hiring who accounted for a fifth of all male manufacturing employees surveyed by the Ministry

[38] The Yang di-Pertuan Negara's (Head of State's) speech to the Legislative Assembly, 29 November 1963. *Legislative Assembly Debates*, State of Singapore, Vol. 22, 1963, p. 128.

Table 1.13 Average weekly hours worked and average weekly earnings
in Singapore manufacturing industries, 1959–65

	Adults		Young persons[a]		All workers
	Male	Female	Male	Female	
Average hours worked during the week					
1959	46·4	44·9	45·7	42·9	46·1
1960	46·6	45·4	44·5	45·0	46·4
1961	46·5	46·7	50·3	44·9	46·6
1962	48·3	45·0	44·8	44·3	47·7
1963	48·3	44·7	45·1	46·5	47·7
1964	47·7	45·7	45·0	48·0	47·3
1965	47·9	44·9	44·0	45·0	47·2
Average earnings for the week $					
1959	40·66	21·09	21·07	14·91	36·95
1960	43·95	22·88	18·43	16·09	39·72
1961	44·03	21·90	22·57	12·66	39·54
1962	47·49	23·61	24·44	15·93	43·03
1963	48·52	24·36	18·95	15·87	44·05
1964	50·20	23·04	24·00	16·40	44·47
1965	50·83	23·99	21·95	9·67	44·38

[a] Persons under eighteen years of age.

Sources: Singapore, *Annual Reports* of the Labour Department and Ministry of Labour,
1959–65. The figures are based on an annual stratified sample survey, generally taken
in mid-year, covering all manufacturing establishments, including those with fewer
than ten in the workforce.

of Labour from 1963 to 1965 (Table 1.14) were generally entitled to
extra pay for overtime worked over a forty-four-hour week and for work
on public holidays, including Sundays. They received pay for a number
of public holidays during the year, annual holiday pay of one to two
weeks, and sick leave. Many workers received an annual New Year
bonus which tended to rise from year to year under union pressure.
In addition special allowances for housing and travel were not uncom-
mon. Free or subsidised meals were provided in some factories, and the
larger factories also made available medical attention and in some cases
free medicines. Some factories had special provident and pension funds
in addition to making compulsory contributions on their employees'
behalf to the Central Provident Fund which provides old age insurance.
Workers were also insured against injury at work under the Workers'
Compensation Ordinance. Some of the unions were able to negotiate
contracts which restricted a firm's freedom to hire and fire by ensuring
that the union's preferences were followed, and in some cases dismissal
was very difficult and had to be accompanied by severance pay.

Table 1.14   Method of payment of wages in manufacturing industries
in Singapore, 1959–65

		1959	1960	1961	1962	1963	1964	1965
Number of employers								
Questioned		256	211	197	189	226	262	274
Replied		234	195	182	169	202	230	231
Number of workers employed by employers who replied								
	Male	23,493	23,151	23,353	23,169	22,795	22,251	23,404
	Female	5,083	5,052	5,176	5,153	4,646	5,264	6,070
	Total	28,576	28,203	28,529	28,322	27,441	27,515	29,474
Number and percentage of workers at the following rates								
Piece rates	Male	2,193	4,614	4,446	2,391	1,948	1,792	1,771
		(9)	(20)	(19)	(10)	(9)	(8)	(8)
	Female	1,262	1,311	1,525	835	711	1,444	2,067
		(25)	(26)	(29)	(16)	(15)	(27)	(34)
Daily rates	Male	15,817	13,500	13,049	17,294	16,010	15,391	16,405
		(67)	(58)	(56)	(75)	(70)	(69)	(70)
	Female	3,355	3,424	3,229	3,959	3,160	2,984	3,124
		(66)	(68)	(62)	(77)	(68)	(57)	(51)
Weekly rates	Male	1,845	1,498	1,871	204	290	373	616
		(8)	(6)	(8)	(1)	(1)	(2)	(3)
	Female	178	49	56	33	37	80	102
		(4)	(1)	(1)	(1)	(1)	(2)	(2)
Monthly rates	Male	3,638	3,539	3,987	3,280	4,547	4,695	4,612
		(15)	(15)	(17)	(14)	(20)	(21)	(20)
	Female	288	268	366	326	738	756	777
		(6)	(5)	(7)	(6)	(16)	(14)	(13)

Figures in parentheses are percentages of respective male and female totals.

Sources: Calculated from Singapore, *Annual Reports* of the Labour Department and
Ministry of Labour, 1959–65. The figures are based on an annual stratified sample
survey, generally taken in mid-year, covering all manufacturing establishments
including those with fewer than ten in the workforce.

The government was becoming increasingly concerned at the opportunities for featherbedding which the generous fringe benefits allowed,
and it came under considerable pressure from employers, local and
foreign, to tighten employment conditions. An Employment Bill
introduced in May 1968 accordingly increased hours of work of white
collar workers from thirty-nine to the forty-four standard for industrial
employees, curtailed bonus payments to bonuses tied to performance,
reduced public holidays from fifteen to eleven a year, and only allowed
retrenchment benefits after three years' continuous service. Annual paid
leave was restricted to seven days for workmen with less than ten years'

37

Table 1.15   Average earnings and hours of work per week in manufacturing in Singapore, Japan, South Korea, and Taiwan, 1959–65

Year	Singapore		Japan[a]		South Korea[b,d]	Taiwan[e]	
	Hours of work per week	Weekly earnings ($US)	Hours of work per week	Weekly earnings[b] ($US)	Weekly earnings ($US)	Hours of work per week	Weekly earnings ($US)
1959	46·7	12·1	47·3	14·5	1·2	57·0	4·5
1960	46·4	13·0	47·8	15·8	1·0	56·4	5·0
1961	46·6	12·9	47·0[c]	17·1[c]	0·5	55·8	5·9
1962	47·8	14·1	45·8	19·0	5·8	55·2	6·2
1963	47·7	14·4	45·5	20·9	6·4	55·2	6·5
1964	47·3	14·5	45·2[c]	23·1[c]	3·9	55·2	6·6
1965	47·2	14·5	44·3	25·0	4·3	54·6	7·2

[a] Figures include salaried employees.

[b] Figures include family allowances, and for Japan, mid and end of year bonuses.

[c] Sampling design revised.

[d] South Korean earnings rose steadily from 2,350 to 4,700 won per month between 1959 and 1965, but inflation in the late 1950s, currency reform in 1962, and devaluation in 1964, have affected international comparability.

[e] Figures are based on a six-day week and the figures for earnings include family allowances and value of payments in kind.

Sources: Singapore, *Annual Reports* of the Labour Department and Ministry of Labour, 1959–65; and figures for Japan, South Korea, and Taiwan calculated from International Labour Office, *Year Book of Labour Statistics 1967* (Geneva, n.d.), pp. 421, 512–13, 731–2.

continuous service and fourteen days for those with more than ten years' service. Retirement benefits other than those from the Central Provident Fund were only to be paid after seven years' continuous service. There was to be a tightening up of overtime and holiday payments. To spread employment, overtime was limited to forty-eight hours a month, and retirement became compulsory at fifty-five years of age.

In July 1968 amendments to the Industrial Relations Ordinance stipulated that collective agreements could not include more favourable employment conditions than those established by the Employment Act, and enabled employers to insist that managerial and executive staff could only join unions the membership of which was restricted to such positions. The Industrial Court's work in disputes concerning individual employers was streamlined and the Minister for Labour was given greater discretionary powers in such cases.[39]

Such relatively high standards of remuneration with correspondingly high labour costs had a twofold effect on the industrialisation process.

[39] Employment Act, 1968 (No. 17 of 1968) and Industrial Relations (Amendment) Act, 1968 (No. 25 of 1968).

Initially they made the emphasis on import replacement for a domestic market possible. Local effective demand was much greater than it would have been in any other Southeast Asian city with a similar population. The building of flats facilitated a change from nuclear towards conjugal household formation[40] and this stimulated the demand for household goods. However, as Singapore turned to manufacturing for export it could not afford to specialise in labour-intensive products, for labour costs were very high compared to those of such competitors as Taiwan and South Korea. In the early 1960s they were not much below those of Japan. Hours worked were considerably shorter than in Taiwan (Table 1.15). Entering world markets with a relatively high labour cost structure restricted Singapore's choice of manufacturing techniques.

SOCIAL SERVICES

The Singapore government considered that it could provide only limited social service improvements while problems of economic development and particularly of employment overshadowed Singapore. During the implementation of the Development Plan, the duration of which was extended to 1965, it was found that the Health Department program was unrealistic in view of the limited staff available, and some of the proposed improvements were pruned accordingly. The main impact of social service development was therefore concentrated on education and housing (Table 1.8), the two areas most affected by the 1950s' population growth.

During 1961–3 a new school was completed every month, and in 1964 the pace of school building was accelerated so that a new school was built every three weeks. A two-shift system is maintained to accommodate all the children seeking primary and secondary education. Expenditure on education was having an effect on the educational levels attained by 1966. In that year 11·5 per cent of the male and 40·1 per cent of the female population aged ten and over had no education, and the proportion rose to 38·7 per cent of males and 88·7 per cent of females in the fifty-five and over population. But in 1966 nearly all boys and girls aged seven to twelve were attending school, and 47 per cent of the males and 41 per cent of the females aged fifteen to nineteen were attending secondary schools or tertiary institutions. In the secondary and tertiary education age groups these proportions were not only higher than in most developing countries, but were also higher than in

[40] Yeh, *Fertility Decline in Singapore*, pp. 9–10.

many developed countries.[41] The availability of schooling, parents' pressure to obtain education for their children, and poor employment opportunities, all contributed to the relatively late ages for leaving school, but while educational attainments were high, they were not always of the sort required in the economy, and in particular there was a dearth of technical education at all levels. In 1968 the government turned its attention to rationalising and improving tertiary technical education by appointing Dr Toh Chin Chye, then Deputy Premier, Vice-Chancellor of the University of Singapore, the oldest tertiary institution, and at the same time retaining him in the Cabinet as Minister for the new portfolio of Science and Technology.[42] An improvement in the training of technicians at the post-secondary school level is also expected to follow.

The most successful performance was in housing. Until 1959 the Singapore Improvement Trust, a public housing corporation set up before World War II, was responsible for public housing. Its peak year was 1958 when 3,841 housing units were completed, and it had completed 23,019 units and housed 8·8 per cent of the population by 1959. The Trust was replaced by the Housing Development Board which completed a peak of 13,028 dwellings in 1964 and a total of 67,089 for 1961–6. Slum and squatter clearance was far from complete, but by

Table 1.16 Singapore gross domestic expenditure, at factor and market prices, and expenditure at market prices in current and constant prices, 1960–6

Year	Gross domestic expenditure at factor cost $ m.	Gross domestic expenditure at market prices $ m.	Per capita gross domestic expenditure at market prices in current prices[a] $	Consumer price index, Apr.–May 1960=100, at Dec. of each year	Per capita gross domestic expenditure at market price in 1960 prices $
1960	2,016	2,131	1,304	100·9	1,304
1961	2,304	2,428	1,439	100·8	1,440
1962	2,407	2,536	1,464	101·7	1,452
1963	2,745	2,876	1,620	105·3	1,552
1964	2,811	2,956	1,624	105·7	1,550
1965	3,013	3,182	1,706	106·8	1,612
1966	3,187	3,377	1,765	108·2	1,646

[a]Calculated from mid-year population estimates.

Sources: United Nations, *Yearbook of National Account Statistics 1966* (New York, 1967), Singapore Department of Statistics data, and Singapore, *Monthly Digest of Statistics*, Vol. 3, June 1964, p. 122 and Vol. 6, September 1967, p. 117.

[41] You Poh Seng, 'The Population of Singapore, 1966', pp. 79–83.
[42] *Sunday Times* (Singapore), 10 March 1968.

Table 1.17   Singapore gross capital formation, 1960–6

| Year | Gross capital formation | | | Gross capital formation as percentage of gross domestic expenditure |
	Private	Public $ million	Total	
1960	a	a	138·5	6·4
1961	135	92	226·6	9·3
1962	135	120	255·1	10·1
1963	158	165	323·2	11·2
1964	202	212	414·7	14·0
1965	250	214	463·8	14·6
1966	255	199	454·1	13·4

ª Not available.

Sources: United Nations, *Yearbook of National Accounts Statistics 1966* (New York, 1967), and Singapore Department of Statistics data.

1966 24 per cent of the Singapore population was accommodated in government flats or houses.[43] The housing provided was utilitarian, but each flat had a kitchen and bathroom in addition to one, two, or three bedrooms, and terrace houses had been built. Some of the housing development was on reclaimed land. This volume of building activity stimulated building materials manufactures, particularly cement, since most of the public housing was high rise building. The brick, tile, paints, and builders' hardware industries also benefited.

Singapore's per capita gross domestic expenditure at market prices grew from $1,304 in 1960 to $1,765 in 1966 in current prices (Table 1.16), a rate of 5·13 per cent a year. As the consumers' price index only grew at 1·13 per cent a year in this period, most of the gain was real, and per capita gross domestic expenditure at market prices, in constant prices, grew at 3·9 per cent a year.[44] Opportunities for family planning and improvements in education and housing in addition represented a

[43] Singapore, *Annual Report 1965 Housing and Development Board*, pp. 8–10, and Housing and Development Board information.
[44] Professor Oshima estimated that between 1960 and 1965 prices rose slightly less than the official index indicated, and that gross domestic product at market prices rose somewhat more than the official gross domestic expenditure at market prices series (H. T. Oshima, 'Growth and Unemployment in Singapore', *Malayan Economic Review*, Vol. 12, October 1967, p. 49). The official estimates of per capita gross domestic expenditure at market prices, in constant prices from 1960 to 1965, give a growth rate of 4·4 per cent a year, whereas Professor Oshima's estimates of per capita Gross Domestic Product at constant prices give a growth rate of 5·7 per cent a year for this period.

marked advance in the welfare of lower income groups. Domestic gross capital formation, greatly stimulated by public sector activity, at the same time rose from $138·5 million in 1960 when it was 7 per cent of gross domestic expenditure to $454·1 million in 1966 when it was 14 per cent of gross domestic expenditure (Table 1.17). These changes may not be spectacular, but in view of the difficulties which Singapore faced in its first years of independence they represent solid economic achievement.

PROSPECTS FOR MANUFACTURING

The increasing importance of manufacturing had become evident in 1964 when it was able to take up some of the slack due to Confrontation, although construction industries, deliberately encouraged by government spending, were also important in preventing an expected decline in national income.[45] Diminishing activity in rubber processing, which had contributed a peak 23 per cent to value added in manufacturing in 1960, but only 7 per cent in 1964 (Table 1.4), tended to offset the increase in total manufacturing activity, but by the mid-1960s a distinct shift to manufacturing was nevertheless evident.[46]

Because manufacturing productivity was increasing, the numbers employed in manufacturing did not grow as rapidly as value added, but it made a significant contribution to the increase in employment opportunities. Between 1959 and 1966 employment in manufacturing establishments with ten or more workers grew by some 25,000 (Table 1.4). If it is assumed that the 1963 employment ratio between establishments with five to nine workers and establishments with more than ten workers was maintained throughout this period, the additional number employed by establishments with five to nine workers would be 2,500, making a total addition of 27,500 employed in manufacturing. This represented 40 per cent of the increase of 68,000 employed between 1957 and 1966 (calculated from Table 1.7).

[45] Oshima's gross domestic product and official gross domestic expenditure estimates agree that there was slight growth between 1963 and 1964, the year in which Confrontation had the most impact, so that the decline in income per head was negligible.

[46] D. J. Blake and F. Y. Koh, *The Foreign Trade Ratio as an Indicator of Economic Change in Singapore 1949–1965*, Research Monograph No. 1 (Economic Research Centre, University of Singapore, June 1967, mimeographed), conclude that the period 1949 to 1965 saw a significant change in the structure of the Singapore economy with a declining dependence on entrepôt trade and an increasing reliance on manufacturing.

The increase in employment in manufacturing was approaching the early 1960s' target of 5,000 to 6,000 a year annually by the mid-1960s, but, together with the employment growth in other industries, it was not sufficient to prevent the growth in the number of unemployed from 24,200 in 1957 to 52,600 in 1966 (Table 1.7). The unemployed were then at least 9 per cent of the workforce.[47] Prospects for the late 1960s were just as gloomy, for no sooner had Singapore overcome the effects of Confrontation than it was faced with the withdrawal of British armed forces. It was estimated that in 1967 expenditure generated locally by the British military base in Singapore was about 14 per cent of gross national expenditure, and half of this will be phased out by 1971. In addition, 18,000 retrenched military base workers will be thrown on the labour market between 1968 and 1971. During this period 25,000 teenagers will also enter the labour market every year.[48]

The Singapore government has shown outstanding resilience and determination in handling a situation which exacerbates its difficulties afresh. Once again entrepôt trade will not be neglected. A substantial revival of the trade with Indonesia, amounting to exports of $355 million, had been accomplished in 1967, and exports of $300 million a year, albeit mainly petroleum and petroleum products which had few secondary effects on the economy of Singapore, went to the Republic of Vietnam in that year. The Economic Development Board is making a special effort to help foreign firms establish wholesaling and repairing headquarters for Southeast Asia in Singapore to boost entrepôt trade,

---

[47] This is probably a conservative figure. Professor Oshima calculated that the full-time unemployment equivalent of those partially unemployed adds another 8,446 unemployed, making a total of 10·5 per cent of the workforce unemployed in 1966 (Oshima, op. cit., p. 37). Professor You Poh Seng suggests that another 1·0 to 1·5 per cent of the workforce were not looking for work because they did not believe it was available, and this would raise total unemployment to almost 13 per cent (You Poh Seng, 'The Population of Singapore, 1966', p. 89). R. Hirono, 'Labor Force, Employment and Earnings in Singapore', *Seizi Keizai Ronso* [Journal of Economics and Political Science], (Seikei University), Vol. 15, 1965, p. 524, estimated that there were over 60,000 persons, or about 10 per cent, unemployed in Singapore in 1964 out of a workforce of 606,373. D. J. Blake, 'Employment and Unemployment in Singapore', in W. E. Chalmers (ed.), *Crucial Issues in Industrial Relations in Singapore* (Singapore, 1967), p. 182, estimated that unemployment was as high as 15 per cent of the workforce in 1961 and 1962, but that it dropped down to 12·3 per cent by 1965.

[48] Dr Goh Keng Swee, Finance Minister, Budget address to the Legislative Assembly, 5 December 1967. *Parliamentary Debates*, Singapore, Vol. 26, 1967.

and foster further manufacturing developments. Tourism is being encouraged, and plans approved in 1967 are expected to create some 25,000 jobs by 1971.[49] Urban renewal and land reclamation is being undertaken and the government is stimulating private domestic building. But all such efforts are still secondary compared with the emphasis on the growth of manufacturing, the high productivity and multiplier effects of which in further income and employment creation are central to Singapore's economic development.

In his Budget speech in December 1967, outlining the measures the government proposed to take to deal with the situation arising from the British withdrawal, Dr Goh Keng Swee emphasised:

> I want to establish beyond all doubts that to counteract the effects of the military reductions and reduce the large number of unemployed persons, we will have literally to re-double our present efforts to promote industrial growth.[50]

An expansion of manufacturing could only be achieved if more manufactured goods were exported and the government introduced taxation concessions 'designed to provide the maximum incentives to exporters, without at the same time allowing them too much fat.'[51] Profits of approved manufacturing companies from the export of new manufactured goods and additions to exports were to be taxed at only 4 per cent.[52] There was to be a new emphasis on engineering industries which were both capital- and labour-intensive, and for which Singapore's highly educated workforce would be particularly well suited once appropriate improvements in technical education were made. The Economic Development Board should be more adventurous in industrial financing,

[49] Ibid.

[50] Ibid.

[51] Dr Goh Keng Swee, introducing the Economic Expansion Incentives (Relief from Income Tax) Bill's second reading in the Singapore Legislative Assembly, 5 December 1967, ibid.

[52] The Economic Expansion Incentives (Relief from Income Tax) Act, 1967 (No. 36 of 1967), Part IV. The provision was even more generous than it seemed because in order to simplify accounting procedures for the firms and the government, 'established markets' were ones to which a firm had exported regularly for five years, and profits on exports were to be regarded as the same as profits on domestic sales, and total profits were therefore to be simply apportioned between exports and total sales by the share of exports in total sales. Since profits on exports were usually lower than on domestic sales this meant that the actual value of the tax concession was greater than its face value. Firms enjoying these privileges, however, were no longer able to use double deduction for expenses incurred in opening up new export markets.

but above all foreign investors would continue to be wooed and encouraged for they alone had the applied technical knowledge which Singapore's increasingly sophisticated industries would need. The Pioneer Industries Ordinance was accordingly repealed and re-enacted in 1967 with amendments which reduced income tax on earnings from approved royalties, technical assistance fees, and contributions to research and development to 20 per cent instead of the regular 40 per cent company income tax, and remitted them altogether if they were used to acquire share capital in the company from which the payments were received. To encourage foreign firms to finance new installations by loans, interest on overseas loans of at least $200,000 was made tax free.[53]

Foreign investment was thus still regarded as crucial to industrial development. The extent of the total contribution of direct foreign investment to investment, output, and employment in manufacturing, and its importance in less quantifiable aspects of industrial development such as the transfer of sophisticated technology, were not known, but to the Singapore government it seemed that whatever costs foreign investment imposed, the benefits it brought were greater. The chapters which follow endeavour to examine more closely the contribution made by the principal foreign investors to the growth of Singapore manufacturing.

[53] Ibid., Part V.

United Kingdom Investment

Thirty years ago more than 70 per cent of total foreign investment in Singapore and Malaya was United Kingdom investment. Most of this was direct investment in banking and in commerce, in tin mining and in rubber. There was very little United Kingdom direct investment in manufacturing industry. Of the twenty-two United Kingdom manufacturing firms now in Singapore only three were in production before the war and of these one was the subsidiary of a United Kingdom company which resumed manufacturing in 1959 after having closed down that side of its business as far back as 1932.

Another three United Kingdom manufacturing firms established factories in Singapore in 1948, 1949, and 1957, and these were no doubt among the only eight factories in Singapore considered to be 'modern and efficient by western standards' in 1959.[1] It is since 1959 that Singapore has made notable progress in industrialisation, and of the twenty-two United Kingdom manufacturing firms whose experience is described in this paper, sixteen began production between 1961 and 1967.[2]

It is conceivable that the sixteen United Kingdom manufacturing firms established in Singapore in the period 1961 to 1967 were attracted to Singapore by industrialisation itself. It is significant that only four

[1] 'An Industrial Development Programme', Legislative Assembly, Singapore, *Sessional Paper*, No. Cmd 5 of 1959, p. 9.
[2] In recording the fact that information was provided by each of the twenty-two United Kingdom firms mentioned above I would like to express my thanks to the businessmen in London and Singapore, not all of them associated with those firms, who so generously offered comment and opinion about United Kingdom direct investment in Singapore manufacturing industry. Normally courteous, their kindness to me was unfailing.

United Kingdom companies had a manufacturing operation in Singapore on 5 March 1957 when the All-Party Mission to London was instructed, by the Singapore Legislative Assembly, to secure from Her Majesty's government in the United Kingdom the status of a self-governing state for the people of Singapore. Yet neither industrialisation nor political independence seems to have been especially important in attracting United Kingdom direct investment in manufacturing to Singapore, and apart from the minority of United Kingdom companies which regard Singapore as a centre for their Southeast Asian operations most United Kingdom companies appear to have been induced to invest in Singapore manufacturing because other countries were doing so, or seemed likely to do so.

Table 2.1   Manufacturing commencement date of firms with United Kingdom capital investment in Singapore, by industry

	Pre-1957	1957-1960	1961	1962	1963	1964	1965	1966	1967
Metal products	1	1	—	1	—	2	1	—	—
Petroleum products	—	—	1	2	2	—	—	—	—
Electrical products	—	—	—	—	1	—	1	1	—
Other manufactures	3	1	—	—	—	1	—	1	2
Total	4	2	1	3	3	3	2	2	2

According to the *Straits Times* for 5 August 1967, the total paid-up capital in manufacturing industries established in Singapore in the period 1961 to 1966 was $190 million, of which slightly more than half was direct foreign investment. Of this direct foreign investment Japan was said to have a 24·0 per cent share of paid-up capital, Canada 15·3 per cent, the United States 13·5 per cent, Malaysia 11·0 per cent, Hong Kong 10 per cent, the United Kingdom 7·0 per cent, Taiwan 6·2 per cent, Switzerland 3·8 per cent, and Australia 3·2 per cent.[3]

The *Straits Times* report goes on to say that the United Kingdom was associated with fewer than six Singapore manufacturing enterprises in production, under construction, or approved up to the end of December

[3] Some of the discrepancy between these figures and the real situation is due to the fact that several of the British firms covered in this study made their investment in Singapore through other countries, notably Canada and Malaysia. Some is due to the fact that the sum of $190 million appears only to include pioneer firms. Even with these qualifications, however, the figures quoted are inaccurate.

1966. These statistics would not have been quoted were it not that they help to explain why I was told repeatedly in Singapore in the summer of 1967 that the United Kingdom share in Singapore's manufacturing industry was disappointingly small. That it should be so regarded is natural in view of the fact that the United Kingdom continues to hold the dominant share in direct foreign investment in Singapore banking and commerce, but there is more to it than this. As Table 2.2 shows, the book values of net assets attributable to United Kingdom direct investment in Singapore's non-petroleum manufacturing industry do not compare well, in terms of market size as measured by gross domestic product, with the book values of net assets attributable to United Kingdom direct investment in non-petroleum manufacturing industry in most other sterling area developing countries. If, however, we add to the Singapore figure the United Kingdom investment in two petroleum refineries, in brake fluids, in lubricants, and in bitumen manufacture, it is much more likely that United Kingdom direct investment in Singapore manufacturing industry is comparable, in terms of market size, with United Kingdom direct investment in other sterling area developing countries.

Table 2.2   Book values of net assets attributable to United Kingdom direct investment in non-petroleum manufacturing industry in sterling area developing countries, December 1965

	U.K. direct investment (Y) £ m.	Gross domestic product (X) £ m.
Malawi	0·6	52
Singapore	2·1	353
Jamaica	2·9	350
Zambia	3·2	306
Trinidad and Tobago	5·9	240
Hong Kong	6·0	431
Ghana	6·8	670
Ceylon	7·8	580
Pakistan	17·9[a]	3,583
Malaysia	19·8[a]	928
East Africa[b]	23·0	844
India	151·2	17,203

[a] Figures are incomplete.

[b] The data for Kenya, Uganda, and Tanzania are not quoted separately. Until recently British investors regarded these countries as a single investment outlet.

Sources: H.M.S.O., *Board of Trade Journal*, Vol. 194, 26 January 1968, pp. ix–x; United Nations publications and country data.

The above data, plotted on a scatter diagram, would show a very close linear relationship between United Kingdom direct investment and gross domestic product of the form $Y = 2\cdot467 + \cdot008X$ ($R^2 = \cdot9724$). On this basis one would expect British direct investment in Singapore to be about £6 million ($51·4 million) rather than £2·1 million ($18 million). It should be remembered, however, that United Kingdom investment of roughly £5 million ($42·9 million) in Singapore's petroleum industry is not included in the above data, that book values of net assets attributable to United Kingdom investors are not a particularly good measure of the net worth of United Kingdom direct investment overseas, and that United Kingdom direct investment in Singapore has probably been less than it would have been had Singapore not seceded from Malaysia, even allowing for the fact that a number of United Kingdom firms were established in Singapore in the expectation that Singapore would remain part of Malaysia.

It is difficult to explain why a close linear relationship should exist between the book values of net assets attributable to United Kingdom direct investment in non-petroleum manufacturing industry and gross domestic product in the twelve territories listed in Table 2.2, or to explain why there should also be a close linear relationship between United Kingdom direct investment and gross domestic product in sterling area developed countries of the form $Y = 41\cdot122 + \cdot024X$ ($R^2 = \cdot7884$) for the same date. We know, however, that the greater part of United Kingdom direct investment in sterling area developing territories has been undertaken during the past ten years by a comparatively small number of United Kingdom companies with subsidiaries in several of these territories. It is likely that policies similar to those adopted by United Kingdom companies in Singapore have been applied to United Kingdom manufacturing operations in other sterling area developing countries. To generalise from the Singapore experience one would expect United Kingdom investment in these countries to be geared to existing market size. Because of the way in which book values are defined we can also surmise that our statistical result might not have been so good had not the growth of United Kingdom direct investment in manufacturing taken place simultaneously in the twelve territories listed in Table 2.2. This suggests that there is a common factor influencing the decision to invest in each sterling area developing country. Singapore experience would lead us to suppose that this common factor is the desire by the parent United Kingdom company to retain a market, opened up by exports, which is in danger of being lost to foreign, or more exceptionally locally-owned, competitors. There is also an implication that foreign competitors have become more active in sterling area developing countries during the past ten years, partly as a consequence of the liberalisation of restrictions on capital flows from the main investing countries.

THE OPERATIONS OF UNITED KINGDOM FIRMS IN SINGAPORE

Companies based in London have a controlling interest in the twenty-two United Kingdom manufacturing firms at present in Singapore. They hold directly, or through their Malaysian subsidiaries, majority shares in fifteen of the firms.[4] In seven firms British minority capital is combined with third country capital in such a way as to ensure control over company policy by the United Kingdom partner.

Included among the twenty-two firms are two of Singapore's three oil refineries and concerns manufacturing brake fluids, lubricants, bitumen, metal and plastic containers, crown cork closures, water meters, welded wire mesh, cold drawn steel wire, roll formed galvanised steel sheets, industrial batteries, electric light bulbs, television aerials, ceiling fans, electric irons, industrial gases, paints, gramophone records, cosmetics, and cigarettes, in addition to the ship building, ship repair, and general engineering done since 1929 by the United Kingdom company which owns the oldest British manufacturing enterprise in Singapore.

Excluded from the survey are firms owned wholly, or in part, by former Singapore residents who now live in England, and firms owned wholly, or in part, by Singapore agency companies in which United Kingdom residents have a substantial portfolio interest. While a complete survey of these firms was not possible it does seem that the Singapore agency firms are actively seeking a stake in Singapore's industry because of their desire to extend their investment by participating in Singapore's industrialisation. For these agency firms the preferred form of investment in manufacturing appears to be the joint venture in which a foreign or local partner manages the firm whose products the agency will market.

[4] Three Singapore manufacturing firms are wholly owned by the Malaysian subsidiaries of three United Kingdom companies. One of these Malaysian subsidiaries is wholly owned by the United Kingdom parent company, the other two are public companies in which Singapore and Malaysian citizens have a minority interest. For the purpose of this survey each of these three Singapore manufacturing firms is regarded as the direct subsidiary of a United Kingdom company.

50

Joint ventures involving United Kingdom and Singapore capital are the exception rather than the rule. A reason for this, apart from the stated preference of most United Kingdom companies for sole ownership of subsidiaries, is that many British companies had marketing subsidiaries in Singapore long before they began manufacturing in that country, dating back in the case of one United Kingdom company to the turn of the century. In such circumstances there is no very compelling argument for United Kingdom companies to combine on their manufacturing side with a Singapore partner contributing local marketing experience to the joint venture. Even among the minority of United Kingdom companies which had no previous sales organisation in Singapore only one United Kingdom company had allied itself with an agency company, and with this exception, the local participation in issued capital in all joint ventures involving United Kingdom and Singapore capital represents no more than a residual holding in a Singapore manufacturing firm acquired by a United Kingdom company as an alternative to establishing its own factory in Singapore.

Singapore and Malaysian citizens are also minority shareholders in the two United Kingdom subsidiaries in Malaysia which have wholly-owned Singapore subsidiaries. These Malaysian subsidiaries became public companies some years before independence because it is the policy of the two parent companies in the United Kingdom to allow local participation in issued capital in all of their operations overseas; both companies are financially capable of sole ownership of their subsidiaries.

With the exception of the above companies the United Kingdom companies now operating in Singapore have a preference for sole ownership of subsidiaries. This form of ownership of subsidiaries is said by most executives greatly to simplify management problems. Although few executives felt it necessary to elaborate on this theme, possibly because this advantage of the sole ownership principle was to them self-evident, it does seem that sole ownership makes it much easier for United Kingdom management to plan operations internationally without having to account separately to their own shareholders, or to a third party, for the current profitability of each of their subsidiaries in overseas markets.

Bearing in mind that United Kingdom companies generally expect to generate cash for expanding their Singapore operation from the sales of the product manufactured by their local subsidiary, it is clear that an overly generous dividend policy could be an important constraint on the growth of the Singapore firm. Here again the sole ownership is an

51

advantage if, as is asserted by a number of executives on the basis of their experience in other countries, a local or third country minority partner is more likely to demand an immediate return on capital than the United Kingdom parent. Unfortunately, however, the sample of British firms in Singapore is so small and their operation so recent that it is difficult to decide whether this would be the case for Singapore. It is true that there are only a handful of British firms in Singapore which declared a dividend in 1966 in contrast to the very much larger number of firms which retained profit in the business, but there is no very clear association between ownership and dividend policy in the sense that dividend policy seems to be the more conservative the greater is the United Kingdom company's share in the issued capital of its subsidiary. Perhaps the only comment that it is safe to make is that a conservative dividend policy is on the whole characteristic of United Kingdom firms in Singapore, although one or two firms have remitted substantial profits overseas.

The chief executive of one United Kingdom company investing in Singapore said that his board 'paid attention to the deposition of capital, investment policy, the return on capital and the related appraisal of results among all their overseas subsidiaries'. Similar remarks were made by other executives. Typical was the executive who described the principal controls which his company used in respect of its overseas operations as follows:

1. The approval of annual budgets, trading profits and capital expenditure;
2. Monthly reporting against these budgets showing itemised sales by departments, gross profit margins, net profit and cash flow statements; significant diversions from budget to be taken up in correspondence;
3. Specific approval on capital expenditure projects which come up during the course of the year and which have not been foreseen at the time of budgeting;
4. The provision of finance;
5. The appointment of the managing director and the finance director.

Although no United Kingdom company would object to appointing a local man to head its Singapore operation 'if he had the right experience' none of the companies had done so, and at present each United Kingdom manufacturing firm in Singapore is managed by an expatriate who is either the managing director of the Singapore manufacturing subsidiary or the chairman of its board by virtue of his position as chief executive of the Singapore marketing subsidiary of the parent company. This situation is not expected to alter in the immediate future.

With this exception few United Kingdom manufacturing firms employ expatriates, and of the two thousand persons employed by these firms only forty-one are not Singapore or Malaysian citizens. Seven United Kingdom manufacturing firms employ no expatriates at all, although in the case of these firms the local manager is directly responsible to the expatriate chief executive of another Singapore subsidiary of the United Kingdom parent.

Not surprisingly the firms said that they were not under any pressure from the Singapore government to employ local citizens, and all of them were of the opinion that they could employ more expatriates at top managerial and technical level if they wanted to. They added that nowadays it was difficult to recruit suitable staff overseas and that the question of doing so seldom arose.

Less expected was the fact that the degree of control exercised by the United Kingdom parent over its overseas subsidiaries in general, rather than over its Singapore subsidiary in particular, was said to be greater than it had been a few years ago. Several reasons were given for this trend. One was the increasing sophistication of business management practice. Another was the greater volume of business directly attributable to manufacturing operations overseas. A possible reason hinted at by one executive concerned recruitment of senior executives for overseas subsidiaries. It was said that in the past it was quite usual for the local managing director to be an expatriate who had joined the overseas subsidiary as a junior executive. More recently junior executives had been recruited locally, and since few of these had much experience in the firm it was to be expected that an increasing number of senior executives would be expatriates transferred from other subsidiaries within the group or seconded from the parent company. In these circumstances it was reasonable to expect that head office would keep a closer watch on the activities of its various subsidiaries than had seemed necessary, or indeed possible, in the days when their overseas operations had been headed by men whose entire career had been made in a particular foreign country. Recruitment policies for senior management do appear to have changed in recent years, but there is not much evidence that it is this which has brought about the changed company policy towards control over subsidiaries rather than the increasing sophistication of business management practice or the growing volume of business done by overseas manufacturing subsidiaries. Control is anyway too strong a word to use for it implies that the board of the United Kingdom parent company actually initiates policy for its various overseas subsidiaries. On the contrary the Singapore evidence suggests that the chief executive of the subsidiary controls all the day-by-day activities of the company's operations in a particular country and that it is he who, through the local board of directors, initiates major capital expenditure, product development, sales, wages, and employment policy. It is, however, usual for all such policies to be submitted to London for approval. As one executive put it 'each subsidiary is in large measure autonomous, its management being concerned with the business of that company and very much a part of the environment in which it operates although the Board of the parent company has to strike a balance, taking account of all circumstances, to achieve the best results for each subsidiary within the framework of total capital and other resources available'.

In the task of reconciling local interest with overall company policy the United Kingdom companies may have been more successful than most. In Singapore I was told by many businessmen that the managing director of the average United Kingdom manufacturing firm has considerably more room for manoeuvre than his American or Japanese counterpart in initiating changes in company policy. Granted that this is the case it must be remarked, however, that United Kingdom firms in Singapore are normally product rather than market orientated and that it would be a most unusual firm which would invest in products and processes not identifiable with those of the parent company. Indeed the overwhelming majority of United Kingdom firms in Singapore manufacture only a very small range of products, and some only produce a single commodity. In such circumstances the opportunities for independent action are limited. The most likely reason for the concentration of United Kingdom firms in a limited range of products is simply that the Singapore market is too small to allow them to use the highly capital-intensive methods of production with which they are most familiar for anything other than an extremely limited range of products. This is why, for example, the fragmentation of markets through the introduction of tariffs between Singapore and Malaysia has seriously reduced the growth potential of a number of United Kingdom firms in Singapore.

It was said earlier in this paper that most United Kingdom companies appear to have been induced to invest in Singapore manufacturing industry because other countries and, more exceptionally local businessmen in Singapore, were investing in competitor firms, or seemed likely to do so. It is necessary to review some of the evidence that leads to this conclusion in more detail.

We can begin by noting that no United Kingdom company gave the desire for profit as the immediate cause of its decision to invest in

Singapore. One company even went so far as to say that it was concerned merely to break even on its Singapore operation. By this it probably meant that its investment in Singapore manufacturing industry was in the nature of a 'loss leader' to ensure the continued importation into Singapore of those products of the parent company which were not manufactured in Singapore. There were other companies which said that profits in Singapore were less than profits in the United Kingdom, but in this case it is much less certain that the companies had from the first regarded their investment in Singapore as being in any sense a 'loss leader'. By contrast it is known that there are two United Kingdom firms in Singapore which made a profit retained in business plus dividends equivalent to between 15 and 20 per cent of the value of their sales in 1966. Such returns are, however, greatly in excess of the average profit made by the thirteen United Kingdom firms for which data are available. In 1966 their profit was 8 per cent of sales. Other evidence suggests that there has been a fall in the average rate of return to United Kingdom direct investment in Singapore expressed as a percentage of the book values of net assets attributable to United Kingdom investors (Table 2.3).

Table 2.3   Average rates of return[a] on book values of net assets attributable to United Kingdom investors in Singapore, Hong Kong, and Malaysia, 1960–5[b]

	1960	1961	1962	1963	1964	1965
Singapore	30·0	32·7	26·7	c	c	14·8
Hong Kong	22·4	20·7	20·7	13·7	14·6	21·5
Malaysia	17·8	17·1	14·8	15·3	15·8	14·5
All sterling area developing countries	10·8	9·7	9·1	9·4	9·7	9·0

[a] After overseas tax.

[b] Includes book values of net assets in non-manufacturing industry but excludes direct investment in petroleum manufacturing industry.

[c] Figures not available.

Source: H.M.S.O., *Board of Trade Journal*, Vol. 194, 26 January 1968, p. xvi.

The figures quoted in Table 2.3 are much higher for Singapore between 1960 and 1963 than I would have expected them to have been on the basis of the material I collected in Singapore. I am not able to account fully for this discrepancy; to some extent the sharp fall in recorded profit in 1965 was brought about by Confrontation and the break-up of Malaysia. In 1965 the average rate of return on United Kingdom direct investment in Singapore was practically the same as that in Hong Kong and Malaysia in 1964 and in Malaysia in 1965.

Although the statistics for other sterling area developing countries have not been quoted there is no easily discernible relationship between recorded profit and the book values of net assets attributable to United Kingdom investors in these countries.

The four United Kingdom companies whose manufacturing operations in Singapore were started before 1957 are companies the principal products of which carry the natural protection of high freight cost because output is bulky in relation to input.

We cannot be certain why the above companies came to Singapore but it is believed that one United Kingdom company was induced to make a fairly large initial capital investment in Singapore in order to retain its hold on a market which might otherwise have been lost to the newly-established Singapore manufacturing enterprise of its principal foreign competitor. A second United Kingdom company, whose Singapore operation dates from 1948, was apparently induced to make a very much smaller initial investment to test an expanding market in manufactured cans for the Malayan pineapple canning industry which had hitherto been supplied by less efficient local producers. It will be recalled that in the period of dollar shortage immediately after the war there had been an attempt by the British Ministry of Food to discourage the importation into the United Kingdom of products, such as canned pineapples, from hard currency areas.

For the majority of United Kingdom non-petroleum manufacturing companies which have started production in Singapore during the past ten years the immediate reason for having a Singapore subsidiary was said to be the desire to prevent a market opened up by British exports from being lost to local or foreign-owned manufacturing firms in Singapore. Typical of the comments made are the following:

> If we had not gone in someone else would have, which made the decision inevitable, although we would much prefer to carry on treating Singapore as an export market.
>
> The reason for acquiring manufacturing facilities in Singapore was the progressive exclusion of imports of our products and our desire to maintain sales in Singapore and to expand our operation in the area generally.
>
> Our main competitors were building factories in Singapore and we felt that we should be represented in the market.
>
> The decision to invest in local manufactures in Singapore is the same as that which applies to other territories, that is if we do not go into local

manufacture we lose what business we have, because of the introduction of local manufactures from other sources and/or the imposition of penal import duties.

The main fear was that, once established, the local or foreign-owned competitor firms in Singapore might be afforded tariff protection. There was also some feeling that in a market as small as Singapore's the company which came into local production first could almost certainly monopolise that market because no competitor company could hope to achieve reasonable returns to investment in a divided market. As far as is known no United Kingdom company decided to start manufacturing in Singapore in order to obtain for itself tariff protection for a product which was being priced out of the Singapore market by cheaper imports from other countries, although it is believed that one company, whose Singapore factory is export oriented, might have been hoping to secure a greater measure of protection by locating its subsidiary there. With this and perhaps one other exception no United Kingdom non-petroleum manufacturing firm in Singapore can be said to be export oriented in the sense that the immediate cause for its establishment in Singapore was the desire to cater to markets outside Singapore and Malaysia. It is significant that of all the United Kingdom companies now manufacturing in Singapore one of these two companies was the only United Kingdom company which admitted to having considered another Asian location for its factory.

As far as the petroleum manufacturing companies are concerned, geography probably played the major role in attracting two United Kingdom petroleum refineries to Singapore, for although both refineries sell most of their current output in Singapore they were planned as 'export refineries' with a balancing role in meeting the product requirements of other United Kingdom subsidiary and associated companies in Southeast Asia.

The granting of pioneer status may have been an important contributory factor leading to the establishment of United Kingdom firms in Singapore from 1961 to 1967, for in spite of such comments as 'we would have come in anyway', fifteen of the sixteen United Kingdom firms established in Singapore in these years are, or have been, pioneer industries. The firm which is not is one of the very few United Kingdom firms in which the United Kingdom participation in issued capital is unusually small. It could be conjectured that the absence of pioneer status would make the Singapore market a much less attractive investment prospect for United Kingdom capital.

57

Important advantages of pioneer status are accelerated depreciation and exemption from corporate tax for a period of up to five years from the date in which commercial production is started by approved firms. Six United Kingdom pioneer firms with an investment in fixed assets of more than $1 million received the full five-year tax exemption; the other nine United Kingdom pioneer firms received tax exemption for shorter periods depending on the size of their capital investment.

It can be argued that profits are unusually low during the first few years of a firm's operation and that firms will not gain much from a five-year tax holiday, but near capacity producers of a limited range of products for a known domestic market are as likely to make profits in the first year of production as in any other. To such firms a tax holiday can be an important concession.

In Singapore there are United Kingdom companies which have made gains from the tax holiday. Some companies chose to expand their Singapore operation by establishing additional 'pioneer' manufacturing subsidiaries instead of enlarging the size of their existing manufacturing subsidiaries, in spite of the fact that the share capital in their new enterprise was held in a form identical with that of the first of their manufacturing subsidiaries in Singapore. But although the desire to obtain an extension of tax holiday concessions probably caused an increase in the number of United Kingdom firms in Singapore we do not know what effect it had on the overall size of United Kingdom direct investment in Singapore. This investment probably would, as is usually claimed, have come in anyway because of the need to protect a market threatened by foreign or locally-owned manufacturing firms. Nevertheless there is some ground for believing that had pioneer status not existed a few United Kingdom companies would have waited longer before coming to Singapore. Some may have decided to stay out of the market altogether.

Like pioneer status, the existence of the Jurong industrial estate may have helped in attracting foreign firms to Singapore. Its effect on United Kingdom investment is, however, small, and only a handful of United Kingdom firms located in Jurong. It can be no surprise, therefore, that British businessmen in Singapore are much more critical of the facilities offered by the Jurong industrial estate than are the American or Japanese businessmen whose main investment in Singapore is at Jurong.

The main criticism of Jurong is that it is difficult of access from Singapore and, by implication, that it has encouraged investment outside the urban area where its marginal social, as well as private, net product would have been greater.

With the above exception British businessmen in Singapore are uncritical of the methods adopted by the Singapore government to promote industry in Singapore, although there are British businessmen who are of the opinion that the Economic Development Board may have involved itself unnecessarily in the continuing dialogue between industry and government. Such a dialogue, however, lies at the heart of an effective development strategy.

CONTRIBUTION TO SINGAPORE'S ECONOMY

It is not our purpose to examine Singapore's development strategy, but we need to say something about the contribution made by United Kingdom manufacturing firms to employment, value added, and exports in Singapore.

In August 1967 the twenty-two United Kingdom firms with which this paper is concerned provided employment for slightly over two thousand persons, or about 4 per cent of the manufacturing workforce in establishments with ten or more workers, and 0·4 per cent of the total workforce. Two United Kingdom firms employ between them more than one thousand persons. By contrast thirteen United Kingdom firms had fewer than fifty employees (Table 2.4).

Table 2.4 Size of manufacturing firms with United Kingdom capital investment in Singapore, by number employed and industry, August 1967

	1–50	51–100	101–200	201–400	Over 400
Metal products	4	1	—	—	1
Petroleum products	1	3	1	—	—
Electrical products	3	—	—	—	—
Other manufactures	5	—	1	1	1
Total	13	4	2	1	2

Older firms are generally the main employers of labour, but it is noteworthy that there has been almost no increase in the number of persons employed in United Kingdom firms since 1964. With the exception of the firms which started production in 1967, no United Kingdom company of which this question was asked expected an increase in its labour force over the next two years. On this evidence it cannot be said that the United Kingdom firms will make much of a contribution towards solving Singapore's problem of unemployment in the foreseeable future.

The contribution made by United Kingdom firms in training Singapore workers in industrial techniques is not measurable. In one sense this contribution has been small, for although United Kingdom firms have brought new techniques and processes to Singapore these techniques involve an extensive use of capital and are almost invariably specific to the particular firms concerned, with the result that the simple skills demanded of production line workers are of little direct use in other factories. In another sense the chronic shortage of technical staff and managers in Singapore, coupled with their high cost elsewhere, has created a situation in which many United Kingdom firms have needed to do far more than they expected to provide facilities for training senior staff. A notable example is the United Kingdom firm which as early as 1957 had sent ten of its senior local staff for training in England.

The contribution of United Kingdom firms to value added in manufacturing in Singapore depends on the size and the nature of these firms. An indication of the nature by outlay of thirteen of the United Kingdom firms is given in Table 2.5. It has been presented in this form to avoid disclosure of individual company accounts. For the same reason specific comment is withheld about particular items in Table 2.5. More generally under the heading 'retained in business' we learn, for example, that such profits averaged 4·9 per cent of the sales of the thirteen United Kingdom firms, that four of these firms added more than 4·9 per cent of their sales revenue to reserves, and that retained profits ranged from a loss of 4 per cent to a gain of 20 per cent.

Table 2.5   Outlay as a percentage of sales of thirteen firms with United Kingdom capital investment in Singapore in 1966–7

Outlay category	Average firm	Number of firms ranked as above average in outlay category	Range of outlay category
Materials and services	76·1	8	36 to 90
Wages and salaries	8·2	4	1 to 18
Fringe benefits	1·0	4	Nil to 4
Retained in business	4·9	5	— 4 to 20
Dividends	3·1	4	Nil to 16
Taxation	1·2	3	Nil to 9
Depreciation	5·4	3	1 to 14

Total sales by the thirteen United Kingdom firms included in Table 2.5 amounted to about $220 million in 1966, representing a value added in production by these enterprises of roughly $40 million.

The value of goods exported from Singapore by the thirteen United Kingdom manufacturing firms included in Table 2.5 was about $70 million, or 31 per cent of their total sales in 1966. The share of exports to sales in individual firms ranged from 1 to 93 per cent. In total they represented about 2 per cent of Singapore's exports, including re-exports, in 1966. Most of the exports of United Kingdom firms were sold in Malaysia and neighbouring centres of Southeast Asia.

It would be desirable to quantify the current and long-term effects of United Kingdom direct investment in Singapore manufacturing industry on Singapore's balance of payments. In the absence of any very great direct or multiplier effect on employment or the development of human capital in Singapore the case for or against United Kingdom direct investment in Singapore manufacturing industry must rest on the continuing impact that such investment can have on Singapore's balance of payments. No such assessment can be made on the basis of the information now available, although it is believed that in Singapore's special circumstances the value added in Singapore to the products of United Kingdom manufacturing firms is a fairly satisfactory, if crude, measure of the balance of payments effect at the present time on the not unreasonable assumption that materials and services used by United Kingdom firms are largely paid for in foreign exchange, and that price and income effects can be ignored. It is, of course, no guide to the future impact of the United Kingdom manufacturing sector on Singapore's balance of payments position. By pursuing a policy of protectionism Singapore has made significant short-term balance of payments gains from United Kingdom direct investment in Singapore manufacturing industry, but this may be at the cost of a long-term distortion in her industrial structure because of the introduction into the country of techniques and processes more appropriate to countries with a large domestic market. The highly volatile export markets of Southeast Asia are a very poor substitute for such a market.

3

Helen Hughes

Australian Investment

AUSTRALIAN BACKGROUND

Australia is a capital-importing country with a net inflow of $US664 million in 1965–6. Compared to the inflow of direct investment the outflow from Australia is negligible, and only a very small proportion of Australian foreign investment goes to developing countries.[1] Singapore together with Malaysia is, however, the most important of these, and Australian investment in Singapore manufacturing is the largest single block of Australian investment in manufacturing in developing countries,[2] although the total amount is small compared to Australian investment in New Zealand or the United Kingdom. Australian investment is also small compared to other countries' investment in Singapore, but Australian factories were among the first in Singapore, and they are still among the largest. Australia is the developed country closest to Singapore and this geographical proximity has tended to offset its smallness and inward orientation as an industrial producer. The first Australian

[1] For the six years 1960–1 to 1965–6 the average annual direct investment inflow into Australia was $US536·7 million, of which an average of $US232·9 million came from the United Kingdom, and an average of $US229·4 million came from the United States and Canada. The average annual outflow for the six years was $US16·9 million. (Calculated from Australian Commonwealth Bureau of Census and Statistics, *Annual Bulletin of Overseas Investment in Australia, 1965–1966*.)

In 1964–5 and 1965–6, the only years for which figures could be obtained, $US1,834,000 and $US641,000 respectively went to Southeast Asia, which includes Burma, Cambodia, Indonesia, Laos, the Philippines, South Vietnam, Thailand, Malaysia, and Singapore. (Letters from Commonwealth Statistician, 7 October 1965 and 20 December 1966.)

[2] Estimated from survey of Australian investment in manufacturing in Southeast Asia and the islands of the Southwest Pacific.

manufacturing firm came to Singapore in 1928 when one of the owners of Humes Ltd, manufacturers of concrete pipes and other civil engineering products, visited a distant cousin, Sir Hugh Clifford, the Governor of the Straits Settlements, for a holiday. High transport costs ensured a measure of local monopoly and Humes later added asbestos cement board (which they did not manufacture in Australia) to take advantage of the Singapore and Malay markets. Another Australian manufacturer came to Singapore before World War II and a third one soon after, both in pursuit of markets they had developed as exporters. From the late 1950s Australian interest in Singapore and Malaya grew, and by December 1966 a total of at least fifty-eight Australian firms had shown a serious interest in manufacturing in Singapore and Malaysia.[3]

Australian interest in Singapore manufacturing has been part of a slow outward turning in manufacturers' attitudes. Firmly entrenched

---

[3] Most of the Australian firms which were interested in Singapore at the same time investigated the possibilities of investing in Malaysia, and a list of fifty-nine Australian-domiciled firms which had established subsidiary or associated enterprises in Singapore and Malaysia or had made inquiries in Australia, Singapore, or Malaysia about doing so, was drawn up as a basis of a survey of Australian investment in Singapore. The survey was conducted in two stages. A leading executive of each firm was interviewed in Australia to establish the reasons for interest in Singapore and Malaysia, whether investment was undertaken or not, and what, if any, were the results. All of the fifty-nine firms identified were contacted and fifty-eight were interviewed between June 1966 and June 1967. They all answered the questions put to them, although, of course, not all were able to answer the questions equally fully. The second part of the survey was carried out in Singapore and Malaysia in October 1966 and July 1967. The local managers of seventeen of the twenty-one enterprises established were asked in a personal interview about the course of development of their factories. Some questions asked in Australia were repeated for the local point of view. Where relevant the enterprises also filled in a questionnaire with figures of their investment, output, and employment. Two managers were absent from Singapore and could not be interviewed, one had failed and one was not yet established. Information about these firms was therefore obtained in Australia. The survey was supplemented by interviews with other businessmen in Australia, Singapore, and Malaysia interested in trading and manufacturing links between the two areas, and with Singapore, Malaysian, and Australian government and other public officials. To all these I am greatly indebted for the unstinting and patient way in which they answered my questions and questionnaires, for their ideas, their courtesy, and frequently their hospitality. A preliminary analysis of the results of the survey, covering Malaysia as well as Singapore, was published as 'Australians as Foreign Investors: Australian Investment in Singapore and Malaysian Manufacturing Industries', *Australian Economic Papers*, Vol. 6, June 1967, pp. 57–76.

behind high tariffs, Australian manufacturers have traditionally supplied domestic markets and New Zealand, and rapid expansion of the Australian economy in the late 1940s and in the 1950s intensified their concern with domestic rather than export markets. Only a handful of firms was exporting manufactured products from Australia in the mid-1950s when the Department of Trade initiated a vigorous policy of export promotion to diversify the composition and geographical distribution of Australian exports.[4] Increasing Australian business interest in Singapore and Malaysia was part of a growth in awareness of the economic and political importance of geographical propinquity to Asia. Australian manufacturers were often influenced by their own vision of political responsibility as well as by hopes of profit when they began to think of selling their products to Southeast Asia and then of manufacturing them there. Singapore and Malaysia where English was the language of business and government seemed the most favourable areas to investigate, although Hong Kong, the Philippines, Thailand, and Indonesia also came into most of the investors' field of inquiry. Only Hong Kong could match Singapore and Malaysia in the quality of public services and administration, but while Hong Kong was becoming rapidly developed industrially, Australian businessmen met severe competition from local manufacturers, high land prices, and an uncomfortable proximity to China. Singapore and Malaysia placed fewer restrictions on the foreign ownership of business enterprises than the Philippines or Indonesia; they were among the first Asian countries to guarantee the free repatriation of profits to foreigners; they offered additional attractions in pioneer status with tax holidays which only Thailand attempted to match; there was

[4] The Department of Trade undertook a promotion program for exports through the Trade Commissioner Service, through trade fairs and specially equipped trade ships, and encouraged the formation of an export promotion council of Australian businessmen. Two tax concessions are available for export promotion. Manufacturers receive a rebate of their entire payroll tax for increased exports. For every increase in exports amounting to 1 per cent of a firm's gross receipts (usually total sales) the manufacturer is entitled to a refund of $12\frac{1}{2}$ per cent of the payroll tax he pays in that year. When the increase in exports equals 8 per cent he thus earns a complete payroll tax rebate on his entire earnings. Merchants as well as manufacturers are eligible for a 'double deduction' market development allowance. This means that for every $A1 spent on export promotion such as travel abroad they are entitled to claim $A2 deduction from assessable income. The maximum tax saving under the legislation is limited to 80 cents in each $A1 of assessed income. (Commonwealth of Australia, Department of Trade, *Overseas Trading*, Vol. 13, November 1961, pp. 525–6 and Vol. 13, December 1961, pp. 548–9.)

easy access to land on industrial estates; and their promises of import licensing and tariff protection seemed more realistic than those of other countries.

Since Singapore and Malaysian markets were approximately equal for most of the products in which Australian manufacturers were interested in the 1950s and early 1960s, almost all were initially inclined to choose Singapore as the manufacturing site for the area because it offered better port and other public and urban facilities than Malaya. But when the People's Action Party was elected to power in Singapore in 1959 several Australian firms became doubtful about investing in Singapore. During 1957 and again in 1959 and 1960 labour unrest appeared to Australians in Singapore to threaten life as well as property. Nationalisation seemed a danger. Some firms abandoned their interest altogether and others switched their investigations to Malaya which now appeared more favourable to foreign investment because, while offering incentives to foreign investors which were similar to those available in Singapore, it seemed to have much better long-term domestic market prospects. Within a short time, however, Australian businessmen thought that Singapore's political climate had improved to such an extent that with a prospective economic union between the two countries, it again became as attractive as Malaya. When Malaysia was formed in 1963 the Australian Department of Trade put the weight of its encouragement for manufacturing in Asia behind it: Australian investors began to contemplate production for a protected market of some ten million people.

Industrial location interest swung back to Singapore to some extent, but there were now arguments in favour of Kuala Lumpur as the capital of the new country. Confrontation weakened business confidence in Singapore, affecting the outlook of Australian businessmen already settled there. Australian firms attempting to set up manufacturing enterprises during this period encountered repeated delays in dealing with government departments and local associates, and their own sense of caution was underlined by the Department of Trade's pessimistic evaluation of the area's prospects. At the very time when trade adjustment and a more realistic evaluation of the effects of Confrontation were overcoming this lack of confidence, the split between Singapore and Malaysia precipitated a new crisis. But investors had become inured to crisis. While the instability of the area may have discouraged new Australian investors, separation of Singapore from Malaysia appeared to have no appreciable effect on those already interested in Singapore. When Confrontation finally ceased and economic conditions began to return to normal in mid-1966 potential manufacturers found themselves operating in a new framework. They considered that a common market for the area, although still highly desirable on economic grounds, seemed quite unlikely, at least in the time of the current generation of leaders. Malaysia could still hope to pursue a policy of industrialisation which would rely heavily on its domestic markets, and this was attractive to Australian manufacturers accustomed to the comforts of tariff protection. Singapore's future clearly lay in the much more difficult task of creating an export-oriented manufacturing economy, and for this most of the Australian firms interested in the area were not well suited.

REASONS FOR INVESTING IN SINGAPORE

Table 3.1 shows the principal reason for going to the area given by the fifty-eight firms which either showed interest in establishing a manufacturing enterprise in Singapore and Malaysia, or had actually done so.

The reasons for interest in manufacturing overlapped to some extent, but the most important incentive was to follow up a market opened by exports, and exports were also relevant in most of the other categories.

Table 3.1   Reasons for establishing, or investigating the possibility of establishing, manufacturing activities in Singapore and Malaysia

Principal reason for establishing, or interest in establishing, enterprises	Firms which established enterprises		Firms which showed an interest in establishing enterprises in Singapore or Malaysia
	in Singapore	in Malaysia	
To exploit a market protected by transport costs from imports	3	4	5
To exploit a market already established by exports from Australia	11	12[a]	12
To exploit a market which was expected to follow the imposition of protective tariffs	3	1	8
To provide a market for Australian raw materials	2	2	1
To take advantage of low labour costs to supply exports goods to Australia	2	—	—
Total number of firms[b]	21	19	26

a In three cases the market in Malaysia was established by the Singapore subsidiary of an Australian firm.

b Eight Australian firms established enterprises in Singapore and in Malaysia.

Eight of the twelve firms which were taking advantage of local protection afforded by transport costs were able to explore their market with exports, and all of those which wanted to take advantage of tariff protection did so because, having explored the possibility of exporting from Australia, they had found this uneconomic. Firms seeking a market for raw materials were anticipating a decline in exports of their raw materials or finished products from Australia, and were, in fact, all finding a similar decline in exports to other industrialising countries. Only the two firms which were attracted to Singapore by low labour costs had an interest totally independent of exports.

Exporting from Australia to Singapore and Malaysia was thus crucial to investment in manufacturing, but it was difficult. Shipping freights were usually higher between Australian ports and Singapore than between Singapore and London, Rotterdam, Tokyo, and New York, so that Australian manufacturers derived little advantage from their geographical closeness. Australian manufacturers found it difficult to compete with prices which tended to reflect the marginal costs of production of highly industrialised countries, particularly if these prices were supported by government assistance which Australian manufacturers did not enjoy.[5] The smallness of Australia's domestic market was a serious handicap in the export of manufactured goods. Many Australian industries were rendered uncompetitive internationally because domestic production was not large enough to allow full advantage to be taken of economies of scale or technological advances. The reason was partly that the domestic market was too small and partly that it had been carved into too many production units with the assistance of more or less made to measure tariffs. In this situation very high monopolistic profits sometimes enabled Australian firms to subsidise exports at rates as great as, or even greater than, those of companies in large countries which produced on a more economic scale, but firms in more competitive industries could not afford to do so. In capital-intensive industries which priced their goods in international markets according to principles of discriminating monopoly, the comparative advantage lay with exporters operating from a large domestic market. In those industries Australia was at a disadvantage, and in labour-intensive products, as a high wage country, it could not compete at all. Foreign ownership of Australian manufacturing has also proved a handicap to the development of exports since some, though

[5] The Australian firms said that the principal form of government support they lacked was cheap credit.

perhaps a declining proportion, of foreign firms restrict exports from their Australian subsidiaries.[6]

It took time for the Australian Department of Trade's encouragement of exports to have effect. Most Australian exporters sought Singapore and Malaysian markets only when times were relatively poor at home, dropping their endeavours in boom years to concentrate on supplying the more profitable and more easily served Australian market. Thus while Australian exports of manufactured goods to Singapore and Malaysia grew from $US5·8 million in 1948–9 to $US32·8 million in 1964–5, the rate of growth until 1961–2 varied inversely with the rate of growth of national expenditure in Australia.[7] In boom times Australian exporters sometimes failed even to supply firm orders, losing markets already developed, damaging their commercial reputation, and bringing Australian products generally into disrepute. Australian manufacturers long accustomed only to their domestic markets were for the most part slow to adapt their trade marks, packaging, and labelling to the needs of multilingual Singapore and Malaysia. Because they were not accustomed to handling shipping for export they had difficulties with packing and documentation, and this caused problems to importing agents when goods arrived in Singapore.

Considering the difficulties of exporting, the growth of Australian exports has been quite creditable, although the total volume of exports has never been commensurate with the opportunities the area offered. The range of products is still narrow, few firms are involved, and the very small share that Australian firms have of the Singapore market makes it difficult for Australian manufacturers to identify manufacturing opportunities there.

The fifty-eight firms interested in manufacturing in Singapore and Malaysia seemed to be typical of the firms interested in exports and foreign investment. All either exported or had made the attempt, and

[6] H. W. Arndt and D. R. Sherk, 'Export Franchises of Australian Companies with Overseas Affiliations', *Economic Record*, Vol. 35, August 1959, pp. 239–42, analysing a Department of Trade survey, found considerable restrictions on foreign companies' rights to export to Asia. D. T. Brash, *American Investment in Australian Industry* (Canberra, 1966), showed that for American companies restrictions on exports appeared to be less important than had been thought, and that American subsidiaries' exports of manufactured goods were growing quite rapidly so that 'a great many American affiliated companies are rapidly assuming a major role in the expansion of Australian manufactured exports' (p. 240).

[7] Hughes, op. cit., p. 61.

twenty-eight had one or more subsidiaries or associated companies in other countries. But they were not typical of firms which might be expected to have resources to engage in foreign trade and foreign investment. In size, by their number of employees, they varied from eighteen to more than 45,000, but only seventeen of the firms had more than 1,000 employees. (Table 3.2).

Table 3.2   Distribution of firms which established, or were interested in establishing, manufacturing enterprises in Singapore and Malaysia, by number of employees

Number of employees per firm	Number of firms
Fewer than 100	10
100 to 500	23
500 to 1,000	7
1,000 to 5,000	10
5,000 to 10,000	4
More than 10,000	3
Total[a]	57

[a] In one case, where a primary product marketing board was the Australian entrepreneur, this classification did not apply.

Only six of the firms were subsidiaries of foreign-owned companies, so that these were also poorly represented.[8] Only three of these companies had actually invested in Singapore and Malaysia. The Australian associate of one of these foreign companies was responsible for the Southeast Asian area; one of the Australian associates had been established in Australia for some eighty years and had an Australian management with a local outlook; in the other case a great deal of persuasion and pressure by the Australian executives had been needed to obtain permission to enter the Southeast Asian market.

[8] This proportion is markedly lower than foreign firms' share of Australian industrial production. Brash (op. cit., p. 30) estimated that in 1961–2 foreign subsidiary and associated companies could have accounted for perhaps 20 per cent of Australian employment in manufacturing and conceivably up to a third of the value added. Foreign firms' share of the employment and output of the large-scale, newer industries which might have expected to have resources for exports and foreign investment is almost certainly higher. However, it needs to be said that foreign firms probably performed no worse than large Australian firms in this respect.

Twenty-six of the firms had their head offices in Sydney, twenty-one in Melbourne, eight in Perth, two in Brisbane, and one in Adelaide. The disproportionately high interest from Western Australian firms was partly due to the Western Australian government's promotion of exports and direct foreign investment, but it also reflected the outward interest of a state which has never become quite reconciled to federation with the eastern half of Australia.

Forty of the firms made producer goods, sixteen were consumer goods manufacturers, and two made both consumer and producer goods. The industry distribution of the fifty-eight firms which showed interest in Singapore and Malaysia, and of the twenty-one which were formed in Singapore in association with Australian firms, is shown in Table 3.3.

Table 3.3   Distribution of Australian firms interested in Singapore and Malaysian manufacturing and of Singapore firms with Australian capital investment, by industry group

Industry group	Australian firms interested in Singapore and Malaysian manufacturing	Singapore firms with Australian investment
I Food and beverages	5	2
II Textiles, garments, and leather	4	2
III Wood and paper products	4	1
IV Rubber products	—	—
V Chemicals and chemical products	6	5
VI Petroleum and petroleum products	—	—
VII Non-metallic mineral products	6	3
VIII Metals and engineering	25	6
IX Electrical products	5	2
X Miscellaneous	3	—
All industries	58	21

Twenty-two of the twenty-six firms which did not go ahead with investment projects made their decision because not even the combined Singapore and Malaysian markets, together with possible export opportunities from the area, promised an economic level of operation. Five of these firms decided not to invest only after the division between Singapore and Malaysia fragmented an already small market, and in two cases a failure to invest was due to the expected effects of Confrontation in

Singapore's economy. One company, in its field fairly large by Australian standards, felt that it could not spare a capable executive for an overseas venture. Another found all its available capital services engaged in expansion in Australia, and, being very much a family concern, did not wish to go to the capital market for a 'risky project' such as investment abroad. In the main, however, firms did not regard lack of capital or executive staff as an impediment. Political uncertainties also did not seem to worry the firms once they had seriously committed themselves to a venture, although the fact that most of the planned investment was in the first instance small and could be amortised in a short time was undoubtedly important.

Commercial considerations absorbed the attention of all the firms once they became interested, but the encouragement of both the Singapore and Australian governments had been important in introducing Australian firms to the idea of manufacturing in Singapore.

The process of industrialisation itself stimulated interest, and the attractions of pioneer status, the promotion of Jurong, the prospects of tariff protection, all drew attention to Singapore opportunities, but the work of the Economic Development Board was by far the most important factor. Forty-seven of the fifty-eight firms had some contact with the Board, and all except two of these had found it useful, particularly in the initial stages. Small firms found the Board especially helpful. In two cases it had introduced Australian enterprises to local partners, and in four others it had helped to find local capital to join the Australian investors. There were some complaints, particularly in the period of unification with Malaysia, of long delays in the Board's decisions.

Seventeen of the twenty-one firms which established subsidiaries or associated enterprises in Singapore were able to assess their attitude to the attractions of pioneer status, although only seven of them had pioneer certificates (Table 3.4).

The formal answers tend, however, to be misleading. The impression conveyed by the executives interviewed was that while for the most part they were happy to take advantage of any concessions that pioneer status conferred, such advantages were of relatively minor importance. One of the larger firms expressed the opinion of several by saying that the tax concessions 'were not worth tuppence'. The consensus was that once an enterprise was making a profit the company did not object to paying taxes which it considered 'reasonable', that is no higher than in Australia. The firms which expected to obtain protection felt that they would have obtained it in any case, and those which were interested in government orders felt that a local firm had an advantage whether it had pioneer

Table 3.4   Firms' attitudes to pioneer status

Advantages of pioneer status	No. of firms which considered various advantages of pioneer status important
Taxation concessions	14
Promise of protection	8
Advantage of obtaining government orders	3
Pioneer trade union	1
No advantage	3
Total number of respondents	21

status or not. Seven of the firms grumbled about the amount of red tape involved in having pioneer status. Perhaps most important of all was the fact that in not one case had the attractions of pioneer status been decisive in bringing a firm to Singapore.

The encouragement of the Australian government was important in pushing Australian firms to take an interest in Southeast Asian manufacturing, although the only provision with material benefit—a special insurance against non-commercial risks—evoked little interest among the firms interviewed.[9] Non-commercial considerations were clearly important for all the firms interviewed. Two small manufacturers who had designed their own products said that their desire to show that Australian goods were 'equal to any in the world' was as important in leading to investment in manufacturing in Singapore as it was in establishing exports in the first place. Most of the firms interviewed said that they were seriously concerned to 'do something for Asia' because 'they are our neighbours' and 'whether you like it or not we have got to live with them. Anyway what's good for them is good for us'. All but two of the fifty-eight firms were to some degree influenced by the Department of Trade's attitudes and policies although young executives appeared to be much more motivated by attitudes inspired by the Department of Trade than those close to retirement.

Firms which have started operations in recent years, some of which are nevertheless already showing profits, were unanimous that a much greater effort was needed to begin manufacturing in Singapore than to expand Australian activities to the extent necessary to bring in the same amount of additional profit. Only for firms creating a market for Australian raw

[9] The Australian government's insurance scheme protects investors against risks of expropriation, restrictions on transfer or convertibility, and war or insurrection, which are beyond the control of investors.

materials were there no easier alternatives to manufacturing abroad; for all other manufacturers, the higher risks and difficulties in investing in manufacturing abroad rather than in investing at home were offset by considerations of national interest.

PROFILE OF THE SUBSIDIARY AND ASSOCIATED FIRMS IN SINGAPORE

Fifty of the fifty-eight firms interviewed had given consideration to the nature of ownership of subsidiary or associated companies abroad. Only four claimed that it was company policy to establish wholly-owned subsidiaries abroad. Twenty-five firms had a definite preference for a significant local participation in an associated enterprise from its inception, and the other nineteen firms wished to see various degrees of local participation, some from a new venture's inception, some only after it had been established. For the four companies which wished to control their subsidiaries completely, ease of management was the principal reason, but it appeared that company policy on the issue had not been questioned for some time, and answers were mainly in terms of 'company policy'. The companies that wished to see local participation were aware of the problems this might involve, particularly in management difficulties. Their strong feelings of moral rectitude in advocating local participation seemed due mainly to the refusal of foreign, and particularly United States, firms to give Australians an opportunity for equity participation in highly profitable subsidiary enterprises in Australia. This was echoed in the Department of Trade's strong support for joint ventures, which, however, also owed something to the belief that a venture with a local partner would have a better chance of success than if it was wholly Australian owned. Such evidence as the small sample of firms supplied gave no support to this view. There did not appear to be any correlation between the form of an enterprise and its success. Table 3.5 shows how these attitudes worked out in practice.

Table 3.5   Form of ownership of firms with Australian capital investment

Form of ownership	No. of enterprises
Joint venture with indigenous Singapore firm	4
Joint venture with Singapore agency firm	3
Joint venture with another foreign firm	4
Public company with substantial Singapore share ownership	4
Public company with insignificant Singapore share ownership	3
Wholly-owned subsidiary of Australian company	3
Total	21

Control of the subsidiary or associated company appeared to be very much a matter of management. Ten of the twenty-one enterprises were not managed by Australians but in six of these managers were Europeans who managed foreign-owned agency or other firms. Only in the four other enterprises was management local. Eleven enterprises were managed by Australian expatriates, but it did not follow that there was tight control from Australia. In fact, with the exception of two firms, the Australian expatriate managers had a good deal more freedom than they would have had managing a subsidiary or associated company in Australia where parent company control is traditionally very close. Nine of the twenty-one enterprises had local company boards, but these lacked experience in the manufacturing process and provided little help for the manager. Even when they met frequently they merely tended to confirm his decisions.

The managers' attitudes are perhaps the best guide to the degree of independence they enjoyed (Table 3.6).

Table 3.6   The degree of independence of firms with Australian capital investment in decision-making

Singapore management assessment	Number of enterprises
Completely independent	9
Moderately independent	7
Have little independence	5
Total	21

The sample is small, but it seemed significant that all the large firms and all the well-established ones felt completely or moderately independent of the Australian parent. The limit to independence for those which considered themselves completely independent was with regard to investment which required a new dose of capital from Australia, rather than to undistributed profits. Otherwise the larger firms were free to invest in new products and new processes, and these did not have to be identical with those being developed in Australia, although parent company practice was usually followed. For the joint ventures with local companies, access to Australian company manufacturing practice and product development was in all four cases considered the principal advantage of the association to the Singapore firm. On the other hand one of the companies which had departed from its parent's products was a wholly-owned subsidiary of an Australian company.

The source of finance for additional fixed investment was predominantly internal funds, initially from paid-up capital and subsequently from undistributed profits. Only four of the twenty-one enterprises used outside finance for fixed investment, and all were able to obtain bank loans or overdrafts without difficulty. They felt that interest charges were 'reasonable'. Ten of the twenty-one enterprises relied on bank overdrafts or loans from time to time for working capital, none had difficulty in obtaining such funds, and again all felt that interest charges were 'normal' and 'reasonable'.

Table 3.7 gives an estimate of net annual additions to fixed assets by enterprises with Australian capital.

Table 3.7   Estimated net annual additions to fixed assets[a] by firms with Australian capital investment, 1961–6

Year	Net additions $	Percentage of capital expenditure in Singapore manufacturing establishments with ten or more workers[b]
1961	1,800,000	16
1962	1,700,000	5
1963	2,100,000	12
1964	3,100,000	6
1965	2,700,000	5
1966	2,200,000	3

[a] Investment in land and buildings, plant and equipment, and stocks, minus depreciation.
[b] Calculated from Table 1.4.

In every year, the amount invested from undistributed profits swamped new external capital which formed less than 20 per cent of total new fixed investment in the period 1961 to 1966. The actual inflow of capital from Australia thus made a very small contribution to the growth of total investment from 1961 to 1966. The average investment in fixed assets by firms with Australian capital fell from 16 per cent of total capital expenditure by Singapore manufacturing establishments with ten or more workers in 1961 to 3 per cent in 1966.

Most of the firms which have established manufacturing enterprises in Singapore claim that they have brought new techniques and processes to the area. To some extent this is true in all cases, but it is not always as true as it sounds. Eleven of the twenty-one enterprises were producing for an intensively competitive market, and only four of these had been the first to make their product in Singapore. Another four of these eleven enterprises were producing in an overcrowded market and this was the principal cause of low utilisation of capacity, and, in two cases, of ultimate failure.

Only two of the twenty-one enterprises were dissatisfied with their production equipment. In one case decisions about plant renewal were held up by uncertain market prospects, while in the other the plant manager felt that mistakes had been made in equipping the plant so that it was not sufficiently mechanised. The amount of second-hand equipment bought by the enterprises was negligible in total. Only two enterprises had relied on second-hand equipment for a significant proportion of their investment. It represented 90 per cent of the total value of additions between 1961 and 1966 for one plant, and 22 per cent for the other. Two firms had carefully investigated the possibility of using second-hand machinery and rejected it. The managers of eighteen of the twenty-one enterprises argued that mechanisation frequently paid because of the savings of raw material and improved quality of products. The degree of international competition in Singapore had made for a very sophisticated market which would not accept poor quality products resulting from primitive techniques. Second-hand machinery led to servicing problems and poor spare parts supplies, with consequent delays which in turn led to high production costs. Some spare parts could be made to order locally, but some had to be ordered from abroad. One enterprise regretted that it had installed semi-automatic rather than fully automatic equipment and attributed some of its considerable production difficulties to this decision. Conversely the firms with the fewest factory problems were the most highly mechanised.

Management appeared to be the prime factor in the degree and speed with which success was achieved by a subsidiary or associated enterprise. All but three of the twenty-one enterprises employed expatriate managerial and technical staff at the executive level. There was a total of fifty-one expatriates. The high cost of employing expatriate staff, the shortage of good executives in Australia, and Singapore's policy of limiting immigration permits, tended to limit the number of expatriates employed. After the initial construction period was over, the expatriate staff was reduced to one or perhaps two men for all but the very large firms. In two of the old established firms there were local managers in top management, including one general manager, but the newer firms had not yet been able to train managers locally.

Many of the Australian managers found unexpected difficulties. The business framework differed from that to which they were accustomed, and although the majority of them appeared to be versatile, it took them time to become acclimatised to the business habits and *mores* of their new environment. Some, poorly selected, failed to do so. The manufacturing operation which they controlled in Singapore was often smaller in scale than the one they knew at home, and this in itself presented problems, though the supervision of the manufacturing process itself was generally simple. In most cases they had to deal with all the other aspects of business enterprise with which they were not acquainted from their domestic experience: sales, cost and other accounting, purchasing, the ensuring of regular deliveries of raw materials, spare parts and servicing of plant, and labour relations. In Australia help and advice had never been farther away than a telephone call, but in Singapore the managers often found themselves working long hours in an atmosphere of isolation. To Australian head offices overseas activities were with two exceptions very minor concerns so that they were usually slow to answer their managers' letters and to deal with their problems. Fourteen of the seventeen managers interviewed in Singapore thought that the Australian parent firms underrated the problems of managing factories abroad, and this criticism seemed in most cases to be valid. To some exceptionally strong managers the isolation from head office was a most satisfying challenge, and once a firm was well established distance from head office could be an advantage. But where the manager was poorly chosen in the first place, and where he was inadequately equipped, technically or commercially, the enterprise floundered. The experience of the Singapore firms suggested that Australian firms underestimated the difficulties in starting an enterprise abroad. Thinking mainly in terms of the volume of output, they did not send out sufficiently experienced men. Some felt that they could not afford the high cost of a trainee on the spot in addition to the man in charge. In enterprises so afflicted managerial crises recurred. There were of course firms which were well run and able to train local people so that a good succession of managerial staff was available, but this situation is as yet far from general.

Table 3.8 illustrates the sources of raw material used by the twenty-one enterprises in Singapore during 1966. Two of the firms established to provide a market for Australian raw materials were using them; one of these was a wholly-owned Australian subsidiary while the other had 50 per cent Singapore capital participation. Another firm, although not entirely Australian owned, expected to use Australian raw materials for the most part.

Table 3.8   Source of raw material used by firms with
Australian capital investment

Source of raw material used	Number of enterprises
Singapore	6
Imported from Australia	12
Imported from elsewhere	11

All the firms using Australian raw materials or components thought them competitively priced, adding that otherwise the Singapore enterprises could not compete. Four of the twelve enterprises which used Australian raw materials complained that, because they were a small part of the parent's total operations, deliveries were poor, and there were therefore hidden costs in high stock holding and interruptions to production. In no case, however, was there a formal agreement tying the Singapore enterprise to Australian raw materials. Sixteen enterprises claimed that they would purchase their raw materials in the cheapest market, regardless of the nationality of the suppliers.

Firms with Australian capital only employed about 4 per cent of workers employed in Singapore manufacturing establishments with ten or more workers in 1966 (Table 3.9) and 0·4 of the total Singapore workforce.

Table 3.9   Workers employed by firms with Australian
capital investment, 1961–6

Year	Number of workers	Percentage of employment in Singapore manufacturing establishments with ten or more workers [a]
1961	1,751	5
1962	1,799	5
1963	1,752	4
1964	1,826	4
1965	2,005	4
1966	2,121	4

[a] Calculated from Table 1.4.

In establishing a manufacturing enterprise in Singapore, Australian firms found themselves beset by both shortages and surpluses of labour.

Singapore appeared to be short of managerial and supervisory staff from foreman upwards, and there was a great deal of turnover, with skilled men moving from one firm to another. The situation differed only in degree from that to which the parent firms were accustomed in Australia, but given the small total number of experienced men that degree of difference was very important. Technically-trained men were easier to find, although they too lacked experience. In some of the professions, notably accounting, the supply was greatly in excess of demand, and this was also true for all clerical positions.

When it came to selecting labour for the factory floor the situation was even more difficult. Fully trained men were extremely scarce. Most firms employed men who had some experience in an allied production field and then trained them themselves, unless they could steal skilled workers from government enterprises, British military establishments, or their competitors. The twenty-one enterprises had sent ten key men to Australia for training between 1961 and 1966; two of these were foremen and the others were technical or managerial staff.

There were plenty of unskilled workers, but many problems in employing them. Firms generally chose men from the construction workers who built a plant, and to avoid a rush of applicants, relied upon the employees to bring along relatives and friends when more hands were needed. Several firms gave examples of low technical and high clerical and academic attainment by men and women applying for factory jobs. In five cases trade union agreements limited hiring to men supplied by the union, and, although the firm did not have to hire all the men presented, managers felt that this was a serious limitation on their choice of labour. In these enterprises even greater difficulties occurred when a firm wished to sack an indifferent worker. The firm had to prove that he was redundant before dismissing him, and had to pay severance pay.

Management of labour in the factory naturally presented problems to which Australian managers were not accustomed. Matters of dignity and face had to be considered and these were frequently compounded by strong social differences. Personal relationships between the managers and men were very important in Singapore. Some Australian managers were able to fit into a paternal framework as well as indigenous employers, but others found it a relief when a union was formed in their plant. They could deal with the union rather than the men and rely on it to keep discipline in the factory.

Three of the enterprises had considerable difficulties with unions in the early 1960s but felt that the situation had greatly improved by 1966. Only one enterprise had run into difficulty with the Pioneer Industries

79

Employees' Union, but here industrial strife had forced the company to shut down production. This, however, was an exception and the firm had been as unreasonable as the union. The other six firms which had dealt with the Pioneer Industries Employees' Union found it very similar to Australian unions.

The issues likely to arise in Singapore factories more frequently than in Australian industry were absenteeism, poor time keeping, unwillingness to work overtime, and untidiness in the work place. All were clearly problems of an industrialising society, and the methods of dealing with them reflected this. One firm provided housing near the factory for key workers to ensure regular attendance, while another found that free coffee ensured punctuality in the mornings. All in all labour relations seemed more delicate and complex than in Australia. Australian trade unionists would no doubt be surprised to hear that 'you can't push the men as hard as you can in Australia'.

During a firm's establishment period, labour cost tended to be high, certainly higher than most Australian firms had anticipated. Fringe benefits were considerable, representing between 10 and 40 per cent of base wage rates for the eight enterprises which were able to make an estimate. They included holiday and sick pay, medical attention, subsidised meals, travel and housing allowances, as well as overtime pay. Thus although the base wage rates were about a quarter of comparable Australian rates, the difference shrank if fringe benefits were included. Labour cost per man per day was often a higher proportion again, ranging from a third to a half of Australian labour cost, because labour productivity was often lower than in Australia.[10]

Managers found that considerable unemployment imposed a pressure to find jobs for extra men, and they frequently employed a greater number of workers than they would need in Australia for this reason alone. However, labour output per man was also thought to be lower than in Australia by ten of the twelve enterprises which were able to make a direct comparison. This was thought to be partly a matter of climate. People could not perform as well in tropical conditions as in temperate ones, and air-conditioning costs were said to be too high to make its use possible. Singapore workers also were of slighter build than Australians, and they could not be expected to do the same amount of physical labour. One firm found that whereas a labourer could shift

[10] For the most part the twenty-one enterprises appeared to be paying higher wages than minimum ones for their industry, but the sample was too small to make comparisons with wages and salaries paid in Singapore manufacturing.

80

three 56-pound cases a minute in Australia, two men were required to do this in Singapore. But to some extent, as one Australian manager at least was careful to point out, the employment of more men was due to the differences in the scale of production. Singapore plants tended to be smaller than their Australian counterparts, and the labour force had to be greater per unit of output to achieve the same flexibility of output.

Mechanisation and incentive payments tended to reduce the importance of differences of physique and climate, and familiarity with factory conditions improved productivity fairly rapidly. One firm claimed that output per man did not differ greatly from that in Australia, one found it better than in the United Kingdom, and one thought it higher than in Australia. In one operation exactly comparable in size and degree of mechanisation, a Singapore factory used fewer man hours per unit of output than its Australian counterpart, although the manager claimed that overall output per man was lower in his Singapore plant than in Australia.

Most managers found local workers very adaptable to given tasks, but reluctant to act freely on their own initiative. There was much discussion of the particular aptitudes of the various races, but there were as many exceptions as there were rules. Where productivity was lagging a long way behind comparable Australian factories after several years of operation and the cause was not climate, size of enterprise, or the need for heavy manual labour, the fault seemed to lie with the organisation of production.

The average contribution of firms with Australian capital to value added in manufacturing establishments with ten or more workers in Singapore fell only slightly from 7 to 6 per cent of the total value added between 1961 and 1966; labour productivity was at least up to average for Singapore manufacturing, and probably somewhat better than average (Table 3.10).

The supply of public services was universally thought to be adequate, and prices were thought to be reasonable although only one firm could compare the cost to the cost of similar services in Australia, finding it approximately the same as a proportion of total production cost.

Seven of the twenty-one enterprises had chosen a site on the Jurong industrial estate, but not all were happy with their situation. One firm complained at the high cost of putting in an electricity substation, and there were complaints of the handicaps of a factory situation far from Singapore's commercial centre. Managers found that they wasted at least half a day if they had to make a business call in Singapore. The greatest problem at Jurong was transport for the workers, particularly

Table 3.10   Estimated value added in production by firms with
Australian capital investment, 1961–6

Year	Value added	Percentage of value added in Singapore manufacturing establishments with ten or more workers[a]
1961	13,400,000	7
1962	21,200,000	9
1963	20,200,000	7
1964	19,600,000	7
1965	22,900,000	6
1966	24,300,000	6

[a]Calculated from Table 1.4.

if they worked overtime. One firm had solved the problem by lending all its workmen the money to buy a motor cycle, and all the other firms had to pay a transport allowance. There were also minor grumbles about excessive red tape and unnecessarily high standards imposed by the fire department and the health department. It was felt by all the firms that Jurong was rather too much a showpiece than a working factory area, but there was also some pride in being pioneers on the estate. Firms which had remained in the older industrial areas had done so mainly because they were already established there, and felt the advantage of being close to areas where their workers lived. Some of the newer firms stayed outside Jurong mainly for this reason, though fear of 'red tape' was also a factor.

SALES

To all the Australian enterprises selling their products presented much greater problems than producing them. One of the twenty-one firms failed during 1966 and one early 1967, and marketing problems were the principal reason for failure in both, although they had production difficulties as well. Ten enterprises could make an estimate of their use of capacity during 1966: four were producing at 50 to 60 per cent of capacity, three were producing at 70 to 80 per cent of capacity, one was producing at 90 per cent of capacity, and two were producing at full capacity. One of the latter was working three shifts, two of the others were working two shifts, and otherwise one shift was the normal measure of capacity.[11]

Seventeen of the twenty-one enterprises found prices intensely competitive for most of their products, because they had to sell against other local producers of the same products or their close substitutes, or against imports. Three firms which had expected to find shelter behind tariffs found that they had great difficulty competing with 'back yarders' who, they claimed, paid lower wages and did not carry overheads. There was no evidence of restrictive practice in pricing. One manager, accustomed to an industry which can claim more than a hundred years of restrictive practices in Australia, was frankly irritated by Singapore manufacturers' inability to act together to fix their prices and restrict their outputs.

Only one of the enterprises had restrictions on export sales imposed by the parent. It could not export to neighbouring countries where the parent company had established subsidiaries. Otherwise there appeared to be no restrictions on sales by product or area, and all the other firms expressed an interest in exporting.

Only four of the twenty-one enterprises confined their sales to Singapore. Three of these were producing tariff protected goods, and the fourth a product which did not carry well and for which it had established another factory at Kuala Lumpur. Eight of the twenty-one enterprises had associated firms in Malaysia which had been established to overcome the trading barriers between Malaysia and Singapore. In all but two cases this fragmentation of production had raised production costs, but it was thought necessary either to take advantage of tariffs or to forestall other competitors. Most firms selling both in Singapore and Malaysia from their Singapore production found their market evenly divided between the two, with a slight advantage for Singapore sales, so that the normal sales break up was 60 per cent of 'domestic' sales in Singapore and 40 per cent of 'domestic' sales in Malaysia.

Ten of the twenty-one enterprises exported beyond Singapore and Malaysia. The proportion of exports to volume of production ranged from 10 to 70 per cent. The three old established firms were the major exporters, and in each case the management was given complete freedom by the parent to find export markets. In two of these cases the Singapore enterprise seemed considerably more export-minded than the parent

[11] The firms were asked to consider full capacity as the output they could achieve over a long period of time with existing equipment, working the number of shifts they regarded as normal for their industry.

company, and in the third case the parent company's policy of exporting from the cheapest manufacturing base favoured Singapore over Australia.

While the export performance seemed creditable, all the firms engaged in exporting noted that finding export markets was difficult. Most of the exports went to other Southeast Asian countries, to East Africa, and to the Middle East, and some of the firms were afraid that exporting would become more difficult as these countries also industrialised. Others, however, were confident that new export opportunities would be found elsewhere.

All these exports were achieved before the Singapore government introduced its export incentive scheme. The Australian firms looked forward to receiving taxation concessions on exports as they did to any opportunities to make extra profits, but their principal reasons for exporting had been to keep down unit production costs by keeping up the volume of production and the desire to be 'good citizens', and these seemed likely to continue to be the main driving forces in exports.

CONCLUSIONS

In terms of the value of investment, production, and employment, Australia's contribution to manufacturing development in Singapore is small, and in view of its size in relation to the major industrial countries investing in the area, it will probably remain so. On the other hand geographic proximity and political interest should enable Australia to maintain a contribution significant even in these terms, and one that may perhaps be more important than appears at first sight in the development of manufacturing skills.

Perhaps the best contribution of Australian managers has been their attitude to work. Like the old-fashioned small-scale indigenous employer, and frequently to an even greater extent, they often work in overalls side by side with the workers on the factory floor to get a plant into production, providing instruction in industrial attitudes as well as technical skills. One Australian manager added evening classes for his employees to such informal training. Where undue weight is placed on white collar and professional work and too little pride is associated with manual work, such attitudes should be helpful to the industrialisation process.

The number of firms was too small, and few had operated long enough, to make profit evaluation meaningful. The few firms which have been established for a long period were profitable, and in some cases were showing a better return on capital than on comparable Australian investment. Good profits are needed to attract and keep foreign investors, but because they are foreign such investors also have to show good will by not being unduly restrictive in their purchase of raw materials, in their sales, and, above all, in allowing local equity participation in their success. Perhaps because Australia is on balance a capital-importing rather than a capital-exporting country, Australian entrepreneurs in Singapore for the most part qualified as good foreign investors by these criteria.

4

Japanese Investment[1]

JAPAN'S MANUFACTURING INVESTMENT OVERSEAS

Before World War II Japan had large private foreign investments in China and Manchuria, but defeat in the war stripped the country of every overseas asset. In the immediate post-war years Japan concentrated its capital formation at home for fast economic recovery and growth. Striving to catch up with the level of industrial technology and personal consumption attained by Western Europe and North America, Japan was on balance a capital-importing nation between 1958 and 1964. In 1965, however, capital outflow became greater than capital inflow (Table 4.1).

Table 4.1   Capital inflow and outflow, Japan, 1957–66

Year	Long-term capital Inflow	Long-term capital Outflow	Balance $US million	Short-term capital balance	Total
1957	43	53	— 10	— 84	— 94
1958	149	59	90	—125	— 35
1959	132	159	— 27	182	155
1960	156	155	1	676	677
1961	384	211	173	456	629
1962	476	179	297	29	326
1963	765	298	467	107	574
1964	558	451	107	233	340
1965	33	447	—414	— 62	—476
1966	—103	706	—809	— 64	—873

Source: Compiled from Japan Economic Planning Agency, *Nihon Keizai Shihyō* [Japanese Economic Indicators], October 1963, p. 16, and August 1967, p. 20.

[1] I would like to thank the then Japanese Ambassador to Singapore, His Excellency Mr Ueda, Mr Y. Shinojima of the Japanese Embassy in Singapore, and Mr Sakurai, President of the Japanese Industrialists' Association of

On reaching the pre-war level of industrial production and per capita personal income around 1955, Japan began to look for foreign investment opportunities. Private investment abroad grew rapidly from $US8·6 million in 1955 to $US92·8 million by 1960, and in 1966 it was $US224·9 million.[2] This investment was spread over all five continents. By 1967 equity investment accounted for $US572 million, loans $US481 million, and branch investment $US266 million, a total of $US1,320 million.[3] North American countries have had the largest share of this gross private foreign investment ($US377 million) followed by Central and South American countries ($US354 million), Asian countries ($US256 million), Near and Middle Eastern countries ($US234 million), European countries ($US44 million), and Oceania ($US36 million). African countries had the smallest share ($US17 million). Equity investment alone followed the above ranking except for the Near and Middle East which had the smallest share of all. In number of foreign investment projects, however, Asia ranked first, followed by North America, Central and South America, Europe, Oceania, and Africa. The Near and Middle East also had the smallest number of projects. Altogether, Japan's private sector has so far invested most heavily in the developing regions of the world where it committed $US899 million, or 68 per cent of its total investment. This is in marked contrast to the regional distribution of private foreign investment shown by the United States, United Kingdom, and the Federal Republic of Germany. More than half of the direct private foreign investment of these countries went to

---

Singapore, for introducing me to Japanese managers in Singapore, and the managements of all the companies associated with Japanese firms who extended the fullest co-operation by filling in my questionnaires and giving me ample time in repeated interviews with them. I am also grateful to executives of the parent companies in Osaka and Tokyo for giving me an opportunity to check the quantitative data collected in Singapore, and filling out the details of investment motives and programs from the head office point of view.

[2] Japan, Ministry of International Trade and Industry, *Kigyo Shinhitsu no Genjo to Mondai* [Japan's Overseas Investment: Its Present Status and Problems] (Tokyo, 1968), p. 3. Figures are of government approvals of foreign investment, not actual investment figures which may be somewhat lower.

[3] Ibid., pp. 11–12. Japanese investment statistics classify direct equity investment with portfolio investment under the heading of 'portfolio investment', but the bulk of investment in this classification is equity investment. The 'real estate' investment category in Japanese investment statistics mainly covers investment in the overseas branches of Japanese companies and has therefore been called branch investment.

other developed countries.[4] Thus there appear to be significant differences in foreign investment patterns between the early starters in industrialisation and Japan, reflecting differences in the economic structure and international trade patterns.

Branch investment, in which oil production in Saudi Arabia and Kuwait with an investment of $US231 million took the lead, accounted for 20 per cent of Japan's gross private investment abroad.[5] Mining investment was also important, clearly showing that one major motive behind growing private foreign investment by Japan was the procurement of a regular supply of high grade, low cost, industrial raw materials essential to the continued growth of its economy. Yet Japan has been even more interested in investing in manufacturing which took up 38 per cent of its total gross private foreign investment, whereas the mining sector took 31·9 per cent of the total (Table 4.2). Commercial investment has also been important because of its role in the continued growth of foreign trade. The basic motivations of Japan's growing private foreign investment have thus been: (1) to maintain and improve exports to overseas subsidiaries through shipments of industrial raw materials, semi-finished products, machinery and equipment, (2) to improve supplies to overseas manufacturers and importers through foreign branch operations, and (3) to secure a supply of industrial raw materials which was stable in quantity, quality, and prices.

Japan's manufacturing investment in Asia ranked second by regions following Central and South America, but in 1967 it had by far the largest number of mining and manufacturing investment projects (435), followed by Central and South America (120), North America (34), Africa (34), Oceania (30), Europe (21), and Near and Middle East (6).[6] Small domestic and overseas markets in the Asian region, reflecting relatively low per capita incomes and smaller mining deposits, led to small-sized investments.

Japanese investment in manufacturing in Asian countries averaged $US338,000 per project, following an average of $US2,031,000 for Central and South America, an average of $US1,959,000 for North America, Europe, and Oceania combined, and $US422,000 for Africa. The average size of all the Japanese private manufacturing investment overseas was $US850,000 per project for all regions at the end of 1966.

[4] R. Takagi, *Nihon Kigyo no Kaigai Shinhitsu* [Overseas Operation of Japanese Industries] (Tokyo, 1967), pp. 97, 113, and 125.
[5] *Kigyo Shinhitsu no Genjo to Mondai*, pp. 11–12.
[6] Ibid.

Table 4.2   Gross private foreign Japanese investment by industry,
December 1967[a]

Industry	Gross investment $US million	Percentage of total
Agriculture and forestry	22·1	1·7
Fishing	10·0	0·8
Mining	420·7	31·9
Construction	33·9	2·6
Manufacturing:	500·6	38·0
Food processing	38·8	2·9
Textiles	81·5	6·2
Chemicals	23·7	1·8
Non-mineral products	10·6	0·8
Iron and steel and metal products	70·5	5·3
Machinery	128·8	9·8
Electrical machinery	20·9	1·6
Miscellaneous manufacturing	125·8	9·5
Services:	332·8	25·2
Commerce	146·7	11·1
Finance, insurance and services	165·7	12·6
Emigration	20·4	1·5
Total	1,320·1	100·0

[a] Figures are of government approvals of foreign investment, not actual investment figures which may be somewhat lower. Figures have been rounded.
Source: Japan, Ministry of International Trade and Industry, *Kigyo Shinhitsu no Genjo to Mondai* [Japan's Overseas Investment: Its Present Status and Problems] (Tokyo, 1968), Appendix Table 1, p. 13.

Machinery industries attracted the largest share of Japanese investment in manufacturing, followed by iron and steel and metal products, and textiles. These three industries alone shared 57 per cent of the gross private manufacturing foreign investment (Table 4.3), reflecting Japan's domestic resource availability, the particular shape of its industrial structure, and the importance of foreign trade to the modernisation and continued growth of the Japanese economy. In Asia, however, these three industries only accounted for 41 per cent of manufacturing investment, while investment in food was relatively high at 22 per cent.

Though not among the first comers to Singapore, Japanese manufacturers have played an important role in its industrialisation. At the end of 1966 there were twenty manufacturing firms with Japanese affiliation in Singapore. One had not yet begun to implement its plans, five were constructing factories or installing machinery, and fourteen were in

Table 4.3   Gross private Japanese foreign investment
in manufacturing industry, by industry and region, 1951–66[a]

	Central and South America	Asia	Africa	Others	Total	% of total industries
Food processing						
No.	11	40	2	8	61	14·4
$US m.	3·4	20·3	1·4	4·1	29·2	8·1
Textiles						
No.	12	50	17	3	82	19·3
$US m.	34·0	19·5	6·7	0·8	61·0	16·9
Iron and steel and metal products						
No.	7	19	2	1	29	6·8
$US m.	49·9	10·5	1·1	0·4	61·9	17·2
Machinery						
No.	24	26	—	7	57	13·4
$US m.	68·7	7·6	—	4·4	80·7	22·4
Electrical machinery						
No.	10	30	1	5	46	10·8
$US m.	3·7	5·6	—	0·4	9·7	2·7
Chemicals						
No.	9	39	—	7	55	13·0
$US m.	1·2	5·7	—	5·3	12·2	3·4
Miscellaneous						
No.	15	67	1	10	94[b]	22·3
$US m.	17·8	22·3	0·5	64·9	105·5	29·3
Total						
No.	88	271	23	41	424[b]	100·0
$US m.	178·7	91·5	9·7	80·3	360·2	100·0

[a] Figures are of government approvals of foreign investment, not actual investment figures which may be somewhat lower.

[b] Includes one very small project in the Near and Middle East.

Source: Japan, Ministry of International Trade and Industry, *Kigyo Shinhitsu no Genjo to Mondai* (1966), Appendix Table 1, p. 1.

production.[7] Nineteen of the firms were pioneer firms. These had contributed 13 per cent of the total paid-up capital in pioneer industries by 1966, and represented the largest amount of foreign investment by any one foreign country in pioneer firms. Firms with Japanese capital

[7] The top managers of these fourteen firms were interviewed in Singapore in 1966 and 1967, and details of Japanese experience in Singapore in the following discussion are largely based on the information and opinions they provided.

were also among the largest in Singapore, although the average size of the Japanese-affiliated Singapore pioneer firm amounted to only $1,275,000 in equity participation. This was smaller than that of the pioneer firms with United States affiliation but larger than for firms with Hong Kong or Taiwan affiliation.[8]

Japan's manufacturing investment in Singapore was widely distributed by industry group. Metals and engineering industries were responsible for 44 per cent of the total paid-up capital invested by Japan in pioneer firms,[9] accounting for the large scale of the firms with Japanese affiliation. The Japanese affiliated firms also tended to have some export orientation and this made their average size relatively large even in light and non-durable goods industries.

Japanese firms, aiming at the anticipated expanded market of Malaysia rather than Singapore alone, were established one after another in 1963. In fact fifteen of the nineteen pioneer firms with Japanese capital were granted a pioneer certificate in that year. The unfavourable economic climate which followed Confrontation and separation from Malaysia was reflected in delays among pioneer firms in constructing their plants. Only four of the fifteen firms which received pioneer certificates in 1963 began to construct factories in that year, six in the following year and another in 1965. Three other firms delayed their factory construction by nearly three years: one started in 1966, the second in 1967, and the last in 1968. The unfavourable economic conditions facing Singapore also forced many Japanese-affiliated firms to scale down the intended size of their plant and equipment. Where such adjustment was impossible or difficult to make on technical grounds, and even where it was made, below capacity production became normal, further curtailing the level of production and employment which had originally been anticipated.

Among the thirteen Japanese affiliated pioneer firms interviewed, only two firms reported that they had at one time or another reached capacity level production. Average production ranged from 70 to 80 per cent of capacity, but a majority of firms reported running their plant at the rate of only 35 to 70 per cent capacity. In one instance, a plant's output fell to as low as 12 per cent of capacity well after the time the plant came into production, driving the company to the brink of bankruptcy. In 1967 the goal of most Japanese-affiliated firms in Singapore was to bring their production up to a level of capacity considered normal in their respective industries. This necessitated reorientation from import

[8] See Appendix Table I.
[9] See Appendix Table I.

substitution to export expansion, and required further streamlining for cost reduction and quality improvements. Firms also thought that along with better internal operations many improvements needed to be made by the government in tax, tariff, and export policies, and that the construction of Jurong harbour should be speeded up.

REASONS FOR JAPANESE MANUFACTURING INVESTMENT IN SINGAPORE

All except one of the Japanese firms which set up manufacturing enterprises in Singapore had some prior business contact there. Some had traded through Singapore, while others had sold goods there. In this trade Japanese commercial houses were in most cases intermediaries, and they quite often became partners in Japanese manufacturing subsidiaries in Singapore, together with Japanese manufacturers and Singapore partners who were wholesale merchants or import and export traders. The functions of the Japanese commercial houses as partners in joint ventures in Singapore were identical with those they had previously exercised as independent concerns, but they now imported industrial raw materials, parts, and machinery and equipment instead of finished goods for Singapore, and exported products manufactured by their own subsidiaries. Domestic distribution was left to the subsidiaries themselves or to their Singapore partners.

The most important reasons for starting manufacturing in Singapore were to gain access to the Malaysian market, to use it as a centre for regional distribution, and to reap the benefits of government protection and assistance. Many Japanese firms also stated that they had come to Singapore to avoid losing ground to their competitors in Japan and abroad. Because Japanese commercial houses and manufacturers tended to engage in cut-throat competition in Singapore as elsewhere, the establishment of a manufacturing firm with their capital participation tended to reduce excessive competition among them. Only two firms came for 'access to raw materials'. None gave 'presence of cheap labour' as a major reason for coming to Singapore, and none replied that either 'higher profit potentials' or 're-export to Japan' was its major reason for starting manufacturing in Singapore. The Japanese investors in Singapore were clearly most interested either in protecting or in expanding their existing export market in and around Singapore.[10]

[10] These responses correspond closely to those in a survey of the reasons for Japanese overseas investment conducted by the Japan Export-Import Bank in 1964. The major objectives of the ninety-one firms which responded in this inquiry were found to be: (1) to promote export of industrial raw materials,

Prior to 1961 Japan had been exporting to Singapore at the annual rate of about $300 million, but with the inauguration of Singapore's industrialisation program Japanese manufacturers and commercial houses became fearful of a decline in their exports not only to Singapore but also to its neighbouring countries, and of the permanent loss of these expanding markets to their competitors at home and abroad. The Singapore Pioneer Ordinance of 1959 had given some impetus to the growing interest among Japanese investors in the possibility of manufacturing in Singapore, and the Singapore government's announcements of its intention to introduce protective measures such as higher tariffs and import restrictions precipitated Japanese investment in 1963. The strategic location of Singapore as a regional distribution centre was an attractive factor for the Japanese investors, but without the threat of protective measures it is unlikely that the same number of Japanese investors would have come to Singapore.

Furthermore, the continuing formation of pioneer firms with Japanese interest in Singapore from 1961 to 1966 seems to indicate that the various investment incentives provided by the Singapore government from 1959 did not motivate the entry of Japanese investors into Singapore manufacturing industries as much as government protective measures adopted from 1962. Japanese investors came to Singapore because they thought they had no alternative if they wished to protect and expand their existing market in and around Singapore; they would most probably have come to Singapore even without investment incentives. Decisions on the size of manufacturing investment projects were based primarily on the anticipated size of the local and export market in relation to competition. They did not appear to be much affected by the provisions of the Pioneer Ordinance. No firm objected to the suggestion that the tax exemption period should be extended from five to ten years, but there was no strong support for this idea either. The anticipated formation

---

semi-finished products, and machinery and equipment, (2) to protect the existing export commodity market, (3) to develop new export commodity markets, and (4) to secure dividend, management, and royalty payment from overseas projects. The firms had more than one objective in investing abroad, but the protection of existing export commodity markets and the development of new export commodity markets were the two most important objectives of the Japanese investors in manufacturing operations abroad. Much of Japan's manufacturing investment overseas has been a counter-measure against the threat of export reduction as a result of tariff protection and import restrictions abroad, whether in developing or developed countries. *Yugin Joho* [Bulletin of the Japan Export-Import Bank], Vol. 5, August 1965, Table 2, p. 2.

of the Federation of Malaysia during 1962–3, on the other hand, was a very important motivating factor, not only in bringing manufacturers to Singapore but also in increasing the size of plant and equipment investment; the severance of trade relations between Singapore and Indonesia as a result of Confrontation and the raising of trade barriers between Singapore and Malaysia after 1965 was a great disincentive.

The Economic Development Board was very helpful to Japanese investors in many ways, but only three firms with Japanese affiliation sought and obtained financial assistance from it at the time of establishment. Two obtained loans and the third a loan and equity participation. Most Japanese firms did not need government financial assistance because the parent firms in Japan were large and had ample financial resources. One pioneer firm with Japanese affiliation obtained participation from the Economic Development Board as a measure of official support for its manufacturing operation. This firm has been given the largest single loan commitment and equity participation the Economic Development Board has so far made to Singapore firms. In another instance, however, a Japanese affiliated firm had declined an Economic Development Board loan proposal for fear that the Board should interfere with its business. Eleven of the fourteen firms in production had obtained loans from the Export-Import Bank of Japan to finance imports of machinery and equipment shipped from parent or related firms in Japan. Formally, of course, these loans were granted to the Japanese firms to finance the export of capital goods as a part of Japanese government policy, but the effect was to lessen the need for raising Singapore loan and equity capital.

Japanese-affiliated firms had no suggestions for improved government assistance in their internal operations. There were, however, some complaints of delays in construction due to too rigid a building code and fire regulations, and some firms claimed that the Economic Development Board did not provide enough assistance if a firm was in trouble after it became established.

MANAGEMENT AND TECHNOLOGY

Most Japanese firms have resident Japanese executives working in co-operation with Singapore executives. Only in three cases were there no Japanese in the top positions of managing director, general manager, factory manager, or sales manager. In these firms Japanese commercial houses were important partners in the joint ventures, but they were apparently interested only in the fruits of the affiliated operation. Two

94

of the three firms were small in size, with a majority of shares owned by Singapore partners, but the third was one of the largest Japanese subsidiaries in Singapore, and the Japanese partners held two-thirds of the total paid-up capital. The whole factory operation was, however, simple and repetitive, requiring little technical or managerial sophistication. In one firm, on the other hand, the manager was Japanese although the Singapore partner held majority shares and was long established in importing and wholesaling. This Singapore partner was simply not interested in the manufacturing side of the business, having little technical knowledge of the manufacturing process although it was a simple one.

In the companies run by both Singapore and Japanese managers, the board chairman and sales manager were generally Singaporeans while the managing director and general manager or factory manager were Japanese. In a few companies, however, where the Japanese investors were majority shareholders, the board chairmanship was also held by a Japanese. In a few affiliated firms in which Singapore investors were majority shareholders a Singaporean was a managing director. The position of managing director was clearly the most influential one within the companies. Thus in seven of the eight firms in production in which Japanese investors had majority shares the managing director was Japanese, while in ten of the eleven firms with Singapore investors in the majority, the managing director was a Singaporean. The exception was a firm where Singapore investors lacked the necessary technical experience. Sending top executives from Japan not only provided management for the Singapore firms, but also gave the parent firms an opportunity to train executives in foreign business operations.

All the firms had to seek approval by their parent firms for any major management decisions regarding capital investment, financial loans, product change and diversification, appointment to the board of directors, pricing policy, and disposition of earned profits. Minor decisions, however, were made by the firm's leading executive in Singapore who merely informed his parent firm of such decisions. On issues such as the size of employment, changes in wage and salary rates, hours of work, fringe benefits and other important terms of employment, changes in the source of materials and distribution channels, and pricing of minor items, the Japanese subsidiaries had to secure an understanding from their parent firms in Japan. By and large the management of the firms with Japanese affiliation seemed relatively independent of managerial control by their parent firms but felt that United States and United Kingdom firms left their Singapore management more free. There may be some bias in this

95

judgment, but it seemed true on the whole, reflecting the greater importance attached to Singapore manufacturing operations by Japanese home
offices, the relatively short time their Singapore plants had been in operation, the centralised management traditional in Japanese business, or,
more simply, less experience in foreign manufacturing. Certainly the
more important the manufacturing operation in Singapore was to the
parent firm and the less experience the latter had in foreign manufacturing, the closer its control over the Singapore enterprise. But all
the Japanese firms with Singapore manufacturing interest had some
experience of foreign manufacturing, and the other factors therefore
seemed more important.

Although the Singapore firms with Japanese affiliation sought their
own economic objectives of profit maximisation and growth, they naturally had to take into account constraints imposed by their parent firms,
in Japan, Singapore, and elsewhere if the parent firms' aims and their
own did not coincide. Whereas the Singapore firms would tend to think
in terms of long-run growth, to the parent firms short-run objectives of
recovering their investment as quickly as possible could be important
as well. The centralised pattern of Japanese management could reinforce
the homeward orientation of Japanese managers in Singapore, and,
indeed, in some affiliated companies there was an impression that the
management seemed to be more concerned with pursuing the short-run
objective of the Japanese parent firms than with long-run growth in
Singapore or with the firm's contribution to the Singapore economy. In
most firms with Japanese affiliation, however, the top managers clearly
understood that long-run growth of the Singapore firm was in the parent
firm's interest, and that, moreover, their superiors in Japan also understood the identity of interest between the two firms. The Japanese
managers had faced few difficulties arising from conflict of interest
between the parent and associated firm. The control exercised by the
Japanese parent owed more to the needs of the Singapore firm than to
the imposition of control by the parent. Nevertheless in some instances
Singapore investors felt that the managers had relied too heavily upon
judgments and directives coming from the Japanese parent companies
rather than upon their own decisions.

Japanese firms brought new products and new production processes
to Singapore, although neither products nor techniques were startlingly
new by Japanese standards. It followed that no excessive restrictions
were imposed on the use of the techniques introduced. The re-export of
techniques without the approval of the parent firms was of course
prohibited, but for a period, normally ten years, the Singapore firms

96

could use a technique free of charge or with the payment of technical licensing fees ranging from 1 to 5 per cent of annual sales. Some of these fees ran for a specified period of time while others required a lump sum payment in the first few years of operation. The Singapore firms made little effort to improve their production techniques through research and development activity. They did not have adequate staff for this purpose and at their early stage of development it simply did not pay to do so.

All but one of the firms brought technical experts from Japan to begin production. The number of these experts from Japan varied among companies: one firm had only one engineer for a brief period while another had more than thirty-six Japanese engineers and technicians for some time after production began. The size of the Singapore operation, the time elapsed since production had started, and the technical complexity of the production process, affected the number of Japanese technicians employed. The availability of engineers and technicians in Singapore was another factor. Japanese technical men trained local ones, and Singapore technicians and engineers were trained by the parent firms in Japan. Such training was not merely for technical purposes, but also provided an incentive for Singapore technical employees. It was also intended to show them how to take the leadership in increasing workers' productivity. In some cases these Singapore technical employees and foremen were under a contractual obligation to continue their services with the Singapore firm for some length of time. The Singapore firms in general paid both travelling expenses and salaries of Japanese staff in Singapore, but in a few cases the Japanese parent companies defrayed all these costs for new, struggling firms.

THE SOURCES OF RAW MATERIAL AND CAPITAL GOODS

The Singapore firms relied for much of their durable and non-durable capital goods upon imports from their parent or related firms in Japan. Some of the joint venture agreements between Singapore and Japanese investors had a clause specially mentioning the obligation of the affiliated companies to purchase certain key non-durable capital goods from their parent or related firms in Japan unless this was disadvantageous to them in terms of cost, quality, or time of delivery. The proportion of the total physical inputs imported from Japan ranged from 15 to 100 per cent on major items, though for most of the firms the range was much narrower, averaging 75 to 100 per cent. One firm relied heavily on local materials, and another on materials from a very competitive supplier in the region, but Singapore had not attained a stage where local production could feed manufacturing with industrial raw materials and semi-fabricated products. Some firms also depended on imports from Australia, the United States, and Western Europe, but Japan had a locational advantage which often made its goods more competitive.

A number of managers said that they were willing to purchase their materials from any country or any firm that could deliver the best materials most quickly at the lowest price. It seems that the heavy reliance on Japanese products was largely due to their competitiveness. However, the home office orientation of most Japanese managers and formal joint venture agreements were also factors. Several Japanese managers interviewed emphasised that many of the non-durable goods imported from Japan had attained a world-wide reputation of being high quality products, competitive in price and service. They claimed in fact that there had been no undue favouritism on their part towards Japanese goods. This seems to have been largely true, but there is no denying the fact that the local shareholders had complained in several instances of higher costs of Japanese materials in relation to comparable ones from other countries. If the Japanese goods imported by the Singapore firms were truly competitive in price, quality, and delivery time with goods from other countries, there should be no fear among the parent firms in Japan of possible reductions in the procurement orders for their products even without preference clauses in their joint venture agreements. Japanese investors could therefore strike out such clauses from their agreements and meet the complaints lodged by some Singapore investors about excessive charges on the cost of the physical inputs imported from Japan.

Almost all the durable capital goods installed in Japanese-affiliated firms came from parent or related firms in Japan. The only exception was in a firm in which a third country investor provided the equipment. While the use of Japanese machinery and equipment helped Japanese exports and guaranteed continued purchases of parts and industrial raw materials, the Singapore firms had the advantage of being able to maintain the equipment in operating condition easily because they had ready access to Japanese production managers and engineers.

By and large the equipment was not the most up-to-date by international standards, but rather it was suited to the size and scope of the Singapore manufacturing operation. The Japanese parent firms were themselves short of high level technical and skilled manpower, and this to some extent limited the choice of the equipment installed in Singapore, but the main factor in the choice of capital goods, more important than

98

the availability of technical manpower or other input requirements, was the size of the market. Once machinery was installed, the elasticity of substitution between capital and labour and between labour of one grade and another seems to have been very low. Differentials in productivity between labour-intensive and capital-intensive production processes were large in spite of narrow wage differentials among different skill grades. The narrow margins on which these new manufacturing firms had been operating, particularly in export markets, also limited the elasticity of substitution. There appeared to be no complaints from Singapore investors with regard to the price of equipment.

DOMESTIC AND OVERSEAS MARKETING

With two exceptions the bulk of output, ranging between 50 and 100 per cent of the total sales in any given year, was sold in Singapore. One of the two exceptional firms exported 40 to 60 per cent of its annual sales, and the other exported 90 to 96 per cent, with the proportion exported increasing from year to year in both cases. The high concentration of sales in the internal Singapore market meant that domestic competition was very keen not only among Singapore producers but also with importers who had stockpiled goods in anticipation of protective measures. However, as imported stocks began to fall and as the Singapore government introduced higher tariffs and import quotas favourable to domestic producers, the Japanese-affiliated firms began to feel less competition from the foreign producers abroad except in a few cases where no import quota had been introduced. Their chief concern in Singapore, therefore, was to reduce competition among domestic producers. The Japanese-affiliated firms wished to see a change in government policy which would not allow more than one firm to produce the same commodities in Singapore, but this was opposed by the Economic Development Board for fear of monopoly. Cartel arrangements to maintain price levels were also frowned upon. The Japanese-affiliated firms tried to persuade competitors to specialise in distinct products, but such specialisation was not always possible. In some cases companies succumbed to competition, selling out to their competitors, but in others competition remained very stiff. An inflow of foreign manufactures continued in many cases to ward off the danger of monopolistic domination. Many Japanese-affiliated firms felt that the Economic Development Board and other government agencies had an unrealistic belief in the efficiency of a free market mechanism. Firms needed to strengthen their international competitive ability rather than their competitive strength against each other, and this required government assistance in reallocating economic resources for the benefit of export industries without sacrificing social welfare or the import substituting industries. The greater number of the Japanese-affiliated firms had intended to export much of their output to Malaysia, and their import substitution character was not intentional but the result of circumstances beyond their control. There is no doubt that the Japanese-affiliated firms will adjust themselves to export possibilities when they arise and return to export orientation as originally planned; there was some indication of such change already in mid-1967.

Some 50 to 100 per cent of the goods exported by the Japanese-affiliated firms went to Malaysia, and the rest went to several countries of Southeast Asia, South Asia, the Middle and Near East, Africa, Western Europe, North, Central and South America, and Oceania. The management of Japanese-affiliated firms tended to regard exports to Malaysia as 'artificial exports', usually classifying them as domestic sales in their accounts, but growing trade barriers between Malaysia and Singapore made exporting to Malaysia increasingly difficult. With the assistance of their Japanese parents' international sales network most of these firms were therefore making efforts to increase the number of countries to which they exported. In some cases the Japanese parents even gave their Singapore firms a share of an existing export market to tide them over a difficult period. The Singapore firms were also trying to diversify their products and to rationalise their production to bring their costs down to the level of international prices. Together with Singapore encouragement of exports these efforts were gradually increasing the export ratio of the sales of the Japanese-affiliated firms.

In some cases joint venture agreements between Singapore and Japanese investors restricted the affiliated firms' export of goods by market area, type of product, and prices, so as not to compete with the export activities of Japanese parent companies.[11] To ensure that such clauses were effective the Japanese-affiliated firms were required to consult with their home offices before exporting restricted goods to the so-called restricted markets. Nevertheless export competition among

[11] Restrictions were usually confined to exports to Malaysia and Indonesia, and firms had to negotiate with their parent companies in Japan to export to other countries. With the increase in the number of Japanese manufacturing subsidiaries in Southeast Asian countries, such export restriction will become more important unless parent companies co-ordinate production so as not to produce competing goods within the region.

Japanese and other foreign associated firms in Singapore was increasing, particularly when several manufacturers were making one product. Competition in exports was generally becoming more intensive, with increased export emphasis by Japanese and other foreign manufacturers, for they were by and large concentrating on the same markets, and local production in these markets was also growing. Such competition increased the export income of the various firms but not of Singapore, unless it had a cost-reducing effect through rationalisation which led to an increase in total exports.

Keen competition abroad and a protected market at home led some Japanese-affiliated firms to follow the usual pattern of setting dual prices differentiated between the domestic and export markets. They adopted a cost-plus pricing policy for the domestic market and a variable cost pricing policy for overseas distribution. Lower export prices were made possible by higher domestic prices in a classic case of a partial transfer abroad of the net increase in productivity at home. The dual pricing policy was necessary to enable the Japanese subsidiaries to take advantage of economies of scale, and although in the short run it may have contributed more to the growth of their firms than to the Singapore economy, in the long run it was likely to be also beneficial to Singapore.

EMPLOYMENT, WAGES, AND INDUSTRIAL RELATIONS

Since the Japanese-affiliated firms tended to be comparatively large, the size of employment per firm also tended to be larger than that for other foreign subsidiaries in Singapore. But they also tended to be more capital-intensive and this limited the size of employment. Average employment was a little over a hundred employees, and this was much larger than the average employment in foreign pioneer firms in Singapore.[12]

Of the 2,646 employees in the Japanese-affiliated firms in 1966, 179 were Japanese nationals and of these 36 were in the top management positions, 41 in the middle and lower management positions, and 38 in the engineering and technical positions, with the rest distributed among clerical, skilled, and semi-skilled occupations. Since the Japanese engineers and technicians played a role in lower management, over 60 per cent of the Japanese nationals were working in a managerial capacity. The relatively high ratio of Japanese nationals employed reflected the importance attached by parent companies to Singapore

[12] See Appendix Table VII.

Table 4.4   Composition of employees in Singapore manufacturing firms with foreign capital investment, by ethnic group, age, and level of educational attainment, 1965

	Hong Kong	Japanese	United Kingdom	United States
Total number of firms	2	6	8	2
Total number of employees	360	1,483	3,452	591
		Percentage distribution		
Ethnic group:				
Chinese	94·7	69·1	52·3	94·7
Malay	—	15·4	24·8	—
Indian and Pakistani	—	4·5	10·8	—
Others and unspecified	5·3	11·0	12·1	5·3
Age:				
Under 20 years	68·3	32·0	1·0	68·3
20 to 24 years	25·6	34·4	4·7	25·6
25 to 39 years	2·8	26·9	55·4	2·8
40 to 59 years	—	3·8	32·4	—
60 years and over	0·2	0·2	0·1	—
Unspecified	3·1	2·7	6·4	3·3
Level of education:				
Prim. school drop-outs	31·4	16·1	19·8	31·4
Completed prim. school	25·7	15·6	7·2	25·6
Sec. school drop-outs	30·3	29·9	25·8	30·3
Completed sec. school	6·1	24·2	13·7	6·1
Higher education	—	0·1	0·2	—
Unspecified	6·5	14·1	33·3	6·6

Source: R. Hirono, *Shingapōru ni Okeru Rōdō Idō no Tokusei* [Characteristics of Labour Mobility in Singapore] (Tokyo, 1967), pp. 141, 144, and 151. This information was based on a survey carried out in Singapore in July and August 1965.

operations, and relative complexity of techniques. But wage differentials between Singapore and Japanese executives and technicians were narrower than between the Singapore and American, United Kingdom or Australian executives and technicians, reflecting a lower supply price of such manpower in Japan, and this may also have been a factor. Such differentials between Japan and other developed countries are, however, being rapidly eroded, and this should lead to the steady replacement of Japanese by Singapore executives and technicians as the latter accumulate industrial experience.

A small number of Japanese nationals were employed as clerks in the Japanese-affiliated pioneer firms, mostly as assistants to office managers who were often local employees. There were also some skilled and semi-skilled employees. Of the 1,627 employees in this category only 47 were Japanese nationals.

The local clerical and production employees of the Japanese-affiliated firms were predominantly Chinese and they were younger in age and had better educational qualifications than employees of other firms with foreign affiliation.

The Japanese-affiliated firms adopted a policy of hiring the younger, industrious workers, mostly of Chinese origin, and giving them on-the-job training for technical skills and off-the-job training to instil in them a spirit of team work in factory production. This policy was in part a response to the problem of the high proportion of young people among the unemployed, but there was also a presumption that the young workers were more apt and able to adjust themselves to the new environment of factory technology and team work essential to efficient operation and high manufacturing productivity. The Japanese-affiliated firms used interviews and sometimes written tests as well to find their workers. For semi-skilled jobs they usually had from thirty to forty applicants, for the skilled jobs from among ten to twenty applicants, for clerical jobs from forty to a hundred applicants, and for technical jobs from five to ten applicants. There were usually twenty to thirty applicants for telephone operators' jobs, while newspaper advertisements for office clerks and clerk typists attracted about three hundred applicants. Many of the firms ceased using newspaper advertisements, relying on their own employees to recommend their family members, relatives, or friends for new jobs. Even this 'closed' hiring system guaranteed that the number of applicants considerably exceeded the number of jobs available so that the company could make a choice out of a pool of trustworthy applicants without the burden of sorting through hundreds of applications. The Japanese-affiliated firms indicated that the workers thus hired had turned out to be more stable and hard-working, and more loyal and faithful, than the workers recruited from the open labour market. Basic employment policy and the 'closed' hiring system were almost complete replicas of traditions which prevailed in Japan from the 1910s until a change began to be felt in the mid-1960s when the Japanese labour market made a gradual turn from a surplus to a shortage of labour. It seems that Japan's traditional employment policy and hiring system are not, after all, peculiar only to Japan, but appropriate to the early stage of industrialisation in any Asian country where a modern industrial technology and the factory system are thrust into a traditional

103

socio-economic structure so that they require a committed labour force which will adapt to the new and changing environment under conditions of surplus labour.

Since a majority of the clerical and production workers were in their twenties in Japanese-affiliated firms, the average wages and salaries paid tended to be lower than in those foreign firms where the average age of workers was more advanced. Data based on questionnaires sent to all the Japanese pioneer and non-pioneer firms reveal that the total wage bill for all employees including managers in twelve companies with 2,106 employees amounted to $12,906,000 in 1966. This represents annual pay of $6,128 per employee, or a monthly pay of $510·7 per employee. This was very high by Singapore standards.[13] Unfortunately, there are no total wage bill data specifically for workmen and clerical employees in Japanese-affiliated firms, and therefore we are forced to rely on wage and salary rates and earnings for individual workers of different classifications obtained through interviews with manufacturing firms with Japanese affiliation in Singapore. According to this survey, the daily rates ranged from $3·00 to $4·50 for unskilled, from $4·50 to $6·50 for semi-skilled, and from $6·50 to $15·00 for skilled workmen. For the industrial clerks such as telephone operators and drivers, the monthly salary ranged between $90 and $300, while that for the clerks ranged from $180 to $650. On the average daily wages in the Japanese-affiliated firms, roughly speaking, stood at around $3·50 to $4·00 for unskilled workmen, $5·50 to $6·00 for the semi-skilled, and $9·50 to $10·50 for the skilled workmen. Equally roughly speaking, the monthly salary stood on the average at around $135 to $150 for the industrial clerks and around $300 to $350 for the clerical personnel.

These average wages compared well with those paid in other pioneer firms in Jurong and were probably higher than those paid in other, non-pioneer, firms in the same industry. Relatively high wages and salaries were common among foreign firms. The scale of production was relatively large, and they did not wish to give the impression that they were exploiting Singapore workers, but on the contrary wished to contribute to their welfare. This was also in line with the government policy of building up a welfare state in Singapore.

The wage structure of the Japanese-affiliated companies was very different, and probably becoming increasingly so, from Singapore's

---

[13] The figures for Japanese-affiliated companies are of course inflated by expatriates' salaries, but the average annual remuneration for all employees in Singapore manufacturing in 1966 was only $2,810 per employee.

traditional wage structure. In Japanese-affiliated firms wage differentials between the production and clerical workers were narrower, while wage differentials between different grades of skill among production workers were wider. The traditional pattern of wage differentials between production and clerical workers in the older Singapore firms was established in labour-intensive repairing and servicing industries where in the tradition of a pre-industrial society manual labour was considered inferior to mental labour. The new Japanese-affiliated firms upgraded the technical requirements and made the composition of the workforce more complex. Simple operations were run by the unskilled, intermediate machine tendering operations were run by the semi-skilled, and more technical operations were run by the skilled and maintained by technical and engineering staff. Since wages in Singapore were geared to job contents, technical and other requirements, rather than to personal factors as in Japanese industry, the new technology in Singapore tended to upgrade the wages paid to production workers while making little changes in the salaries paid to clerical workers, thus reducing the extent of wage differentials between clerks and production workers.

Wage differentials among various production skill grades in older Singapore establishments were narrow because their essentially simple, highly labour-intensive methods had a fairly simple and narrow skill mix. A strong labour movement also contributed to the narrowing of skill differentials. Union pressure at the collective bargaining table tended to narrow differentials by claiming across-the-board increases in cents per hour or in dollars per day, week or month, instead of a percentage increase. There was some government support, if not overt, for such demands in the early 1960s. With new technology the skill mix was broadened and became more complicated, resulting in wider wage differentials among production workers. In the mid-1960s changes in government and union attitudes enabled the managements of the new industries to change the wage structure to fit the technical and manpower requirements of their production processes.

Overtime work fluctuated widely in most Japanese-affiliated firms, ranging from 0 to 70 hours per month for workmen, foremen and supervisors on the production floor, but much less for non-production employees. Many firms were running their plant on a one-shift basis, although a few had a two- to three-shift run after the initial test run period. On average workmen earned about 10 per cent of their basic rates in overtime payments and shift premiums, although in one Japanese-affiliated firm the total monthly earnings were recorded as 165 per cent

105

of their base pay for workmen, 135 per cent for both clerks and industrial clerks, and 160 per cent for foremen and supervisors in factory operation. The level of fringe benefits, however, showed a remarkable uniformity at about 20 to 25 per cent of the total wages paid. The types of fringe benefits—sick leave, paid holidays, and some medical benefits—were also fairly uniform. Transportation allowances had been provided only by two firms, and a housing allowance by only three firms. One of the firms transported employees by lorry for a time only, and then gave these men a transport allowance, and the other gave an allowance only to the workmen and foremen. The housing allowance was granted only to employees renting Economic Development Board flats in Jurong on a full or partial subsidy basis. The amount and kind of fringe benefits granted were lower and fewer than in parent firms in Japan, and it was easier to administer such benefits in Singapore. However, there had been some switch in union pressure to fringe benefits when increases in the base rates began to be resisted more strongly in the mid-1960s.

In most of the Japanese-affiliated firms wages, hours of work, and other important terms of employment were decided by collective bargaining between the union and the management, but in five there was no union. Workers in the unionised pioneer firms with Japanese affiliation belonged to the Pioneer Industries Employees' Union. There had been some efforts at militant union organisation in several Japanese subsidiaries, but the workers did not show much enthusiasm for unionisation *per se* and the employers showed no sympathy to these unionists in particular. In four firms all the organisable workers, and in the rest 80 to 90 per cent, belonged to the Pioneer Industries Employees' Union. Labour agreements had been concluded only in six of the nine organised firms and were being negotiated in two others.

On the employer side, the Japanese-affiliated firms organised the Japan Industrialists' Association of Singapore which provided the Japanese managers with a means of communication about various managerial problems including labour management relations. Many also used management consultant services to solve their labour relations problems. Though not directly, the Singapore Employers' Association whose members were mainly older, foreign, non-pioneer establishments and non-manufacturing firms, also provided some assistance to the Japanese-affiliated firms by circulating labour relations information. The Economic Development Board had been quite helpful in solving problems between unions and management. Only one labour dispute had developed into a strike, and with government assistance this dispute came to an end in one day.[14] Another Japanese-affiliated pioneer firm was threatened by a strike but this was averted by the Economic Development Board.[15] In 1966 and 1967 most Japanese-affiliated companies were not faced with any serious labour relations problems, but bonus increases were one of the major issues being negotiated between the union and the management.

CONTRIBUTION OF JAPANESE MANUFACTURING
INVESTMENT TO SINGAPORE

Although during the first three years the contribution of Japanese-affiliated firms to Singapore's gross industrial output did not reach a significant level, the gross value of output increased at a high rate from 1961 to 1962 and from 1962 to 1963, but almost came to a standstill during 1963–4 in spite of an increase in their number. From 1964 to 1965, however, there was a very great expansion in output of the Japanese-affiliated firms and their contribution to the gross industrial output of Singapore establishments with ten or more workers reached 2 per cent. From 1965 to 1966 there was an even greater absolute and relative increase although industrial output now saw a steady increase after stagnating in 1963–4.

The percentage of the national income and industrial gross output contributed in 1966 by Japanese-affiliated companies had in fact become so high that a sudden withdrawal of the Japanese firms would have serious economic effects on Singapore. This of course is extremely unlikely. The Japanese investment has been made in good faith and with long-term objectives in view, and it has been accepted in this light.

[14] The increase in the annual bonus had been a major issue between the union and management for some time, but there were also other demands. The management of the company wished to settle all these issues at the same time. Therefore, when the union came to the management with the annual bonus question, the latter responded by suggesting discussions on the two-shift system first. The talks were deadlocked and the union called a strike on 20 December 1965. On the evening of the following day it was called off at the request of the Labour Minister who issued an order sending the matter to the Industrial Arbitration Court. On the third day the management of the company went to the Court and through it proposed a collective bargaining agreement to the union. After a week's negotiation between the management and the union an agreement was signed.

[15] The company dismissed an employee, supposedly for a fair reason, but the man went to the Pioneer Industries Employees' Union and the latter took up his case and threatened to go on strike. The Economic Development Board suggested the company rehire him, and the company did so, but in a month's time discharged him again for a personal misdemeanor.

Table 4.5   Gross value of output and capital outlay
in fixed assets by firms with Japanese capital investment, 1962–6

Year	Gross value of output[a] $ million	Gross value of output of Japanese-affiliated firms as % of gross value of output in Singapore manufacturing establishments with ten or more workers[b]	Outlay on fixed investment $ million[c]	Outlay on fixed investment by Japanese-affiliated firms as % of Singapore gross capital formation[d]
1962	5·992	0·3	3·497	1·4
1963	9·835	0·6	0·250	0·1
1964	10·589	0·7	42·321	10·2
1965	34·836	2·0	4·907	1·1
1966	87·441	4·4	9·890	2·2

[a] The gross value of output has been used because of the difficulties in obtaining value added figures for the Japanese-affiliated firms.

[b] Calculated from Table 1.4.

[c] Figures show capital outlay in fixed assets by all the Japanese-affiliated pioneer and non-pioneer firms for each year of production start rather than for year in which capital was actually invested. The 1966 figures, however, covered the capital outlay in fixed assets made by two firms which came into production during January and May 1967.

[d] Calculated from Table 1.17.

Nevertheless the importance of the Japanese-affiliated companies' gross output suggests that Singapore should diversify the sources of its foreign investment as much as possible so that unexpected incidents in international relations or unfavourable economic fluctuations in one or more of the major investing countries will have little effect on the continued capital, technological, and managerial inflow which has been contributing to its economic growth.

Table 4.5 gives an estimate of the direct contributions made by the Japanese-affiliated firms to manufacturing investment in Singapore from 1961 to 1966. Fixed investment by Japanese-affiliated firms was quite considerable in relation to manufacturing investment, but there was a wide variation over the years in both the absolute amount of the Japanese manufacturing investment in fixed assets and its contribution to manufacturing investment in Singapore. This was partly a reflection of the smallness of the sample of Japanese-affiliated firms, but more importantly it is due to the indivisibility of fixed capital outlays. Japanese investment, in addition to stimulating Singapore investors to join them in new ventures directly, also stimulated investment indirectly in allied industries, but this of course cannot be measured.

In 1966 firms with Japanese affiliation employed 2,467 local employees, or 4 per cent of total manufacturing employment in establishments with ten or more workers and 0·4 per cent of the total workforce in Singapore.

108

Employment by Japanese-affiliated pioneer firms represented 23 per cent of all the Singapore workers employed in the pioneer firms in Singapore.[16] The Japanese-affiliated firms were less labour-intensive and had higher gross output per employee than all Singapore manufacturing industries, but they were more labour-intensive and had slightly lower gross output per employee than the pioneer industries. Thus for a given level of output the Japanese manufacturing subsidiaries in 1966 contributed more to the creation of employment opportunities than the average pioneer firm in Singapore.

Japanese-affiliated firms helped to improve the technical quality of the Singapore labour force, although the type of industries suited to the Singapore market could not bring particularly advanced techniques. These will only come when sophisticated industries producing synthetic raw materials and components for metal and electrical industries follow the finishing of semi-fabricated goods and the manufacture of simple consumer goods.

Improvements in managerial skills have similarly been limited. Perhaps the greatest contribution Japanese and other foreign firms have

Table 4.6   Foreign exchange contribution
by pioneer firms with Japanese capital investment, 1966

	$'000	$'000
Gross foreign exchange saved	24,824	
Gross foreign exchange earned	20,186	
Gross foreign exchange contribution		45,010
Less: Gross value of materials imported	23,502	
Annual depreciation of machinery imported[a]	7,026	
Net foreign exchange contributions on current account		14,482
Plus: Foreign exchange earnings on capital account[b]	4,715	
Net foreign exchange contribution on current and capital account		19,197

[a] In interviews with the Japanese-affiliated firms it was found that nearly all the machinery installed in pioneer firms had been imported from abroad, mostly from countries of the principal parent firm. The value of machinery installed rather than the total value of fixed assets was therefore used as the base from which to derive the annual import cost of capital equipment. This was computed as one-fifth of the total capital outlays on machinery on the assumption that machinery is replaced in five years.

[b] Foreign exchange earnings on capital account were calculated by dividing into five the total amount of equity participation during 1962–6; they show the average annual amount of paid-up capital contributed by the foreign investors over the five-year period.
Source: Economic Development Board data.

[16] See Appendix Table VII.

made to the quality of Singapore's labour force was improving commitment to modern factory work, reducing the relatively high absenteeism and the irregular pace of work that had hitherto characterised the labour force.

The net foreign exchange contribution made possible by Japanese manufacturing investment is shown in Table 4.6. The net foreign exchange contribution made by Japanese-affiliated pioneer firms in 1966 was substantial on current account alone. When the foreign exchange earnings on capital account in the form of equity capital invested from Japan were taken into consideration, the firms' contributions either came close to, or were greater than, the total value of output they exported in 1966. Compared with the net changes in the foreign exchange reserves held by Singapore in 1966, the gross foreign exchange contributions made by the Japanese-affiliated firms in Singapore were quite significant. The dependence of Japanese-affiliated firms on imported machinery and equipment was typical of all foreign pioneer firms, but they showed a higher ratio of sales abroad,[17] a higher ratio of equity participation from abroad,[18] and relied on imported raw materials to a slightly lesser extent than all foreign pioneer firms,[19] thus contributing more to foreign exchange earnings of Singapore than foreign pioneer firms on average.

The principal problems facing Japanese firms in Singapore are those of markets. Future performance and participation of Japanese capital in Singapore manufacturing will largely depend on the extent to which they can widen their markets both in Singapore and abroad. However, the attempt by Japanese-affiliated firms to expand their domestic markets will only be desirable if it substitutes production in Singapore for imports, lowers the import content of Singapore-produced goods, or lowers prices to consumers. Otherwise it will only cut into the existing shares of other firms in Singapore and add nothing to foreign exchange earnings or welfare.

Export expansion by Japanese-affiliated firms, on the other hand, will be a highly desirable contribution to the government's policy of building a viable and progressive economy. This requires both internal measures by the firms themselves and external measures which must chiefly be taken by the government.

The extent to which the Japanese-affiliated firms can lower costs either by product or process improvement seems to be very limited in

[17] See Appendix Table X.
[18] Economic Development Board data.
[19] See Appendix Table VI.

110

the small internal market. Economies of scale are not attainable. The expansion of export markets is thus an absolute necessity for cost reduction at the plant level. New tax incentives could include rebates of taxes already paid, export subsidies in the form of low interest loans, outright grants of export bonuses, or higher depreciation allowances.

In addition to such government promotional measures, the Japanese parent firms could encourage their affiliated firms in Singapore to increase their exports by lifting restrictions on exports, and by placing the Singapore firms' products on their worldwide sales network. This should not be too difficult since most of the Japanese parent firms are either large-scale manufacturing corporations with international marketing experience, or large-scale commercial houses mainly concerned with overseas market expansion. There may be, however, practical difficulties, as Japanese parent firms themselves are engaged in promoting their own exports. Nevertheless, the pursuit of enlightened self-interest dictates that adjustments should be made to accommodate both claims for export expansion, and it is significant that several Japanese firms in Singapore and their parent firms in Japan have already done so. For Singapore increased exports and foreign exchange earnings will mean a higher capacity for imports and this will afford Japanese parent firms among others greater opportunities for exporting their products to Singapore as long as such products are competitive. Thus the self-interest of Japanese parent firms suggests that they encourage exports from their affiliated firms in Singapore.

Export expansion of Japanese-affiliated firms in Singapore, as of any other Singapore firms, will also increase Singapore's capacity to import the capital and consumer goods necessary for further industrialisation and an increased level of living for Singapore people. The Japanese and, for that matter, other foreign manufacturing investors, could help to a greater extent than they have in the past in the all-important efforts currently being made by Singapore in this direction, so that the competitive position of Singapore manufacturing industries in international markets is enhanced, and the volume and diversity of exports increased.

Japanese and other foreign manufacturing firms would go a long way toward the goals of a continued growth in the per capita real income of Singapore and full employment if they should succeed in helping to enlarge the foreign and domestic markets for the manufactured products of Singapore. They will in turn expect much of the government in improving its assistance to industrialisation by way of more efficient export incentive schemes and other protective measures.

5

Paul Luey

Hong Kong Investment[1]

THE EXTENT OF HONG KONG INVESTMENT

There has always been capital flowing out of Hong Kong for direct investment in industry abroad, though until recently the outflow was occasional rather than regular and its size was not significant enough to attract attention. Since the beginning of the sixties, the frequency and the scale of outflow has increased, and Singapore has become one of the principal receiving countries.

From 1961 to 1966 Hong Kong's investment in industry in Singapore, in terms of aggregate contribution to the paid-up capital of manufacturing firms, was $12·5 million[2] (Table 5.1). In the second half of 1967, largely as a result of the political disturbances which broke out in Hong Kong in May, there was a large exodus of capital to Singapore. Hong Kong concerns were said to have made additional firm commitments to invest $49 million in existing manufacturing firms and new industrial

[1] I would like to thank manufacturers and executives of Hong Kong pioneer firms in Singapore who answered my many questions, and the officers of the Economic Development Board for their help with data on pioneer and Jurong firms.

[2] Capital that has been transferred out of Hong Kong is referred to as Hong Kong capital, and such a transfer is considered to be an outflow of Hong Kong capital. It is irrelevant whether the capital has been transferred from accounts of Hong Kong residents of Chinese or other origin. Some such transfers have been from accounts of Hong Kong residents of nationalities other than Chinese, and some transfers have been from accounts of non-residents. If an Indonesian transferred his funds from his Hong Kong bank account to Singapore, such transfer would be for all intents and purposes equivalent to an outflow of capital to Singapore from Hong Kong. Because of differences in classification, figures in this chapter do not always agree with Economic Development Board data in the Appendix.

112

Table 5.1   Association of Hong Kong capital with capital
from Singapore and other foreign sources, 1961–6

Source of capital	Pioneer firms as at 31 December 1966		Non-pioneer firms during 1961–6[a]		Total Hong Kong investment
	in production or implementing stage $'000	not in production $'000	in Jurong $'000	other[b] $'000	$'000
Hong Kong	3,615	100	160	900	4,775
Hong Kong and Singapore	1,716	811	535	—	3,062
Hong Kong, Singapore, and Taiwan	445	—	—	—	445
Hong Kong, Singapore, and Malaysia	1,815	—	—	—	1,815
Hong Kong, Singapore, Malaysia, and Japan or Taiwan	65	—	5	—	70
Hong Kong, Singapore, Malaysia, and Philippines	1,573	—	—	—	1,573
Hong Kong, United States or United Kingdom or Malaysia	737	—	—	—	737
Total	9,966	911	700	900	12,477

[a] Firms in production, not in production, and in implementing stage.

[b] Assumed to be wholly-owned Hong Kong firms. Paid-up capital of firms is assumed to be all contributed by Hong Kong investors.

Sources: For pioneer firms and non-pioneer firms in Jurong, Economic Development Board data. For non-pioneer firms not in Jurong, company registration information with assumptions given in note b.

ventures in Singapore.[3] This amount may be exaggerated but there is no doubt that from 1961 to 1966 Hong Kong was injecting capital fairly steadily into Singapore's industrial sector, and that the trend would probably have continued into 1967 even if political troubles had not broken out.[4] A large influx of immigrant and foreign capital and the

[3] This was disclosed by Singapore's Finance Minister, Dr Goh Keng Swee: *Straits Times* (Singapore), 3 November 1967; and also *China Mail* (Hong Kong), 5 December 1967.

[4] According to a 1967 survey of some sixty firms by Hong Kong's Department of Commerce and Industry, the twenty-four companies which had already established or were about to establish manufacturing firms in other Asian countries, notably Singapore, Taiwan, and South Korea, stated that their decisions to move to those countries had been made before the disturbances

113

inflows of entrepreneurial and technical skills preceding, accompanying, or following the capital inflow had helped transform the structure of the Hong Kong economy from basically entrepôt activity into an economy in which industry played a very important role; Hong Kong was now in turn assisting other developing economies in their industrialisation through direct investment.

Of the estimated total initial investment made by Hong Kong in Singapore manufacturing, $10,877,000 went to the pioneer industries and $1,600,000 to non-pioneer industries[5] (Table 5.1). There has been some other Hong Kong private direct investment in industry in Singapore, so that total investment was actually larger than $12·5 million, but difficulties in obtaining data have made it necessary to confine this study to investment in the pioneer sector and in the relatively easily identifiable manufacturing firms in the non-pioneer sector.

For an economy which is itself seeking more, and also new sources of, foreign direct investment, Hong Kong appears to have contributed a significant share of foreign capital for Singapore manufacturing.[6] In the main, Hong Kong concentrated its investment on consumer goods industries. By the end of 1966 almost 39 per cent of the capital flow into pioneer industries had gone into textile manufacturing. Food manufacturing took about 28 per cent, while chemical products absorbed almost all the 26 per cent in chemicals and chemical products (Table 5.2). Investment in producer goods industries—chemicals, plywood, rubber products, and cables—did not amount to more than 5 per cent.

One might express surprise that Hong Kong with its expertise and experience in textile manufacturing invested only 39 per cent of its

---

broke out in May 1967. Of the remainder which were alleged to have decided to move, all but two actually had no intention of moving out of Hong Kong or of establishing associated firms overseas (*South China Morning Post* [Hong Kong], 4 January 1968). Hong Kong direct investment in Singapore and other Asian manufacturing industries was a continuous process which had started before May 1967. Journalists' accounts of capital flight from Hong Kong during 1967 have to be taken with some caution.

[5] Data for Hong Kong investment in pioneer industries were supplied by the Economic Development Board, and these have been adjusted to conform to the above definition of Hong Kong capital or investment. Data for non-pioneer firms in Jurong were also obtained from the Economic Development Board. For non-pioneer firms not in Jurong, all of which were in textile industries, the size of investment was assumed to be $150,000 per firm after checking the total nominal capital of the firms given in company registration records.

[6] Hong Kong contributed 10 per cent of foreign capital in pioneer firms: calculated from Appendix Table I.

Table 5.2   Hong Kong investment in pioneer industries,
by industry group, at 31 December 1966[a]

Industry		Paid-up capital $'000	Distribution per cent
I	Food and beverages	2,768	28
II	Textiles, garments, and leather	3,871	39
V	Chemicals and chemical products	2,550	26
IX	Electrical products	552	6
	Other[b]	225	2
	All industries	9,966	100

[a] In terms of Hong Kong's contributions of the paid-up capital of firms granted pioneer status and in production or in implementing stage.
[b] Wood and paper products, rubber products, and stationery products.
Source: Data supplied by Economic Development Board.

pioneer industries capital in the textile and garment industries. The diversification of Hong Kong investment implied in Tables 5.3 and 5.6 is, however, only recent. Until the beginning of 1966 the Colony concentrated its investment in Singapore on textiles, garments, and food manufacturing, with the former two accounting for more than half of the total Hong Kong investment in pioneer industries. In any event, not all of the Hong Kong direct investment was initiated by Hong Kong investors; investment in industries other than textiles and garments seems to have been initiated by other investors with Hong Kong capital playing a responding role. More will be said about this later.

A considerable proportion of the outflow of Hong Kong capital to Singapore's industries went to industrial ventures in association not only with Singapore capital but also with capital from other foreign sources. Between 1961 and 1966 only $4·8 million was invested in the establishment of wholly-owned Hong Kong firms, $3·1 million was invested in ventures jointly with Singapore capital, $3·9 million in multinational ventures with capital from Singapore and one or two other foreign countries, and $0·7 million in ventures jointly with capital from a source other than Singapore (Table 5.1).

Hong Kong's contribution to the total paid-up capital of pioneer firms with Hong Kong investment (whether in production or implementing their plans by constructing buildings or installing machinery in December 1966), was only 35 per cent of the total of $28·2 million. The Colony's contribution of paid-up capital to the joint ventures in the food industry was only 20 per cent of the total paid-up capital, and its share of investment in the manufacturing of wood and paper products, rubber

Table 5.3 Stage of implementation of pioneer firms with Hong Kong capital

Industry	No. of firms granted pioneer status				No. of pioneer firms commencing production						Production ceased		Commencement (termination) of Hong Kong participation		Pioneer firms in production at	
	1961	1963	1965	1966	1962	1963	1964	1965	1966	mid-1967	No.	Year	No.	Year	31 Dec. 1966	1 May 1967
I Food and beverages	2	—	—	—	—	1	1	—	—	—	—	—	—	—	2	2
II Textiles, garments, and leather	10	3	—	—	5	5ᵃ	3	—	—	—	1 1 1	1964 1965 1966	—	—	10	10
III Wood and paper products	1	—	—	—	—	—	1	—	—	—	—	—	1	1966	1	1
IV Rubber products	1	—	—	—	—	—	1	—	—	—	—	—	1	1966	1	1
V Chemicals and chemical products	1	—	1ᵇ	4ᵇ	—	—	2	—	3ᵇ	1ᵇ	—	—	1	1966	5ᵇ	6ᵇ
VIII Metals and engineering	—	—	1	—	—	—	1	—	1	—	1	1965	(1)ᶜ(1966)		0	0
IX Electrical products	—	—	1	2	—	—	1	—	2	—	—	—	1	1966	3	3
X Miscellaneous	1	—	1	—	1	—	1	—	1	—	1	1963	1	1966	1	1
All industries	4	15	6ᵇ	6ᵇ	1	6	8ᵃ	6	8ᵇ	1ᵇ	5	—	5(1)	—	23ᵈ	24ᵈ

ᵃ Including one firm which was subsequently granted pioneer status in 1965.
ᵇ Including firms which are subsidiaries or associates of subsidiaries of companies with head offices in Hong Kong.
ᶜ This firm started off as a firm financed with investment funds from Hong Kong. It was subsequently bought by Singapore investors who converted the company into one manufacturing metal products. It was only then that the firm applied for pioneer status.
ᵈ Without including the firms described in b, the totals for 1965 and 1966 would both have been 22.
Sources: Economic Development Board data and data obtained from the inquiry undertaken in July–August 1967 by the author.

products, and stationery products was only 8 per cent of the total. In these categories Singapore contributed more than half of the total initial investment and other foreign investors more than a quarter.

CHARACTERISTICS OF FIRMS WITH HONG KONG INVESTMENT

Hong Kong capital established a relatively large number of manufacturing firms. Between 1961 and 1966 Hong Kong had an investment in no fewer than forty-three manufacturing concerns in Singapore and at the end of 1966 there were thirty-six firms with a Hong Kong interest, in production or implementing. Thirty-one pioneer firms were set up wholly or partly with Hong Kong capital. At least six garment firms were established in 1964, and there were six non-pioneer firms in production or implementing in the non-textile industries in 1966 (Table 5.4). Not all of the firms set up were in production or implementing in 1966. By the beginning of 1967 only twenty-three Hong Kong pioneer firms were in production and another two were being implemented. As shown in Table 5.3, five firms ceased operation or production of their original products and one firm ceased to have Hong Kong participation between 1963 and 1966. Of the non-pioneer firms four of the non-textile manufacturers had begun production, with the remaining two still in various phases of implementation (Table 5.5). At least two of the non-pioneer garment firms had suspended operations by the end of 1966.[7] Altogether, there were thirty-one Hong Kong manufacturing firms in Jurong,

Table 5.4   Stage of implementation of firms with Hong Kong capital
at 31 December 1966

Pioneer firms	
Firms granted pioneer status	31
Firms in production	23
Firms in implementing stage	2
Firms ceased operation or production for various reasons	6
Non-pioneer firms	
Firms in Jurong in production or in implementing stage	6
Other	6[a]
Total for firms in production or in implementing stage	36

[a] One ceased production.

[7] Three garment firms were reported to have been closed; Kayser Sung and R. H. Leary (eds.), *Asian Textile Bi-Annual 1965–1966* (Hong Kong, 1966), pp. 153 and 158. Two of these were non-pioneer firms.

Table 5.5   Non-pioneer firms in Jurong with Hong Kong capital,
by industry group and stage of implementation at 31 December 1966

	Industry	No. of firms in production	No. of firms in implementing stage	Total
III	Wood and paper products	1	—	1
VII	Non-metallic mineral products	1	—	1
VIII	Metals and engineering	—	1	1
IX	Electrical products	1	—	1
	Other	1	1	2
	All industries	4	2	6

Source: Economic Development Board data.

either in production or implementing (Table 5.6). Twenty-three of the seventy-three pioneer firms with foreign capital in production at the end of 1966 had Hong Kong capital participation.

As Table 5.7 shows, seven of the Hong Kong pioneer firms established during 1961–6 were wholly owned by Hong Kong investors, six were Hong Kong-Singapore joint ventures, three were joint ventures in association with capital from another foreign source, and nine were multinational joint ventures. The wholly-owned concerns and some of

Table 5.6   Firms with Hong Kong capital, by industry group and
stage of implementation at 31 December 1966[a]

	Industry	No. of firms in production	No. of firms in implementing stage	Total
I	Food and beverages	2	—	2
II	Textiles, garments, and leather	10	—	10
III	Wood and paper products	2	—	2
IV	Rubber products	1	—	1
V	Chemicals and chemical products	5	2	7
VII	Non-metallic mineral products	1	—	1
VIII	Metals and engineering	—	1	1
IX	Electrical products	4	—	4
	Other	2	1	3
	All industries	27	4	31

[a] All pioneer firms and other non-textile firms.
Sources: Based on Tables 5.3 and 5.5.

118

Table 5.7   Form of Hong Kong investment in pioneer industries
at 31 December 1966[a]

	No. of firms
Wholly-owned Hong Kong firms	7
Joint ventures	
Hong Kong-Singapore	6
Hong Kong-United States	1
Hong Kong-United Kingdom	1
Hong Kong-Malaysia	1
Multinational joint ventures	
Hong Kong-Singapore-Taiwan	3
Hong Kong-Singapore-Malaysia	2
Hong Kong-Singapore-Malaysia-Japan	1
Hong Kong-Singapore-Malaysia-Taiwan	1
Hong Kong-Singapore-Malaysia-Philippines	2
Total	25

[a] Pioneer firms in production or in implementing stage.
Sources: Economic Development Board data and data obtained from author's inquiry.

the joint ventures with Singapore seemed to have been established on the initiative of Hong Kong entrepreneurs. It appears, however, that Hong Kong investors played a responding role in the establishment of most of the multinational joint ventures. In general Hong Kong played an initiating rather than a responding role in joint undertakings when it held more than 51 per cent of the holdings in joint capital ventures or the largest holding in multinational joint capital ventures.

In the pioneer sector, of the six Hong Kong-Singapore joint ventures, Hong Kong had controlling interest in three; and of the three other joint ventures with another foreign country, it had majority holdings in two. In all but one multinational joint venture Hong Kong had smaller holdings than its major partners. Among the twenty-five Hong Kong pioneer firms in production or being implemented in 1966, Hong Kong capital accounted for more than 50 per cent of the paid-up capital of thirteen firms. In contrast, there were nine firms in which Hong Kong held 25 per cent or less, the minimum being 2 per cent, of the holdings in joint and multinational joint ventures (Table 5.8).

With investment capital spread over a large number of firms (especially the large number of multinational joint ventures), the average amount of Hong Kong capital in a pioneer firm was generally small. In 1966, the

119

Table 5.8   Hong Kong shareholdings in pioneer firms with
Hong Kong capital, by industry group at 31 December 1966[a]

Industry	Number of firms with varying degrees of Hong Kong shareholdings				
	100%	76–99%	51–75%	26–50%	1–25%
I Food and beverages	—	—	—	—	2
II Textiles, garments, and leather	4	—	4	1	1
III Wood and paper products	—	—	—	—	1
IV Rubber products	—	—	—	—	1
V Chemicals and chemical products	2	2	—	2	1
IX Electrical products	1	—	—	—	2
Other	—	—	—	—	1
All industries	7	2	4	3	9

[a] Firms in production or in implementing stage only.
Sources: Economic Development Board data and inquiry data.

size of Hong Kong capital in a pioneer firm ranged from a meagre $5,000 to $1·72 million, with $382,000 being the mean. This range also applied to the non-pioneer non-textile firms, but here the upper limit was $400,000. In sixteen of the twenty-five Hong Kong pioneer firms in production or in the implementation stage by the end of 1966, the amount of Hong Kong capital in the firm did not exceed $400,000; in fourteen, it was at or below the $300,000. Among the six firms within the range of $1,000 to $100,000, four were at or below the $40,000 level. In contrast, the four firms above the $600,000 level were actually at or above the $1 million mark (Table 5.9).

The amount of Hong Kong capital in a firm is obviously not always equivalent to the firm's capitalisation, since Hong Kong is not necessarily the sole owner of the firm. With the large number of joint ventures and multinational joint ventures in which Hong Kong was neither the majority nor largest equity shareholder, one would expect the capitalisation of these firms on average to be larger than the amount of Hong Kong investment per firm. But with the exception of the largest four firms, the capitalisation per pioneer firm with Hong Kong participation was still not very impressive. At the beginning of 1967, the capital size of a Hong Kong pioneer firm ranged from $163,000 to $8·97 million, with a mean of $1·08 million. If the largest two firms with a total paid-up capital of more than $5 million each were excluded, the mean was reduced to $562,500; and if the largest four firms with a total paid-up capital of more than $1 million each were left out of account, the mean paid-up

Table 5.9   Frequency distribution of Hong Kong investment in
pioneer industries at 31 December 1966[a]

Range of investment in terms of Hong Kong's shares of paid-up capital of firms $'000	No. of firms
Over 1,000	2
901 — 1,000	2
801 — 900	—
701 — 800	—
601 — 700	—
501 — 600	2
401 — 500	3
301 — 400	2
201 — 300	3
101 — 200	5
1 — 100	6
	25

[a] Firms in production or in implementing stage only.
Sources: Economic Development Board data and inquiry data.

capital per Hong Kong pioneer firm, was only $425,000. Furthermore, fifteen of the twenty-five firms were within the range of $101,000 to $500,000.[8] The two largest firms, each with a capitalisation of more than $5 million, of which Hong Kong capital accounted for about 20 per cent, were in food manufacturing. The seven wholly-owned Hong Kong pioneer firms each had a total paid-up capital of $1 million or less and all but one had a capitalisation of $600,000 or less.

REASONS FOR INVESTING IN SINGAPORE

The outflow of Hong Kong capital for cotton textile and garment subsidiaries and associated firms in Singapore between April 1963 and June 1964 was largely due to investors' expectation of higher returns on investment there than in Hong Kong, but the circumstances which led investors to believe that they could obtain better profits for their investment by manufacturing cotton textile goods in Singapore than in Hong Kong varied for individual entrepreneurs and firms.

[8] These included seven pioneer firms in the cotton textile and garment industries.

For most of the Hong Kong firms which subsequently established subsidiaries and associated companies in Singapore, the decision to invest in cotton textiles in Singapore was associated with the quantitative restrictions on Hong Kong's exports of cotton textile goods to major markets in the developed countries, and the absence of such controls for Singapore. Yet it was not simply United Kingdom and United States restraints on Hong Kong's exports of cotton textile goods that caused Hong Kong entrepreneurs to invest in Singapore. Indeed, by mid-1963, Hong Kong was already in its fifth year of the 'voluntary' undertaking made with the United Kingdom,[9] the third with the United States and with Canada, and the second with Norway.[10] Hong Kong, by that time, was committed to restrain its cotton textile exports to the United Kingdom under successive bilateral agreements for 1959–62, 1962–3, and 1963–6, to the United States and Canada under the Geneva short-term cotton textile agreement for 1961–2, and under the Long Term Arrangement Regarding International Trade in Cotton Textiles for 1962–7, of which Hong Kong was a signatory government; and to Norway under the Geneva Long Term Arrangement.[11] If quota restrictions imposed on Hong Kong by its major customers for cotton textiles had been the only reason for the capital outflow to Singapore, then the outflow ought to have begun before 1963, although it is true that Singapore had its labour union problems at the turn of the sixties, and that the Economic Development Board did not become effective until 1963–4. But it is also relevant that on the whole the Hong Kong cotton textile industry wore the restrictions on its markets very well. The quantitative restrictions did cause some contractions in the industry, especially in the garment section, during the period preceding 1963.[12]

[9] For a review of the voluntary undertaking given to the United Kingdom by the Hong Kong cotton textile industry, see the review made by the Hong Kong General Chamber of Commerce in 'Halfway for Hong Kong', *Far Eastern Economic Review* (Hong Kong), 27 October 1960, pp. 183–7; and *Nigel Ruscoe's Annual Hong Kong Register 1964* (Hong Kong, 1964), pp. 98–100, in which the agreement operating at the time was discussed.

[10] See ibid., pp. 100–1, for the agreements made with these countries.

[11] The Long Term Arrangement was initiated to give various developing countries a share of world markets without unduly affecting the output of developed countries. For the background to the question of international cotton textile agreements, see G. L. Patterson, *Discrimination in International Trade, The Policy Issues, 1945–1965* (Princeton, 1966), pp. 307–17.

[12] By the beginning of the decade of the sixties, the Hong Kong cotton textile industry, especially in the clothing section, had over-expanded (*Industry in Hong Kong*, Hong Kong, 1962, *passim*). For accounts of the development of

These, together with the cancellations of orders for garments by the United States and Canada in the latter half of 1960, had led the cotton textile industry, especially in the spinning, weaving, and garment sections, to operate at 20 to 30 per cent below capacity in 1960–2.[13] However, after this initial setback it recovered its upward trend in terms of value of exports of cotton textile goods. Production of garments was increased to an unprecedented level by 1963. The quantitative restrictions had been something of a blessing in disguise as far as the American market was concerned. They had turned marketing of cotton textiles from a buyer's to a seller's market.[14] Thus it was probably not the export quota *per se* which finally made some of the cotton weaving and garment firms decide to divert part of their reinvestment funds or surplus resources to Singapore, but the increased categorisation of the United Kingdom quota, particularly in garments. Some firms had been producing principally for the United Kingdom market. As under previous agreements, in the bilateral agreement for 1963–6 the annual quotas were classified into four categories: Cotton Yarns, Cotton Loom-state Fabrics, Cotton Finished Fabrics, and Cotton Made-up Goods, including garments.[15] The specialist manufacturers who had been allocated a large quota based on past performance had no difficulty in operating at full capacity in a broad category such as made-up goods. But in September 1963 the

---

the Hong Kong cotton textile industry during the period 1960–2, see Kayser Sung, 'Shrinking Greys for Lancashire', *Far Eastern Economic Review*, 9 June 1960, pp. 1159, 1222–5; Nigel Ruscoe, 'The Hong Kong Garment Crisis', ibid., 30 March 1961, pp. 572–9; Kester Stone, 'Another Garment Shock', ibid., 11 May 1961, p. 259; and Kayser Sung, 'Crossroads for Hong Kong Textiles', ibid., 18 May 1961, pp. 301, 304–9.

[13] 'The fast-growing garment section, which fared so well in the boom year of 1959, is now in the midst of a storm. Some of its United States and Canadian customers have cancelled contracts worth between $HK70 million and $HK80 million. On top of this heavy claims are being made on account of the failure of producers to be punctual with their delivery dates and to meet the quality specifications', Kayser Sung noted in 'The Cancellation Wave', *Far Eastern Economic Review*, 31 March 1960, p. 695. The Hong Kong Spinners' Association chairman made estimates of the contraction of the Hong Kong textile industry at the end of 1962 in the *Cotton Trade Journal*. The relevant section was reproduced in *Nigel Ruscoe's Annual Hong Kong Register 1963*, p. 172.

[14] Sung and Leary (eds.), *Asian Textile Bi-Annual 1965–1966*, p. 78. Quotas restricted supply, and American buyers, who had to place orders in Hong Kong a season ahead of sales in the United States, were actually competing for Hong Kong factory space to fill these orders.

[15] *Nigel Ruscoe's Annual Hong Kong Register 1964*, pp. 98–100.

United Kingdom requested Hong Kong to consider acceptance of a greater degree of categorisation of the annual quota. Hong Kong eventually accepted with great reluctance. Under the amended agreement, effective from February 1964, the original four categories were split into thirty-four. This meant quotas for more specifically defined items than under the original four categories. The large manufacturers were affected much more seriously than the smaller ones. A contraction of the scale of production seemed inevitable, and worse still, there might be further amendments to the quota arrangement.

Some of these firms found a solution in setting up subsidiaries and associated companies in Singapore, for the island state had certain attractions which Taiwan, the main alternative site, did not have. Since they produced mainly, if not exclusively, for the United Kingdom, Singapore was an ideal location because it qualified for Commonwealth preference. The quota question still had to be resolved, and, for the time being, exports of Singapore-made cotton textile goods to the United Kingdom were not subject to any restraints. The Singapore subsidiaries and associates could enter the United States market or markets in other developed countries, for none of these countries had yet requested export restraints from Singapore under the Long Term Arrangement.

At the time the decision to invest in cotton textile manufacturing in Singapore seemed very sound. The entrepreneurs, individual and corporate, took action quickly, and within a matter of months their Singapore factories began production for exports to the United Kingdom. About fifteen cotton textile manufacturing firms, both pioneer and non-pioneer, commenced production in 1963 and 1964, with twelve starting between July 1963 and June 1964. On the basis of their experience of quota allocation in Hong Kong, they felt they had to move quickly into production so that they would have good performance records should Singapore be placed in a similar position to Hong Kong on quotas. As the Hong Kong investors had brought with them the established markets for their products, there was no difficulty in finding buyers. When the global quota implicit in the British Board of Trade Notice to Importers No. 1070 became applicable to Singapore, the Hong Kong firms in Singapore had no difficulty in obtaining the necessary licences or in finding buyers in the United Kingdom.[16]

But not all of the cotton textile and garment manufacturing firms were established by manufacturers in Hong Kong because of quotas.

[16] Sung and Leary (eds.), *Asian Textile Bi-Annual 1965–1966*, p. 153.

One firm manufacturing cotton knitted outer garments was not affected by the United Kingdom quota for Hong Kong because knitted garments were not included in the quota. This company sought to operate in Singapore to supply the Indonesian market but Confrontation made it impossible to attain its objective, at least during the early period of the Singapore operation.

Two garment firms were established with a view to expanding the overseas operations of the parent companies. One of these had considered Singapore to be a good alternative base for exports to the United Kingdom market; but the other had an eye on the Malaysian common market, although it also started operating in Malaysia.

One of the firms producing fabrics and cotton piecegoods was established in Singapore primarily for prestige reasons, though Hong Kong quotas were also a factor. The parent firm is one of the largest weaving concerns in Hong Kong and is part of a vertically-integrated group.

One garment firm was the venture of an individual enterprising industrialist from Hong Kong who was also associated at the managerial level with one of the largest cotton spinning and weaving mills in Hong Kong. He chose Singapore as a location for his factory because of its good government and what the government could offer. He represented one of the many immigrant entrepreneurs and industrialists who had helped the process of industrialisation in Hong Kong. Another garment firm with Hong Kong participation was set up on the initiative of Taiwan investors so that the Hong Kong quota problem had no bearing, although the cotton textile agreement between Taiwan and the United States probably did.

The non-textile firms appeared to be the undertakings of individual Hong Kong entrepreneurs rather than of parent firms in Hong Kong. Given the protection promised by the Singapore government, there was sufficient internal demand for food manufacturing. One of the firms was an associate of a chain of biscuit manufacturing companies, and it was established in part to implement a vertical integration plan. The other non-textile firms were geared to produce for the Singapore market. Two of the pharmaceutical firms were subsidiaries or associates of Singapore subsidiaries of Hong Kong firms. Their operations were started purely because of the possibilities of local demand. It is noteworthy that few if any of the Hong Kong firms in Singapore were set up in anticipation of a Malaysian common market. If the concept had not been stillborn, the size of the market for these firms would have increased, but its failure to do so did not affect the utilisation of capacity to the same extent as in other firms in Singapore.

125

The reasons for the acceleration in investment in Singapore which took place in 1966 and 1967 seemed to be mainly political. Incidents in Macao in December 1966 were probably a contributing factor, and the exodus of capital to Singapore during the latter part of 1967 was probably due to political insecurity in Hong Kong. It was well known by then among Hong Kong manufacturers that Taiwan was a higher return economy than Singapore. But those who wished to have the option of following their capital felt that they would not be as welcome in Taiwan as in Singapore. Some were not certain of the political future of Taiwan. Singapore is an independent state with Chinese forming the bulk of the population, but it is not adjacent to the People's Republic of China. For some investors this seemed to be sufficient inducement, even at the price of lower profits than they might have earned in Taiwan. It is still difficult to determine whether those who invested in Singapore in 1967 were in fact Chinese normally resident in Hong Kong. Some at least appeared to be Chinese normally resident in Indonesia, and for them Singapore was a better, and politically safer, place for industrial ventures. When Confrontation was over they would be close to Indonesia and well able to do business with it.

ORGANISATION AND PERFORMANCE OF FIRMS WITH
HONG KONG PARTICIPATION

About half of the firms currently operating with a Hong Kong interest were completely independent of Hong Kong firms. Five of the pioneer firms were wholly-owned subsidiaries of Hong Kong manufacturing or distributing firms. In the other firms the form of association varied from majority ownership by a Hong Kong firm or its subsidiary in Singapore to minority shares in conjunction with a number of other shareholders from Singapore and other countries.

The internal organisation and decision-making process of Hong Kong firms in Singapore varied between those firms which were subsidiaries or associates of concerns in Hong Kong and those which were not. In almost all cases, the export-oriented Singapore subsidiaries and associates were in effect branches of the parent firms. They were spared most of the problems and administrative routines of finding the raw materials they required and buyers for their products. What to produce, how much to produce, where to ship the finished product, what raw materials were to be used, how much would be required and where to obtain them, were all decided and ordered by the parent firms. As the products had to be manufactured to the same specifications as those of the parent firms, any changes introduced by the parent companies were invariably applied to the Singapore operations. One price policy was usually maintained. This meant that the finished products were sold at the prices fixed by the parent firms regardless of the costs of producing the goods in Singapore. Only the decisions that had to be made locally were left to the management in Singapore. These were usually related to personnel and local sales. Research and development, if any, and major decisions such as technological adjustment or capital expansion, were largely left to the parent companies in the case of wholly-owned subsidiaries and required prior consultation with the parent bodies in the case of joint ventures.

Firms which were independent concerns also had simple internal organisations. Their limited scale of operations did not warrant a complex structure. In food manufacturing there was some research and development. The basic difference between these firms and those with financial links with firms in Hong Kong was found in decision making. Because the firms were independent operations, they made all short- and long-run decisions. In multinational joint ventures in which another foreign group held the largest shares, decisions on capital expansion, technological adjustments, pricing, export markets, or sources from which raw materials were to be purchased, were usually made by consultation among the foreign parent firms.

In all these cases, in order to look after the Hong Kong interests, at least one resident from Hong Kong was in charge of, or represented on the management of, the Singapore operation.

In the subsidiaries of subsidiaries decisions were usually initiated and made locally, though not necessarily by the firms themselves, for the main Singapore subsidiary usually performed the same functions as a parent company in Hong Kong.

INVESTMENT, EMPLOYMENT, AND SALES

The total investment in fixed assets by the end of 1966 by the Hong Kong non-textile firms, both pioneer and non-pioneer, amounted to $33 million, of which $18·3 million was the cost of machinery. These firms, in 1966, provided employment for 3,163 and produced outputs to the value of $78·6 million. In that year, the value added by the firms stood at $10·6 million.[17]

In the pioneer sector, by the end of 1966, the Hong Kong firms had invested $15·5 million in machinery and a total of $27·9 million in all

[17] Based on data supplied by the Economic Development Board.

types of fixed assets (Table 5.10). The heavy investment in fixed assets by the firm producing plywood and core veneer was the cause of the comparatively large fixed investment in the 'other' category.

Table 5.10 Pioneer firms with Hong Kong capital investment: fixed investment, employment, gross value of output, and value added, 1966[a]

	Industry	Investment in fixed assets at 31 December 1966 $'000		Employ-ment no.	Gross value of output $'000	Value added $'000
		Machinery[b]	Total			
I	Food and beverages	6,688 (43)	13,988 (50)	369 (12)	47,458 (62)	2,109 (21)
II	Textiles, garments, and leather	5,164 (33)	7,787 (28)	2,014 (67)	20,572 (27)	5,627 (57)
V	Chemicals and chemical products	644 (4)	1,293 (5)	114 (4)	1,832 (2)	996 (10)
IX	Electrical products	712 (4)	1,042 (4)	106 (4)	3,164 (4)	941 (9)
	Other	2,308 (15)	3,808 (14)	407 (14)	3,049 (4)	263 (3)
	All industries	15,516 (100)	27,918 (100)	3,010 (100)	76,075 (100)	9,936 (100)

Figures in parentheses are percentages of all industries aggregates.
[a] Twenty-one of the twenty-three pioneer firms in production only.
[b] Does not include cost of installation.
Source: Economic Development Board data.

Firms in the food manufacturing industry used capital intensive methods with half the total investment in fixed assets, but employed only 12 per cent of the total employed in Hong Kong pioneer firms. They contributed 62 per cent of gross value of output and 21 per cent of value added. The textile and garment manufacturing firms were the largest employers with 67 per cent of employment. They contributed 57 per cent of value added ($5·6 million), though only 27 per cent of gross value of output.

Taking all Hong Kong pioneer firms as a whole in 1966 the total sales amounted to $81·9 million, of which about 44 per cent were domestic sales. Their exports to Malaysia were $14·5 million (18 per cent of total sales) and to the rest of the world other than Malaysia, $31·4 million (38 per cent of the total). However, as noted earlier, the firms in the food, chemicals and chemical products, and electrical products industries produced mainly for the domestic market, hence the high proportion of domestic sales in the aggregate total sales (Table 5.11). High percentage of total sales for exports was recorded for the textile and garment firms, and for the plywood producers in the 'other' category. Only a very small proportion of the sales in both of these categories was attributed to exports to Malaysia, less than 1 per cent for textiles and garments and for the 'other' group.

Table 5.11   Direction of sales by pioneer firms with Hong Kong capital investment, 1966, in percentages of total sales[a]

Industry		Sales to Singapore	Sales to Malaysia	Other foreign sales
I	Food and beverages	59·4	25·2	15·4
II	Textiles, garments, and leather	8·1	0·8	91·1
V	Chemicals and chemical products	87·5	5·8	6·8
IX	Electrical products	64·5	29·1	6·3
	Other	0·4	0·5	99·1
	All industries	43·9	17·8	38·4

[a] Twenty of the twenty-three pioneer firms in production only.
Source: Economic Development Board data.

Statistics for returns on Hong Kong direct investment in industry in Singapore are not available. One thing is certain. Only a handful of Hong Kong firms in the pioneer sector and in the non-pioneer cotton textile industry have been making profits consistently since their inception. Little is known of the size or rate of profit, let alone whether the returns have been at a level which makes Singapore a high-return economy compared with Hong Kong or whether they have been sufficiently high for the Hong Kong investors who expect high returns over a short-time horizon.

Those firms which have consistently been doing well are mostly found in the cotton textile and garment industries. Other Hong Kong firms which have been making profits at least some of the time are also cotton textile and garment manufacturing firms, but most of these made substantial profits only during their initial period of operation. These firms received a setback when the United Kingdom imposed a 15 per cent surcharge on imports in November 1964, and this was followed by the imposition of quantitative restrictions on imports of cotton textile products from Singapore by the United Kingdom in 1965 and by the

United States in 1966.[18] The inability of the United States to agree to the net additional quota for 1967 owing to a contraction in the United States textile industry, a step which the United States was entitled to take, unilaterally if necessary, under the Long Term Agreement, further aggravated the depressed state of the Singapore cotton textile industry.[19] These firms were already operating below capacity by 1966 and the weaving firms, as usual, fared much worse than the garment firms. The garment firms could, as some actually did, recover more easily by diversifying their products and by producing better quality goods. The weaving firms had difficulties in making adjustments because their machinery and equipment were less adaptable and did not have the multiproduct characteristic of sewing machines. Fabrics for export to the United Kingdom required looms of different specifications from those for export to the United States. This alone shows the complexity of the problem faced by the weaving firms in handling product diversification with limited machinery and equipment. The effects of the United Kingdom and the United States quotas on the weaving industry were still serious in mid-1967. The quotas for fabrics and cotton piece-goods were so small in relation to capacity production that quota production could be filled in less than six months. Most of the garment firms had nevertheless begun to make profits, even though not all of them were operating at full capacity.

The other firms established with Hong Kong capital during 1961-5 had not yet made profits by mid-1967.[20] Five of these firms in the pioneer sector had ceased production of their original products or ceased production altogether at one time or another during 1963-6. The rest of the firms which still remained in operation by the end of 1966 for the most part produced for the domestic market. Internal and import competition made the going difficult for these firms until tariffs and import quota restrictions were imposed by Singapore. These firms found costs difficult to reduce because their main raw materials were imported at world

---

[18] Kayser Sung and P. H. M. Jones (eds.), *Asian Textile Survey 1967-1968* (Hong Kong, 1967), pp. 155-6.

[19] Singapore International Chamber of Commerce, *Economic Bulletin* (Singapore), 31 May 1967, p. 1. The weaving firms found their production quota for export to the United States reduced by 50 per cent in 1967.

[20] These exclude the firms established with Hong Kong capital since 1966 and the firms established prior to Hong Kong capital participation in 1966. For both of these information is not available.

prices while the shortage of skilled labour made it difficult to lower labour cost. The limited internal demand prevented the firms from reaping economies of large-scale production. These firms which have been given protection from competing imports have fared better than those which have not, but even in the protected market there was the problem of internal competition. Flour and cement capacity exceeds internal demand, and with domestic prices controlled by the Economic Development Board the only means to profits as well as to full capacity production is to find new markets overseas. Indonesia seems to be a good potential outlet in which existing surplus capacity could be absorbed and capital expansion would seem justifiable if the market became available.[21] Already by the beginning of 1967, some demand from Indonesia helped firms with Hong Kong participation to increase production, and some of these, notably in the food industry, had begun to expand their capacities in anticipation of increased demand from Indonesia.

Some of the reasons why firms went out of production are known. One pioneer garment firm ceased production because it had not been able to establish a good performance record to qualify for large quota allocation in 1964 owing to a long drawn labour strike lasting one year just before the imposition of quota restrictions by the United Kingdom. Other non-pioneer garment firms closed in 1965, apparently because of the 15 per cent surcharge on imports by the United Kingdom in 1964 and the United Kingdom quota restrictions in 1965.[22] One pioneer non-textile firm suspended operation in 1965 because it could not compete with rival producers in the domestic market. One pioneer garment firm which ceased operation in 1966 was indirectly a victim of the banking crisis in Hong Kong in the previous year and its closure had little to do with the conditions in Singapore.[23]

---

[21] Singapore's Ministry of Finance (Trade Division) drew up a list of export potentials to Indonesia. Three categories of goods were listed: (I) essential commodities; (II) semi-essential commodities; and (III) non-essential commodities (Singapore International Chamber of Commerce, *Economic Bulletin*, 30 June 1966, pp. 2–3). The commodities under Group I which might be of relevance to Hong Kong manufacturing firms in Singapore include wheat flour, rubber tyres and tubes, cement, textiles, and caustic soda; those under Group II: printing ink, pharmaceuticals, garments, and plywood; and under Group III: household textiles and garments and television sets.

[22] *Singapore Year Book 1965* (Government Printing Office, Singapore), p. 2.

[23] The parent company was associated with a bank which went bankrupt in 1965.

PROBLEMS CONFRONTING HONG KONG FIRMS IN SINGAPORE

Hong Kong manufacturers feel that the central problem of production, particularly in comparison with Hong Kong, is the high cost of labour.

Yet the level of wage rates although important is not a crucial factor in putting Singapore at a disadvantage in relation to Hong Kong. Indeed, few Hong Kong manufacturers believe that earnings, including all fringe benefits, are higher in Singapore than in Hong Kong. On the contrary piece rate daily earnings per worker appeared to be comparable with Hong Kong, if not higher than in Singapore.[24]

The reason for the relatively high labour cost content of products lies in low productivity per man hour. The Hong Kong managers argued that at a given level of skill the Hong Kong worker has a higher productivity than a Singapore worker. Another factor in low labour productivity in Singapore manufacturing may be due to the fact that unskilled and semi-skilled workers form the bulk of the labour force employed. The proportion of skilled workers in the total employed of course varies between industries. In the pioneer firms manufacturing cotton textile products the proportion was higher than in all industries in 1966, being about three skilled to two unskilled compared with the overall average of almost one to one.[25] It should be possible to speed up training and increase the supply of skilled workers. Most factory workers in the Singapore cotton textile industry, like those in Hong Kong, are young people of Chinese origin, but the Hong Kong firms have found that it takes a slightly longer time to train their workers to the level of skill required than in Hong Kong.

There seems to be a difference in attitudes to work and earnings between Singapore and Hong Kong workers. In part the difference lies in the way of life. Hong Kong managers suggested that life in Singapore is relatively simple and less sophisticated than in Hong Kong and that Hong Kong people are more materialistic in outlook than those in Singapore. Many Hong Kong managers claimed that Hong Kong workers had to work mainly because of economic necessity while the

[24] This was the view of some of the managers of the firms. It appeared in 1967 that a skilled Singapore worker on average had a 'take home' pay and fringe benefits of $6 per day. The wage rates in Hong Kong's manufacturing industry at the end of 1967 were said to be in the ranges of $5 to $15 for skilled workers, $3 to $11 for semi-skilled workers, and $2·6 to $7·3 for unskilled workers (*Hong Kong: Report for the Year 1967* [Hong Kong, 1968], p. 27).

[25] Economic Development Board, *Annual Report '66*, Appendix Table IID, p. 65.

Singapore workers work because they wish to have pocket money. They were, of course, referring to the young workers, and particularly to young women. Even if Hong Kong workers are not the principal breadwinners, they contribute substantially to their families' support, whereas the Singapore workers are in many cases still dependent on theirs. Although these views may reflect prejudice as well as facts, absenteeism was found to be higher among the female workers in Singapore than in Hong Kong, notably in the garment industry. Most Singapore workers are union members and they are well protected by their unions. Firms could not dismiss workers without union agreement, and even then had to pay substantial severance pay. It was much easier to dismiss workers by suspending operation and re-employing some of them on resumption than to dismiss a worker outright. One garment firm had actually done this as a result of a genuine grievance and with the tacit approval of the government authorities. Managers claimed that they could not do much because their workers had little incentive to supply effort beyond a certain level, even though their take home pay, based on piece rates, would have been increased if they had put in more effort. One of the firms in the garment industry would not consider increasing piece rates in order to induce workers to more effort; it argued that labour cost per unit output was already too high. In any event, the workers seemed to be quite happy with the take home pay.

Such a view was widespread in the garment industry, but it is only a part of the explanation of low labour productivity and high labour cost. The high labour cost per unit output is also due to the relatively small scale of production. A number of Hong Kong weaving and garment firms in the pioneer sector thought that if they had full capacity production they could lower the labour cost per unit output, even if the quality of skill and the physical productivity of their workers remained the same. The limited size of overseas markets meant that export-oriented manufacturing firms could not utilise capacity fully. If their exports were not subject to quota restrictions they met with severe competition from rival foreign producers in the latter's established markets. In those markets where competition was less severe, the demand was usually small. These were mainly markets in developing countries where aggregate purchasing power was low.

The firms found it difficult to increase efficiency with existing scales of production. Very few of the garment firms were able to specialise in one or two lines of products. Most produced a variety of sizes of the same product and a variety of products at the same time. Workers were

133

therefore required to adjust their routines frequently even if they were performing broadly similar tasks, and this considerably reduced their productivity and, with piece rates, their earnings.[26] For the weaving firms which had to change looms once production for a United Kingdom or a United States quota was completed, costs were particularly high. The parent firms in Hong Kong escaped such changes because their scale of production was so large that the utilisation rates of both types of looms were high and the switching of machines therefore unnecessary. Most of these problems were inevitable for a newcomer to world markets which were already severely restricted by quotas. There was some evidence that since Singapore branches and subsidiaries were small they tended to receive the parent firms' small orders, thus no doubt justifying relatively unprofitable investments for firms which wished to keep the goodwill of existing and potential customers even at the cost of taking small, relatively unprofitable orders.

The finding of new markets and the enlargement of existing markets in countries with high purchasing powers were therefore seen as the principal solution to the high labour cost per unit output even by those managers who complained about Singapore attitudes to work. They thought that goods could be produced and sold at competitive prices if they were produced on a larger scale, and that labour cost per unit of output could be lowered through economies of scale, despite problems of skill.

The Hong Kong firms have been trying hard to gain access to new overseas markets, in particular in the developed countries of Western Europe and North America. Firms with parent companies in Hong Kong depend on the parent to find them markets, and the others with limited resources mostly depend on the Economic Development Board to provide them with information on the market potential of various countries. One pioneer firm in the garment industry, however, enlisted the services of a market research specialist to make a survey of the market potential for its products in Western Europe.

Attitudes towards Singapore's effort in assisting the development of new firms were mixed, depending on whether the firm produced for the domestic market or export, and on whether the firm had access to over-

---

[26] In Hong Kong this is a well-known phenomenon which has its repercussions in the labour market. Highly skilled piece workers, much sought after by manufacturers because of their high productivity, switch jobs according to rumours of orders. A manufacturer has to get large orders, not only to keep his plant running, but to retain skilled workers.

seas markets at its inception. For most of the firms which produced mainly for the domestic market, government effort was generally appreciated. But for those producing mainly for export, particularly the cotton textile and garment firms, the government had been of little assistance. They, like the firms engaged in production for the local market, recognised that the Economic Development Board had been doing its best with the resources at its disposal, but Hong Kong industrialists often found a frustrating lack of experience among the Economic Development Board staff. They admitted that the Board's officers were hardworking but thought them too young and unaccustomed to problems of industry. One export-oriented firm, informed of a local order which had been found for it by the Economic Development Board, thought it too ludicrously small for serious consideration. In another case an overseas outlet was found for a manufacturer who was assured he would encounter little competition. It was discovered that the reason the market was not competitive was that Hong Kong had withdrawn from it because it did not pay.

Some manufacturers were very critical of the government for its inability to negotiate with the United Kingdom or the United States for larger cotton textile export quotas. They had placed high hopes on Singapore because they felt that an independent rather than a colonial government would carry more weight in international negotiations. This was not, of course, the case.[27] The firms concerned ought by then to have learned their lesson. Repeated protests by the Hong Kong cotton textile industry against the series of requests from developed countries for voluntary export restraints had borne little fruit. The investors also ought to have realised that Hong Kong, in spite of its colonial status, was in a stronger position than Singapore if only because it had a large textile industry and was a signatory government to the Long Term Arrangement. In establishing subsidiaries and associated firms in Singapore the Hong Kong manufacturers ought to have foreseen that a repetition of Hong Kong's experience of fruitless protests was probable. The government itself could not hope that Singapore would be given special consideration since the Arrangement had been designed to limit exports from developing to developed countries; other exporting countries in the developing world with much more at stake had to subscribe to the international agreement.

---

[27] Sung and Leary (eds.), *Asian Textile Bi-Annual 1965–1966*, pp. 153–9; and Sung and Jones (eds.), *Asian Textile Survey 1967–1968*, pp. 155–6.

All the Hong Kong firms said that the government had provided adequate public utilities in the areas where the factories were located. Very few thought that the costs of these services were too high. Firms with factories in industrial estates or areas other than Jurong were glad that they had not gone to Jurong. The food manufacturing firms had to be close to the existing harbour. Firms requiring a large number of workers, such as those engaged in garment manufacturing, wanted to be close to the source of the labour supply, and this meant setting up factories in the thickly-populated parts of the island. The eighteen Hong Kong factories in Jurong found difficulties in recruiting workers. Four of the pioneer cotton textile and garment manufacturing firms established in 1963–4 not only experienced difficulty in recruiting unskilled workers, but also had problems in finding replacements for those skilled workers who left their employ. It appears that these skilled workers did not move from one factory to another within the same industry as much as from one industry to another, even at the price of having to acquire a new skill. The Hong Kong manufacturers felt that it was a mistake that housing had not been provided in Jurong before industries came there. In Hong Kong, resettlement estates and low-cost housing estates were placed around Kwun Tong before it became an industrial area. The lack of social amenities in Jurong was thought to have been overlooked, and people would not move out to Jurong, a long way from their friends and neighbours, while the rental of flats there was the same as in the more central areas.

Pioneer legislations and other fiscal and economic incentives for investors were generally approved, though these seemed more important for the firms producing for the domestic market than for those exporting. Since the Pioneer Industries Ordinance was already in force when the firms were being established, most of them, especially those producing for exports, simply jumped on the band wagon. They would have come to Singapore anyway even if there had been no preferential treatment. Firms not doing well, however, appreciated tax holidays or tax rate reductions and other preferential fiscal measures which allowed a breathing space and helped to make them profitable earlier than they would have been otherwise. But the manager who said that what was important was high output and profit, and that tax holiday and other forms of preferential treatment for industry made little sense for firms not making any profits during the first five years of production, presented a typical Hong Kong view.

136

CONTRIBUTION OF THE HONG KONG FIRMS TO THE SINGAPORE ECONOMY

Whatever the problems faced by the Hong Kong firms in industry in Singapore, their presence has contributed in many ways, and in many cases more than other foreign firms, to Singapore's industrial development. Firstly, Hong Kong direct investment in pioneer industries helped to mobilise domestic capital for investment in industry in the pioneer sector. By the end of 1966, the amount of Singapore capital associated with Hong Kong pioneer firms was of the order of $12 million. By the end of 1966, firms with Hong Kong capital accounted for 7 per cent of the investment in machinery of the pioneer sector, and 9 per cent of the total investment in fixed assets by all pioneer firms.[28] Secondly, it would not be an exaggeration to say that Hong Kong had established an export-oriented cotton textile industry for Singapore. Hong Kong textile and garment firms still dominate Singapore's light industrial scene. The Hong Kong firms with parent companies in Hong Kong or firms established by individual entrepreneurs from Hong Kong brought with them established markets and the foreign connections of the parent and associated firms in Hong Kong. Thirdly, at the end of 1966, 27 per cent of employment in the pioneer sector was provided by Hong Kong firms, although these firms provided only about 5 per cent of foreign capital in pioneer firms. It is clear that one of the most important advantages of Hong Kong direct investment from Singapore's standpoint has been the fact that Hong Kong investment is mainly in light industries which require a large labour force. The Hong Kong firms also brought about an inflow of technical skill to the pioneer sector. In 1966 there were at least forty-five skilled men from Hong Kong training Singapore workers. On an industry basis the Hong Kong firms accounted for 77 per cent of the employment in the cotton textile and garment industries in the pioneer sector, 30 per cent in food manufacturing, 20 per cent in electrical products industries, and 16 per cent in chemicals and chemical products industries.[29] Fourthly, twenty-one of the twenty-three pioneer firms with Hong Kong participation produced 16 per cent of the total gross value output of all pioneer firms in 1966 and accounted for 8 per cent of the total net value added in the pioneer sector in that year. On the basis of individual industries, Hong Kong firms' contribution in the pioneer sector is even more striking. In 1966 the firms contributed 86 per cent of the total value added in cotton

[28] Calculated from Table 5.10 and Appendix Table V.
[29] Calculated from Table 5.10 and Economic Development Board, *Annual Report '66*, Appendix Table IID, p. 65.

textile and garment industries, 34 per cent in food manufacturing industries, 36 per cent in electrical products industries, and 21 per cent in the chemicals and chemical products industries.[30] Finally, in 1966, they were responsible for $46 million of manufactured exports, $31 million of which were exports to foreign countries other than Malaysia.

Hong Kong direct investment in industry is much sought after by Singapore. Apart from the entrepreneurial and technical skills associated with Hong Kong capital, most of the capital is owned by people of Chinese origin. Hong Kong investors can easily be assimilated if they decide to reside in Singapore. As migrants they may help to repeat the Hong Kong experience of structural transformation for the economy in Singapore.

The preference for Hong Kong direct investment was implied in two legislative enactments of 1967. One of these was general in character, but it was clearly directed at Hong Kong investors of Chinese origin. Under a mid-1967 change in the migration law, foreign investors depositing a minimum of $250,000 in productive enterprises in Singapore would qualify for permanent residence and for citizenship after residence of five years.[31] This was enacted at a time when political troubles were at their height in Hong Kong and the Colony was experiencing a flight of capital for the first time since World War II. The Singapore government also announced that from 28 July 1967 Hong Kong residents would be allowed to transmit their Singapore funds freely without prior approval from the Controller of Foreign Exchange in Singapore.[32] The effects of these legal changes have yet to be determined.[33]

Whether there will be a continued outflow of Hong Kong capital for direct investment in Singapore nevertheless largely depends on whether Singapore is a high-return economy compared with Hong Kong. Singapore will also be competing with investment in Taiwan, which, other things being equal, is a high-return economy compared with Singapore. The Hong Kong entrepreneur is shrewd and resourceful under normal circumstances. He may lack vision, as entrepreneurs in developed countries are inclined to suggest, and his economic judgment

[30] Calculated from Table 5.10 and Economic Development Board, *Annual Report '66*, Appendix Table IIE, p. 66.
[31] William Campbell, 'Singapore's Battle for More Jobs', *Straits Times*, 5 August 1967.
[32] *Straits Times*, 28 July 1967.
[33] *Far Eastern Economic Review*, 14 September 1967, p. 535.

may be affected under political strain,[34] but his aim remains profit maximisation. Unless the problems being encountered by the Hong Kong firms in Singapore are resolved, however favourable the investment climate in terms of public probity and government assistance in obtaining sites, loans, immigration facilities and fiscal and other economic incentives, Taiwan, where labour cost is relatively low and labour unions practically non-existent, will have an advantage.

[34] That the Hong Kong entrepreneur lacks vision was the view of an American businessman, who, however, also admitted that Hong Kong businessmen are shrewd and resourceful (Joseph Z. Reday, 'Hong Kong Manufacturing— Asset or Liability?', *Far Eastern Economic Review*, 14 June 1962, pp. 573-4).

6

Taiwan Investment[1]

THE NATURE OF TAIWAN INVESTMENT

The inflow of Taiwan investment into Singapore manufacturing began in 1963 at a time when the Republic of China's policy of encouraging foreign investors to come to Taiwan was beginning to bear fruit.[2] By the end of 1966 Taiwan investors had an equity interest in sixteen manufacturing firms in Singapore. Thirteen of these were pioneer firms and it is with these firms that this study of Taiwan investment is largely concerned.[3]

Tracing the flow of investment from Taiwan to Singapore is more than usually difficult. Some funds were brought into Singapore by businessmen who had been residents of Taiwan but who changed their domicile upon investment in Singapore. Taiwan investment is also difficult to measure because there was considerable movement of funds in and out of firms between 1963 and 1966. However, if the amount of Taiwan funds from external sources channelled into Taiwan joint ventures as paid-up capital is used as an approximation of the actual inflow of Taiwan capital into Singapore manufacturing,[4] then the size of the capital inflow from Taiwan for investment in the pioneer industries

[1] The authors are indebted to the managers of the firms with Taiwanese affiliation for their co-operation during the survey.

[2] Republic of China, Council for International Economic Cooperation and Development, *Annual Report on Taiwan's Economy, 1964*, August 1965, p. 47. The total inflow of direct foreign investment into the Republic of China was $US18·28 million in 1963.

[3] They include all firms with Taiwan capital participation, and figures in this chapter therefore do not always agree with Economic Development Board data in the Appendix.

[4] Paid-up capital has been used as an approximation of capital inflow in the absence of better information. This of course leaves out of account retained

during the period of 1963–6 amounts to $4·9 million, with another $1·2 million flowing into non-pioneer firms situated in Jurong. Compared with the total inflow of foreign private capital during 1961–6 Taiwan investment has not been large. In pioneer firms it constituted only 5 per cent of the total foreign investment.[5]

The relatively small capital inflow from Taiwan was spread over four principal categories of pioneer industries: textiles, garments, and leather; wood and paper products; chemicals and chemical products; and electrical products. The Taiwan investors also had investments in stationery products, feather industries, and plastic products, all in the 'miscellaneous' category. There was a bias towards investment in the chemicals and chemical products industries and the wood and paper products industries, because by the end of 1966 the former category absorbed 53 per cent of the total investment funds for the pioneer industries from Taiwan, and the latter category another 21 per cent.[6] One of the three non-pioneer firms was also engaged in the manufacture of electrical products, one was producing cement and one was making builders' hardware. One of these firms acquired a pioneer certificate in 1967 and the two others appeared to be in the process of doing so.

Although only 5 per cent of the foreign investment flows for the pioneer industries came from Taiwan, Taiwan accounted for a more significant proportion of the foreign capital invested in the five categories of pioneer industries mentioned above. A little over half of the foreign capital invested in the wood and paper products industries and 38 per cent of the foreign investment in the chemicals and chemical products industries were Taiwan capital.[7]

In the main, Taiwan investors concentrated their investment funds in consumer goods industries. Sixty-two per cent of their capital brought into Singapore for investment in the pioneer industries was invested in enterprises engaged in the production of textile goods, pharmaceutical products, detergents, domestic electrical appliances, stationery products, feather products, and footwear. The other 38 per cent was invested in producer goods industries such as those manufacturing plywood, core veneer, acids and sulphates, electric cables, and lead acid batteries.

---

profits accruing to the Taiwan investors and credit facilities extended by Taiwan financial institutions. It also assumes that shares issued to Taiwan parent and associated firms represent market values.

[5] Calculated from Appendix Table I.
[6] Calculated from Appendix Table I.
[7] Calculated from Appendix Table I.

About three-quarters of the Taiwan capital inflow was found in industries oriented towards import substitution. With the exceptions of the manufacturing of garments, plywood and core veneer, and processed feathers, all of which were export-oriented, production in the Taiwan pioneer firms seemed to be geared towards the Singapore market. Since hitherto Singapore had been dependent on external sources of supply for these goods, their production meant replacing the corresponding imported items. Some of these import replacement goods have also been exported, but the quantities sold abroad formed only a small proportion of total production.

Thirteen firms with Taiwan participation had been granted pioneer certificates by the end of 1966, and twelve had commenced production with another one almost ready to do so.[8] This was a large number in relation both to the seventy-three pioneer firms with foreign participation in production and to the total amount of Taiwan capital committed. The firms themselves were small, ranging from a total paid-up capital of $60,000 to $1,600,000.

All thirteen Taiwan pioneer firms in production or implementing were joint ventures but, if there were special reasons for Taiwan investors' preference for joint ventures rather than for wholly-owned enterprises, they were not apparent. The prevalence of joint ventures is not due to Singapore's company legislation, for there is no discrimination against foreign-owned companies either in company law or in pioneer legislation. While the Singapore government has frequently expressed its preference for joint ventures, there has been no policy opposition to the establishment of wholly or largely foreign-owned companies.

There are, of course, certain advantages for foreign investors in associating with local capital. Such an association reduces the risk of capital loss and this seemed to be important to the relatively small Taiwanese investors. Local participation in management which came in association with Singapore capital was useful in dealing with local problems. Taiwan investors were not familiar with Singapore's labour and distribution and allied problems. The presence of Singapore personnel on the management of the Taiwan pioneer firms is very much in evidence and, as will be shown later, most of the Singapore managers are in charge of local aspects of operations, namely, personnel and marketing.

[8] The following analysis is based on information obtained from the survey carried out by the authors in 1967. Eleven of the thirteen pioneer firms in production or implementing and two of the three non-pioneer firms were interviewed.

142

For Singapore investors interested in manufacturing activity, there were many advantages in a joint venture with Taiwan investors. As they had little or no experience in manufacturing, an association with foreign investors not only helped to spread risks of capital loss but also ensured the necessary managerial skills and technical experience. The flow of entrepreneurship and technology was not necessarily confined to personnel. If the responsibility of making decisions on finance, production, and technological adjustment rested with the parent or the associated company abroad, this should be considered as inflow of entrepreneurial skills and technical knowledge to the host country. Eight out of the twelve Taiwan pioneer firms in operation had either a parent company or an associated company in Taiwan.

In those pioneer firms in which the Taiwan investors held a majority interest in 1966, the parent or associated companies in Taiwan were always consulted on matters concerning the financial aspects of the Singapore operations. They also undertook the responsibility of making long-run decisions on changes in capital structures, borrowing, and plant expansion. In some cases the firms in Taiwan also exercised some degree of control over short-run decisions such as those pertaining to annual budgeting and annual sales planning, and, in a few firms, even to routine operations. As for the non-financial aspects of the Singapore operations, while the Singapore company was usually given the responsibility of looking after personnel and production, approval of the parent or associated company generally had to be obtained for changes in policy. On matters such as product improvement, change of organisation of the Singapore company, and technological adjustment, the parent company or the associated company was always consulted and in a few cases its approval was necessary.

The degree of responsibility undertaken by the parent company or the associated company in Taiwan did not appear to be dependent on the degree of financial control exercised by the firm in Taiwan. Entrepreneurial skills and technical knowledge flowed from Taiwan even though the Taiwan investors' shares of the total capital of the joint ventures were small compared with the Singapore or other foreign investors' shares. In pioneer firms in which the Taiwan investors did not have financial control, all long- and short-run decisions concerning both financial and non-financial aspects of the operations were nominally, of course, the responsibilities of the companies in Singapore. However, in many instances the parent or associated companies were nevertheless consulted, particularly on problems concerning product improvement and technological adjustment.

143

In all but one of the Taiwan firms, at least one top manager from Taiwan was resident in Singapore, and the effective control of a company's operations seemed to fall on these managers. Whether Taiwan investors had financial control in these firms was immaterial. The Taiwan managers were responsible for matters relating to finance and production, and this was true even of those firms in which the Taiwan investors held minority shares.

The Singapore managers, whether in Taiwan- or Singapore-controlled firms, were usually responsible for the control of the labour force and, in some cases, for domestic sales. But in some of the pioneer firms in which the Taiwan investors held the majority shares, even these functions were performed by the resident Taiwan managers.

Physical inflows of technology are reflected in the presence of foreign engineers and other technical personnel. In the Taiwan firms, almost all of the technical personnel came from Taiwan and a few from other foreign countries. Highly skilled technical staff would return to their respective home countries on completion of their tours of duty in training Singapore workers. In September 1967 there were about forty engineers and technicians from Taiwan in the Taiwan pioneer firms. One firm also offered to recruit local workers who were prepared to undergo a period of training in a Taiwan factory.

Although Taiwan's wood and paper products industries have been criticised in recent years for their small and inefficient units of production, Taiwan is the world's largest exporter of plywood.[9] This is a field in which it has acquired considerable expertise, which has been passed on to the Singapore plants. Taiwan firms producing knitted goods and detergents in Singapore are associated with leading Taiwan manufacturers. The Singapore firm producing detergents, for example, is associated with the Taiwan firm licensed to produce Tide and allied products from the United States.

In the field of organisation, it cannot be said that the Taiwan investors had made any distinctive contribution. The organisational structure of the Taiwan firms was fairly simple because the scale of operation was generally small. Several of the Taiwan firms were too small to have separate departments for different purposes. Some firms even let the parent or associated companies in Taiwan handle the purchase of raw materials, though they retained the responsibility of specifying the items required. This arrangement proved particularly convenient for a parent

[9] M. F. Perkins, 'Taiwan: Development that Works', *Finance and Development*, September 1967, p. 172.

company which was also the source of raw materials. There were instances where the firms in Taiwan ordered the required raw materials from other manufacturers and traders in Taiwan or from another country on behalf of their Singapore associates.

Not all Taiwan pioneer firms had their own sales departments although some made direct sales. A number of reasons seemed to account for this, for example following the customary practice of their parent or associated companies in Taiwan, or keeping the distributive margins to themselves. In one particular case, the firm claimed that it could do the job better than the local agents as it had more experience in selling its particular type of product, but the other firms preferred sales through an agent. As many of these firms produced mainly for the domestic market, sales through a local agent were considered desirable and less costly. A few firms sold directly as well as through agents.

The small scale of operations prevented the Taiwan firms from engaging in research and development. This does not mean that the Taiwan entrepreneurs were ignorant of the need for research and development. Indeed, half a dozen firms enlisted the help of the parent or associated companies in Taiwan to undertake such work on their behalf, and demand forecasting in a limited way was attempted by one of the Taiwan firms in Singapore.

IMPACT ON THE SINGAPORE ECONOMY

Among the twelve Taiwan pioneer firms in production by the end of 1966, seven were jointly owned by Taiwan and Singapore investors, and in two of these the Economic Development Board had equity holdings. The remaining five firms were multinational joint ventures: three were jointly owned by Hong Kong, Taiwan, and Singapore investors; one was established with Japanese, Malaysian, Taiwan, and Singapore capital, and one with capital from Hong Kong, Malaysia, Taiwan, and Singapore. All of the twelve joint ventures were registered as private limited companies. Two of the non-pioneer firms had multinational foreign ownership and in one of these Taiwan held a majority share; the third firm was an equal share Taiwan and Singapore joint venture.

The presence of joint capital ventures is in itself evidence of the success of channelling domestic investment funds to industry. By the end of 1966, Singapore capital invested in pioneer firms with Taiwan participation amounted to $3·92 million or 41 per cent of the total paid-up capital of all Taiwan pioneer firms which had commenced production

145

or were at an advanced stage of implementation. These pioneer firms also attracted $775,000 capital from Japan, Hong Kong, and Malyasia.[10]

In addition to attracting direct Singapore equity interest the Taiwan firms mobilised local loan funds, for they drew on the Economic Development Board's funds and on commercial banks in Singapore.

At the end of 1966 the Taiwan investors had a controlling interest in only four of the seven Taiwan-Singapore joint ventures. They held the largest shares of capital in only one of the five multinational firms, with Singapore investors holding the largest share in each of the other four.

The total investment in fixed assets by the pioneer firms in which Taiwan was the principal foreign shareholder amounted to $12·07 million by the end of 1966; this represented 4 per cent of the total fixed investment by all pioneer firms. Investment in machinery and other capital equipment by the Taiwan firms amounted to $7·47 million. The Taiwan firms had a large share of the total fixed investments in the main four categories of pioneer industries in which Taiwan had invested. They ranged from 11 per cent in the textiles, garments, and leather industries to 36 per cent in the wood and paper products industries, with an average of 19 per cent in all five categories (Table 6.1).

Table 6.1   Investment in fixed assets by pioneer firms[a] in which Taiwan was the principal foreign shareholder at 31 December 1966

Industry	Machinery $'000	Total fixed assets $'000	Total fixed assets as percentage of fixed investment by all Singapore pioneer firms in industry group
II Textiles, garments, and leather	791	1,436	11
III Wood and paper products	3,172	5,505	36
V Chemicals and chemical products	2,963	4,254	23
IX Electrical products	459	708	12
X Miscellaneous	89	168	2
All above industries	7,474	12,071	19

[a] Including ten firms in production and one in implementing stage.
Sources: Economic Development Board data and Economic Development Board, *Annual Report '66*, Appendix II C, p. 64.

[10] Economic Development Board data.

146

In the main the Taiwan pioneer firms turned abroad for raw materials. Singapore imports most of its raw materials. In 1966, the cost of imported raw materials constituted 92 per cent of the total cost of raw materials used by the Taiwan pioneer firms. The raw materials for the wood and paper products, and the electrical products, industries were almost entirely supplied by foreign countries. Only in the case of the 'miscellaneous' category was there a higher local component in the raw materials required (Table 6.2).

Table 6.2   Value of local and imported raw materials used by pioneer firms[a] in which Taiwan was the principal foreign shareholder in 1966

Industry	Local $'000	Imported $'000	Total $'000	Imported raw materials as percentage of total raw materials
II Textiles, garments, and leather	135	1,324	1,459	91
III Wood and paper products	3	2,574	2,577	100
V Chemicals and chemical products	282	2,644	2,926	90
IX Electrical products	8	1,892	1,900[a]	100
X Miscellaneous	346	337	683	49
All above industries	774	8,771	9,545	92

[a] Ten firms in production.
Source: Economic Development Board data.

Only in one case could a basic raw material be obtained from another firm locally and the supplier happened to be another Taiwan pioneer firm. One firm purchased its raw materials from its parent company in Taiwan. Japan, Malaysia, and the United States also provided raw materials required by the Taiwan firms in Singapore. Synthetic fibres came from Japan because the Japanese fibres were considered to be of better quality than others, they were cheaper in price, and Japanese deliveries were punctual. Malaysia is a close and cheap source of timber for the wood and paper products industries. The United States has been the major source of raw materials for the production of chemicals and chemical products. Singapore itself could have been the source of raw materials for feather products but, paradoxically, owing to competition from Hong Kong for Singapore duck feathers, the firms in Singapore found it necessary to import the raw materials from Malaysia instead.

The pioneer firms in which Taiwan was the principal foreign share-holder at the end of 1966 provided employment for 1,204 people (Table 6.3). The largest employers were the wood and paper products industries, followed by the textiles, garments, and leather, and the chemicals and chemical products industries. The Taiwan firms account-ed for 11 per cent of the total number of people employed in pioneer industries and 21 per cent of the number employed in the five categories of pioneer industries discussed above. They provided 36 per cent of the jobs available in the wood and paper products and 35 per cent in the chemicals and chemical products industries. Unlike the pioneer firms with capital from the developed countries like the United States or United Kingdom, the Taiwan pioneer firms are mainly engaged in production which requires labour-intensive techniques, and this explains the relatively large number of workers employed by the Taiwan firms.

Table 6.3   Employment in pioneer firms in which Taiwan was the principal foreign shareholder at 31 December 1966

Industry		Employment	Percentage of employment in all Singapore pioneer firms in industry group
II	Textiles, garments, and leather	269	10
III	Wood and paper products	480	36
V	Chemicals and chemical products	264	35
IX	Electrical products	157	29
X	Miscellaneous	34	7
	All above industries	1,204	21

Source: Economic Development Board data.

The gross value of output of pioneer firms in which Taiwan was the principal foreign shareholder in 1966 was estimated at $13,900,000, or 3 per cent of the gross value of output of all pioneer firms.[11] Their value added was $4,026,000, or 3 per cent of the value added by all pioneer firms.[12]

Not all of the goods currently produced are sold immediately and not all of the goods sold have been produced during the same accounting period. Exports by firms in which Taiwan was the principal foreign

[11] Economic Development Board data and Table 1.9.
[12] See Appendix Table VIII.

148

shareholder amount to $9,147,000, or 56 per cent of their total sales. Five per cent of these exports went to Malaysia. Domestic sales accounted for $7,108,000, or 44 per cent.[13] The wood and paper products industries made almost all their sales in the developed countries. The United States and the United Kingdom were the chief buyers, absorbing more than 95 per cent of the plywood and veneer products manufactured and sold by the Taiwan pioneer firms. The Middle East absorbed the rest. Two-thirds of the sales by the Taiwan pioneer firms manufacturing textile and garment products were made to foreign countries. Almost all of the garments sold abroad went to the United States. Domestic consumers absorbed the other third. They took 70 per cent of the nylon knitted goods sold and consumers in Malaysia and Thailand took the rest. Export sales accounted for about 60 per cent of the sales by Taiwan firms manufacturing 'miscellaneous' products. These were mainly exports to neighbouring developing economies like Malaysia, Thailand, South Vietnam, and Hong Kong, but processed feather and allied products were sold entirely to Western Europe.

In contrast, the chemicals and chemical products, and the electrical products industries, sold more of their products locally than abroad. Chemical and chemical product firms accounted for 47 per cent of all domestic sales by all Taiwan firms, and firms engaged in manufacturing electrical products were next largest suppliers to the domestic market. In both cases, domestic sales represented 76 to 80 per cent of the total sales, but the Taiwan pioneer firms in the chemicals and chemical products industries found some foreign markets for their products in Malaysia, Thailand, and Hong Kong.

For all pioneer firms in which Taiwan was the principal foreign shareholder the total value of sales at $16·3 million was higher than the total gross value of output of $13·9 million in 1966. Only five firms, however, in the main in the chemicals and chemical products industries, actually had sales values exceeding gross value of output. Some manufacturers complained that they had stockpiles of finished goods. Apparently they had difficulties in making sales due to the size of the domestic market and internal and external competition. Some Taiwan pioneer firms had difficulties with all three. One such firm was in the chemicals and chemical products industry. But the small size of the domestic market was the chief limiting factor for firms manufacturing import replacement goods, including some of those firms whose sales value exceeded gross value of output.

[13] See Appendix Table X.

There were two basic reasons for establishing Taiwan pioneer and non-pioneer firms: the anticipation of the Malaysian common market and access to raw materials. Most of the firms which were primarily interested in Singapore and Malaysian markets had opened up these markets in the early days by exports from Taiwan, and their Singapore distributors became their manufacturing partners. But the firms which came into existence because of the possibility of a market which extended beyond Singapore into the present Federation of Malaysia have since found that their main market is going to remain Singapore. In spite of Singapore's high per capita income its demand for import replacement goods has not been large enough to provide for full capacity production by the Taiwan pioneer firms concerned. The Singapore government's protective commercial policy has helped to eliminate almost entirely the foreign competitors in the domestic markets for import replacement goods they produce, but tariffs and import quotas are regarded as a poor substitute for a Malaysian common market. Fortunately, with the exception of one firm which has to compete with other, often larger, firms in the same field, these firms have so far experienced little competition in the domestic market, and where the domestic market was protected they were all able to adopt 'cost plus' pricing policies which, they felt, gave them a fair return.

The other group of Taiwan pioneer firms, established primarily because Singapore is situated near the raw materials, consists of export-oriented firms. The size of the market has not been a limiting factor, but to these firms the competition in foreign markets is the key problem. The manufacturers of wood and paper products faced competition in all their markets. South Africa, Finland, and Yugoslavia were the main competitors in Europe. In the United States, local producers, Philippine exporters who were favoured by a preferential tariff, Canadian exporters, and exporters from Taiwan itself made the market particularly competitive. In the United Kingdom, the Commonwealth preferential treatment accorded to Singapore goods made competition less severe. While the quality of the Taiwan firms' products was of international standard, their prices, when based on their usual 'average cost plus profit margin' calculation, were not sufficiently competitive. They had to lower their profit margin to sell at competitive prices.

One of the benefits export-oriented Taiwan firms have brought to Singapore has been established access to foreign markets. The firms manufacturing wood products and garments regard their Singapore operations as extensions of their Taiwan operations. In the case of one company the Singapore venture appears to be an offshoot of a Hong

Kong operation as well. All these firms had marketing connections with overseas buyers before coming to Singapore.

Comparisons of data for the actual and prospective full production employment, and for actual and prospective full production levels of gross value output, showed that none of the Taiwan pioneer firms had reached the level of full production by the end of 1966, but this is not surprising since only nine firms had been in full operation for more than twelve months by the end of 1966. Information on the utilisation rate of machinery and plant was not available, but the fact that most firms worked less than the maximum possible number of shifts in the third quarter of 1967 also suggested that the firms were not operating at full capacity. The export-oriented firms fared better than those producing mainly for the domestic market; among the latter the firms producing consumer goods worked at fuller capacity than the firms manufacturing producer goods.

It is difficult to evaluate the efficiency of the Taiwan pioneer firms because only five had been in operation for two full years or more by the end of 1966. Statistical data were also limited but the figures available suggest that some of the firms have been doing well for their early stage of development. In contrast one firm not only had a negative return to investment in 1965 and 1966 but also a negative figure for value added.

Little is known of the outflow of funds for distribution as dividends and interest to the Taiwan investors or to royalty payments. Since few have yet been able to make substantial profits the problem of an outflow of funds has scarcely arisen. It follows that the question of a loss of tax revenue to the host government due to tax holiday provisions does not arise either.

Whether the Taiwan investors are satisfied with the performance of their investments in the pioneer industries is another question.

PROBLEMS CONFRONTING TAIWAN FIRMS

For the firms which produce for export, the major problems seem to be concerned with selling their products at competitive prices, for they do not consider their rate of return to be reasonable when these prices are competitive. Their profit margin would have been higher had they been producing the goods in Taiwan. The problem, then, is inability to lower costs of production. In one case, the firm complained that while raw materials, owing to their proximity, were cheaper by 20 per cent, labour cost was 100 per cent higher, electricity and power costs were 40 per cent higher, and water charges were also higher than in Taiwan. Most of the

151

manufacturers concerned implied, although they were unwilling to say so overtly, that labour cost per unit output was high and could not be lowered because of stringent labour union regulations. They emphasised that productivity of even skilled labour was low. The fact that they claimed they had good relations with the labour unions does not seem to mean that they could work with the unions towards higher labour productivity or greater efficiency.

Some of the export-oriented Taiwan pioneer firms encountered difficulties in selling in markets where Hong Kong or mainland Chinese producers had established a foothold. The Hong Kong producers could sell at low prices primarily because their labour cost per unit output was low and the mainland Chinese producers could do so because cost was not a consideration. Other Taiwan firms, mainly manufacturers of producer goods, were competing with more efficient producers from developed countries. It is true that the Taiwan investors had brought to their Singapore firms ready markets for their products, but they claim that additional, new, and less keenly competitive markets have to be found. Most manufacturers expect the government to help out in this direction, as the cost of market search is high for an individual firm.

For firms producing principally for the Singapore market, the central problem is the limited size of the domestic market itself. Although almost all of these firms receive protection in the form of an import quota, tariff, or both, the existing capacity, designed for the Malaysian common market, is still too large for Singapore. There was some slight evidence that firms could take advantage of protection by charging monopolistic prices in spite of the Economic Development Board's attempts at price control, and it could be argued that increased demand might be induced by lowering prices. This, however, assumes both increasing returns to scale and a price elastic demand. Several of the firms producing import replacement goods had large stocks of finished goods but it is by no means clear whether they could sell these stocks if they were prepared to lower their prices. These firms, of course, also export their goods whenever possible, and this perhaps helps to explain their willingness to hold large stocks. If they could sell in the Malaysian market, the existing capacity might be fully utilised, but high tariffs unfortunately prevent many Singapore goods from entering the Malaysian market. At least one of the Taiwan investors in Singapore set up a joint venture to manufacture in Malaysia to overcome tariffs.

Why, then, do these Taiwan pioneer firms producing import replacement goods maintain their operations in Singapore? Part of the explanation seems to be that they hope to enter the Indonesian market, and this certainly seemed to be the principal motivation for the three non-pioneer firms which came in 1966–7. With the end of Confrontation, the prospect of selling Singapore goods in Indonesia seemed bright, but as diplomatic relations were not formally normalised until 1967, it remains to be seen whether the expectation can be realised.

What are the prospects of the Taiwan pioneer firms in Singapore? Much depends on whether new overseas markets can be found. This applies both to the firms producing for export and to those producing primarily for the domestic market. The Singapore government is contributing to the search for overseas markets by sending trade missions abroad, and if such missions are successful there is no reason to suppose that prospects for the Taiwan pioneer firms would not be better than they are now. Since, however, there do not appear to be prospects of marked improvements in output per man hour, in markets where Singapore competes with Taiwan, at existing wage levels, Taiwanese investors would probably still make higher profits in production in Taiwan than in Singapore.

7

Peter H. Lindert

United States Investment[1]

THE CHARACTER OF UNITED STATES INVESTMENT

The character of America's manufacturing investment in Singapore reflects the international positions of both countries. The comparative advantage of the United States is evident in the list of commodities currently produced with American participation. Particularly prominent are the petroleum products being turned out by a major refinery and two lubricant blending plants, all three of which are subsidiaries of large United States oil companies. Singapore's principal motor vehicle assembly plant is appropriately also American. The absence of any textile enterprises, in which American capital and management typically do not excel, is conspicuous in contrast with the number of textile mills recently established by Japanese, overseas Chinese, and local capital.

At the same time the flow of goods from the fourteen currently operating American plants is consistent with Singapore's role as an international distribution centre for Southeast Asia. Three factories process tropical resource products (gum, rubber, and plywood and veneer) for export to the United States, while Southeast Asian markets are supplied with a wide range of manufactured goods.[2]

---

[1] In preparing the present chapter I have benefited greatly from comments and other assistance generously provided by executives of the nineteen firms interviewed and by Mrs Linda W. Lindert, Mr Albert K. Ludy, Professor Theodore Morgan, and the staff of the Economic Research Centre of the University of Singapore.

[2] In addition to the petroleum and motor vehicle products mentioned, American concerns in Singapore process and manufacture batteries and related electrical supplies, sanitary napkins, paint, chocolate confectionery, oil drums and water heaters, finished photographic products, and cosmetics and pharmaceuticals for markets throughout Asia. Five additional firms, still under

In Singapore American manufacturers have exhibited the relatively strong preference for majority ownership that has been their trait the world over. United States residents hold majority shares in thirteen out of the twenty Singapore manufacturing concerns employing American capital,[3] and ten of these are wholly-owned subsidiaries. While joint ventures occupy a larger part of this sample than they have in United States direct investments in other countries,[4] the American firms, for the most part large and sophisticated corporations with plants on all continents, have allied with Singapore and third country capital less readily than any other major investing country except the United Kingdom.[5] The high percentage of United States ownership and control appears to have been motivated not by any scarcity of complementary local funds but by the recognition that relations with wholly- or almost wholly-owned subsidiaries are simpler, more easily manipulated, less formal, and less subject to the risk of disclosing any technical or managerial secrets the company may wish to retain.[6] The joint ventures involving Americans, on the other hand, consist for the most part of those firms that have felt a need to combine the talents of a technically experienced partner and a partner long versed at marketing the particular

---

construction when interviewed, will soon produce paper, phosphates, condensed milk, adhesive tapes, and cylinders for bottled gas.

Six of the fourteen firms currently in production are pioneers, as are two of those under construction. One current non-pioneer will soon begin turning out a new product with pioneer certification.

[3] In addition to the nineteen firms whose experience this chapter relates, American funds represent 20 per cent of the paid-up capital of a Japanese-run net and twine producer.

[4] An extensive survey of United States direct foreign investments in manufacturing in 1957 found over 90 per cent of all firms more than half owned by Americans, while 70 per cent of the total were wholly owned (United States Department of Commerce, Office of Business Economics, *U.S. Business Investments in Foreign Countries* (Washington, 1960), p. 102). These figures, however, fail to cover enterprises with less than 25 per cent United States ownership.

[5] While between 70 and 85 per cent of the total paid-up capital of the American-affiliated firms is held in the United States, only 60 per cent of that of all pioneer firms with foreign participation is held in all foreign countries combined.

[6] For a more thorough treatment of American ownership patterns in a different context, see D. T. Brash, *American Investment in Australian Industry* (Canberra, 1966), Chapter IV.

product in and around Singapore, even when one or both partners have been financially capable of complete ownership.

Although the sample is small and heterogeneous, the usual American capital intensity and large scale of production nonetheless emerge from the available figures for Singapore. The average capital-labour ratio of the American plants exceeds that of the pioneer and Jurong non-pioneer firms with foreign participation, with only the British- and Canadian-affiliated concerns roughly matching the American ratio. The American-affiliated concerns also tend, on the average, to employ more workers and to produce larger values of output. In view of such contrasts and the smallness of the domestic market, it is not surprising to find a greater export orientation among United States-affiliated producers; in 1966, for example, nine of them exported 57 per cent of their sales value,[7] while pioneer firms with foreign participation exported 31 per cent of theirs.[8]

Two further features of the United States participation in Singapore manufacturing unavoidably constrain the analysis that follows. Firstly, most of the nineteen enterprises studied were relatively new: although six of them had been established before 1946, none of the rest began operations until 1964. Reaching conclusions about the nature and impact of United States direct investments in Singapore thus requires judging an edifice the foundations of which are still being laid. Secondly, the small number of firms to be studied and the modesty of the amounts involved (2,300 employees and around $25 to $30 million in paid-up American capital at the end of 1966), when viewed in the larger context of United States foreign investments, would seem to reduce the significance of a detailed treatment. But concern over prematurity and sample size is less compelling than the importance of appraising as accurately as possible the contribution that recent and future inflows of American capital, technology, and management might make toward Singapore's growth and employment efforts. The present chapter accordingly attempts to identify the patterns already evident in the American experience in Singapore as these may govern future investments. More specifically, attention will be given to the factors attracting American investors to Singapore, the problems of marketing in and through Singapore, the experience of the United States-affiliated firms regarding managerial and production problems, and the overall quantitative contribution of

[7] Of these nine firms, the six with pioneer status also exported 57 per cent of their total sales.

[8] See Appendix Table X.

these investments toward satisfying the country's employment, income, and foreign exchange needs.

For several American investors the crucial inducement to manufacture in Singapore has been provided by the same advantages that make the island the chief entrepôt of Southeast Asia. The strategic location at the region's maritime hub has seemed especially attractive to those firms whose products seek widely dispersed markets, or draw on a number of different Asian supply sources, or carry a costly freight bill. Inseparable from Singapore's role as a commercial centre are its excellent harbour, loading, and docking facilities, advantages eagerly sought by most of the same firms emphasising the importance of distributive convenience. It is thus not surprising to find the American processors of petroleum products, plywood and veneer, phosphates, marine paints, and rubber located not only in Singapore but also within yards of the Jurong or downtown docks.

The often advertised adaptability and abundance of Singapore labour have exerted a positive, but apparently not decisive, attraction for most firms that have decided to come. The importance of this factor clearly depends on the alternatives being pondered by the prospective investor. A firm weighing manufacture in Singapore against export from the United States, or from an Australian affiliate, would naturally mention abundant (that is cheap) labour as a strong argument in favour of the former choice. In comparisons with Malaysian or Hong Kong sites, on the other hand, labour abundance in Singapore would be less likely to stand out. Such was in fact the pattern of opinions on the subject of labour.

Most American investors attach considerable importance to the 'pro-business climate' created by the government, with special praise being reserved for the efforts of the Economic Development Board. By offering to guide new firms through administrative red tape, arranging for the provision of utilities, and helping to recruit a labour force, the Board has earned favourable comparison with other governments in Southeast Asia. Favour with American investors has also been won by the high integrity of Singapore officials.

Widespread as this acclaim may be, there is a striking contrast between the emphasis it receives from firms in the construction stage and the more qualified endorsements voiced by firms that have been in production a while. Within a few months of the beginning of production, any of a host of minor grievances—one or two per firm—typically arise regarding government treatment. Various official actions relating to land use, electric power rates, taxes, prices, and factory design have been criticised by one firm or another. Such a shift in mood is hardly surprising. The first few months of production divert managerial attention from long-run profit hopes to immediate production problems, and thus from the help given by officials to the help that has not been given. For their part, Economic Development Board officials understandably devote more of their scarce time to the task of attracting new industry than to that of negotiating minor grievances with the firms already attracted. Any courtship is a bargaining process, and bargaining positions change once the key commitment is made. It must be stressed, however, that the complaints have been minor and in no case have they involved an official breach of promise.

The concessionary tax rates offered to recent arrivals, while naturally appreciated by the incoming firms, have had little or no demonstrable effect on the extent of the American commitment on the island. The five-year tax holiday for pioneer firms, for example, was not crucial to the establishment or success of any of the nine American pioneers. Describing the holiday as interesting but inconsequential, the American-affiliated managers have stressed that longer run cost and sales prospects far outweigh any temporary tax concessions, the more so since profits typically remain abnormally low in the first few years of operations. Only one manager has acknowledged a major contribution made by tax reductions to subsequent plant expansion, and conditional pioneer status persuaded one other incoming firm to settle for the particular site preferred by the Economic Development Board. With these exceptions, the pioneer managers seem to have been genuinely unimpressed by their tax holidays; it must, however, be borne in mind that any executive would naturally be reluctant to admit that his concern owed its existence to a tax concession.

From such reactions it does not follow that the five-year exemptions have resulted in a fruitless sacrifice of tax revenues. A balanced appraisal would in fact seem to argue in favour of Singapore's retaining the tax holiday feature of pioneer status. While the tax favour is lightly regarded by its recipients, it is also cheaply dispensed: since profits during the initial years of pioneer production are usually low,[9] Singapore is liable

[9] Exceptions to this pattern can, of course, be found; one American firm reaped extraordinarily large profits during the tax holiday, and the bulk of these was apparently remitted abroad.

to lose relatively little revenue by waiving taxes for a short period. Furthermore, the fact that several other Southeast Asian governments extend similar holidays suggests that the professed indifference of pioneer firms toward the exemption must be interpreted with caution. Any favour that has become a standard promotional device in the area is not likely to focus attention on any one country, but its omission by Singapore alone might noticeably compromise her bargaining position with firms considering several Southeast Asian sites. In such competitive situations there is much to be said for adopting a posture of matching any standard offer—'making every reasonable effort'—to welcome foreign capital.

The announcement of a tax reduction from 40 to 4 per cent on corporate income related to export sales, like the pioneer tax holiday, has failed to evoke any enthusiastic approval or extra commitment of resources by American firms. It is too early to judge the overall response, however, since the incentives were announced only at the end of 1966. The net foreign exchange and income gains to be derived by Singapore from this concession will depend upon the difference between the domestic content in any extra sales and the share of the extra net profits on all sales that is remitted abroad,[10] and any difference between the marginal social benefits of private and government investment outlays. The export incentive may prove on balance to promote Singapore's development less satisfactorily than the five-year holiday, since the percentage of sales revenue constituting profits remitted abroad will be considerably higher after the first few years of operations. The export

[10] The difference between these two magnitudes will be positive (favourable) if it can be shown that the incentive will raise the sales of all eligible firms by more than some critical percentage. For example, if the domestic content share of the induced extra sales ($\triangle S$) were 25 per cent, and the share of the sales without the incentive (S_o) to be remitted abroad as extra net profits under the more lenient tax rate were 1·5 per cent, the relevant condition would be whether

$$\cdot 25 \triangle S > \cdot 015\ S_o,$$
i.e. whether $\triangle S/S_o > \cdot 06$.

That is the foreign exchange and income gains to Singapore would be positive only if the tax reduction produced an increase of more than 6 per cent in the sales and output of the firms qualifying for this concession. The same comparison would be appropriate regardless of whether the analysis is static or allows for dynamic income and price repercussions. (Underlying this illustration is the assumption that the domestic content of domestic sales replaces imports and therefore represents an equivalent foreign exchange saving.)

incentive is not necessitated by comparable offers throughout Southeast Asia, and unlike the tax holiday it covers many firms that are already located in Singapore and are therefore likely to respond with smaller percentage sales increases.

Singapore's industrial estates have clearly facilitated the task of drawing American firms to the island. The only American-affiliated manufacturing concerns not located in industrial estates are five small operations which have been ancillary to the firms' distributive activity, and have thus developed on their bunkering or sales premises. Since most future arrivals will settle in one industrial estate or another, the most pertinent locational question concerns the relative merits of estates near the city and more remote estates like Jurong. Of ten American-affiliated firms that had a reasonable opportunity to choose between Jurong and another site, eight have established in Jurong. They were attracted primarily by the generous allotment of cheap land and access to the Jurong harbour; the combination of these two features has sufficed to make Jurong compare favourably not only with estates closer to town but also with estates in other countries. The supply of services has also proved satisfactory to American firms in Jurong. Initial difficulties were experienced in recruiting a labour force willing to move or commute to Jurong, but these have been overcome with travel allowances,[11] car pools, co-operation from the Economic Development Board, and the passage of time. To be sure, some extra labour cost is involved. Even without travel allowances, the Jurong firms offer slightly higher starting wages than the comparable pair of United States-affiliated plants recently established on sites closer to the urban labour pools. Whether the extra labour cost exceeds the rental savings offered on Jurong leases depends, of course, on the relative labour and land intensity of each firm's techniques of production.[12] Most Jurong firms, at any rate, have suffered no serious disillusionment with the estate that helped attract them to Singapore.

The advantages afforded by Singapore's industrial estates, tax relief, and official hospitality toward foreign investors are viewed by most of the American firms as merely permissive conditions, rather than essential motivations, for their interest in producing there. Their central

[11] The Jurong travel allowances apparently run from 5 up to 10 per cent of base wage rates. For the percentage assumed by all fringe benefits, see p. 168.
[12] Labour cost need not be the only drawback related to Jurong's remoteness: one firm choosing a site closer to town has emphasised the importance of proximity to markets, primarily because its product is perishable in transit.

purpose in establishing plants in Singapore has allegedly been to protect their stake in growing Southeast Asian markets by getting into the area ahead of their chief international rivals. The feeling of racing for markets has been manifested in statements to the effect that 'in this business, if you don't get in, someone else will', and 'being the first company here has been a very big help'. Sentiments of this sort conform to the classic pattern of 'defensive investment', especially when existing or expected official trade barriers play a large role in delineating the relevant markets.

Assertions about the necessity of defending markets, however, must be interpreted carefully and with reference to other information pertaining to the same firms. In what sense is pursuit of local or regional markets an explanation for manufacturing in Singapore instead of supplying the same markets from plants in Hong Kong, Sydney, or San Diego? As will be noted again in the section on marketing, most firms were already marketing in and through Singapore before producing there. Clearly, the nature of the competitive advantage being sought must be specified, and the question of 'markets' becomes instead a question of the relative importance of the advantages of minimising the time and cost of shipping finished goods, other cost economies to be reaped by producing in Singapore, and protection. The importance of the first two factors has already been noted in previous references to the country's central geographic position, its adaptable labour force, and related cost features. Protection merits further scrutiny.

The lure of protection and the threat of its bestowal upon industrial rivals have combined to convince a number of American firms to set up plants in Singapore. Had they not felt that independent Singapore (or Malaysia, if plans were laid between 1963 and 1965) would soon put barriers around one incoming manufacturer or another, some would have continued supplying their products from the outside. Singapore protection, defined to include the threat as well as the actual erection of barriers, has thus tended to raise the country's manufacturing output, employment, and costs. More relevant to policy, however, are the effects of only those tariffs and quotas that were in fact erected around the incoming firms. Their impact on Singapore's industrialisation depends on the extent to which they have succeeded in augmenting employment, output, and foreign exchange earnings by attracting firms that would have stayed away in their absence. Conversely, in those instances in which essentially the same productive facilities would have been set up and operated (by the same firm or a rival) with less or no protection, the main effect would simply be to raise domestic costs and redistribute income.

161

The effects of the various tariffs and quotas sheltering fourteen of the American-affiliated firms, like the commercial policies themselves, have varied greatly from one product to another. Certain goods would probably not have been produced without protection, while others would have; some tariffs have imposed a substantial extra cost on domestic purchasers, while others have not; and so forth. To illustrate the kinds of considerations that have complicated the relationship between protection and individual investments in manufacturing, it is convenient to survey the experiences of two of the largest and four of the smallest American-affiliated firms.

The two large concerns fail to fit the stereotype of infant industries struggling to become efficient and competitive in a strange environment. Both are subsidiaries of technological pacesetters in their respective industries and produce at respectably low unit costs with up-to-date equipment. Both serve as their parents' Asian 'swing plants', exporting a large share of their output to meet fluctuating demands in a long list of countries. Both are able to sell at competitive prices abroad. Why then were their Singapore sales sheltered by specific tariffs? The information available is insufficient to reveal the underlying official reasoning. In one case protection was definitely not crucial in bringing the firm to Singapore, though subsequent expansions have allegedly been financed in part by protected domestic profits; the role of protection in attracting the other firm cannot be determined.[13] While the official motives for imposing tariffs are thus not clear, there is no overlooking the positive contributions made by both plants to Singapore's development. Their value added and their foreign exchange earnings have been sizeable enough to offset any extra costs imposed on domestic purchasers. One employs a large labour force, and the second has served as a showpiece advertising Singapore's growing industrial sophistication. If protection has contributed in any significant way to the scale of operations of these firms, it can be tentatively concluded that Singapore has not paid an inordinately high price to promote these enterprises.

For eight of the other protected American firms, the effects of protection—greater production and employment, higher domestic prices, and so on—can be listed, but no judgment about the net overall benefits of protection can be made. The tariffs and quotas sheltering

---

[13] Because of such uncertainties about the causal link between the tariffs and quotas imposed and the foreign investments attracted, the attempt made below, pp. 173–5, to qualify the impact of the investments will not distinguish between the two factors. Instead, the combined effects of foreign investments and their protection will be appraised for each industry.

certain products produced by the four remaining firms, however, seem clearly to have yielded no net benefit to Singapore. These four processors of consumer goods for the domestic market do little more than mix, cut, package, and ship goods that are imported in a nearly finished state. Their minimal percentages of value added are then consumed at considerable mark-ups on the total price. The four firms will together employ (in the manufacture of these and other products) only 120 workers when and if they reach full capacity. At least two of the four concerns would have manufactured in Singapore even without protection of the products in question, and the products of the other two may have been made locally by other firms. In these instances the benefits of protection have probably failed to offset the extra costs imposed on consumers. Examples like these serve to underline the pragmatism and delicacy which both sides must exercise in negotiations over protection.

MARKETING

From the viewpoint of some of the American investors, the conspicuous instability of Southeast Asian markets is perhaps the most persuasive argument in defence of protection and other measures that secure local markets. The unavoidable vulnerability of Singapore to changes in Asia's political and commercial currents makes the problem of market stability as urgent as that of market growth. The techniques used to meet this challenge are the focus of the present section.

Despite such developments as the impending British military evacuation, domestic demand is considerably less volatile than export demand. The American companies have themselves fostered this stability in a number of ways. They have, with only one or two exceptions, confined the manufacturing activity of their Singapore subsidiaries to those goods that the firm had been selling in the area for several years before local production commenced, thus minimising the risk of inadequate demand for the new output.[14] The goods produced and sold by the local subsidiaries have also tended to be the dependable standard brand-name lines with which both customers and company engineers are most

---

[14] This pattern suggests a promotional tactic to be employed by the Economic Development Board. The Board's representatives might augment the number of United States firms seriously considering establishment in Singapore by approaching additional firms which are currently conspicuous on the list of Singapore's retained imports and re-exports. There are indications that this device has been employed in the past.

familiar.[15] The more specialised or experimental product lines either have not been produced or have been imported directly from the parent company. The desire for well-established local market connections has also been reflected in the formation of eight of the nine joint ventures involving American funds. Each of these eight links a more technically oriented partner with a partner having several years of contact with local customers, the latter usually performing the sales functions of the new manufacturing venture. In all likelihood each of these expedients will continue to be adopted by future American-affiliated firms in order to minimise the danger of unforeseen drops in domestic demand.

Similar precautions have been taken regarding the more volatile export markets of Southeast Asia. Like the Singapore markets, the surrounding areas had previously been supplied with each company's standard brand-name products for several years. A few firms for which Singapore's smallness dictates export dependence have, like the two large firms already described, operated as 'swing plants', filling orders in several countries at once. A widespread network of agents or company-affiliated retailers, and a reluctance to count on any one export market, are both essential to this strategy. Managers budgeting export sales have often prudently refrained from budgeting sales for certain individual markets, especially those in Indonesia.

Past experience has justified this emphasis on flexibility. Political upheavals have frustrated sales plans on several occasions, particularly in the last six to eight years. The Indonesian Confrontation was one such event. More serious in its impact on the American firms, however, was the unexpected separation of Singapore from Malaysia in 1965. One firm, having survived the Japanese occupation in World War II and serious labour agitation of the early 1960s, suffered a severe setback from separation. The prospects for continued union had seemed so secure that the company undertook a major plant expansion early in 1965, only to incur serious capital losses later that year. The loss of Malaysian business has since restricted production to a relatively small scale. One other firm was ready to approve the commencement of

---

[15] The same tendency for American firms to produce their more established and standardised products in developing countries has been detected by other authors. See R. Vernon, 'International Investment and International Trade in the Product Cycle', *Quarterly Journal of Economics*, Vol. 80, May 1966, p. 203; and W. Gruber, D. Mehta, and R. Vernon, 'The R and D Factor in International Investment of United States Industries', *Journal of Political Economy*, Vol. 75, February 1967, pp. 32, 33.

construction of a Singapore plant at its next board meeting, to be held just one week after the day of separation. Malaysian tariffs removed 99 per cent of its projected market, and the entire scheme has remained in abeyance ever since. Nor are these the only firms that have lost sales as a result of separation. On the other hand, Singapore's independence has attracted at least two small American firms that would otherwise have been content to supply its markets from Malaysia. On balance, it appears that the break with Malaysia has not reduced the number of United States firms in Singapore, but has clearly restricted their aggregate investment, sales, and employment.

There is every reason to expect the recurrence of unforeseen restrictions in individual markets. Despite the co-operative gestures attending the creation of the Association of South-East Asian Nations, a continued rise in protectionism in the surrounding countries is anticipated by the exporting firms.[16] In addition, there is no way of predicting how long the Vietnam war will continue to buoy up export sales, or how much demand can be expected from Indonesia. These uncertainties, combined with the British military withdrawal, have reinforced the emphasis of the American firms on resilience and flexibility in their marketing techniques.

MANAGERIAL AND PRODUCTION PROBLEMS

The pursuit of flexibility and risk minimisation have influenced the administrative structure and production techniques adopted by the American companies as well as their marketing strategy. The parent firms have, for example, consistently sought to avoid overcommitment by exercising control over the budgetary and capital-expansion functions of their subsidiaries. Such surveillance has naturally been facilitated by the retention of majority ownership in thirteen of the Singapore affiliates. The degree of subsidiary participation in setting sales goals and planning expansions in capacity has varied somewhat from one company to another. In several cases the financial projections and proposals have been initiated regularly by the subsidiary, while in others the home office has apparently solicited only data on current performance and has itself drawn up the projections. Although some Singapore managers have described approval of their plans by the home office as being routine

[16] One company has made explicit preparations to construct a plant in a nearby country if that country doubles its tariff rate on the firm's exports from Singapore.

165

and virtually automatic, key decisions regarding their investments, the introduction of new products, and export sales have nevertheless emanated from the western hemisphere, and sometimes these decisions have not conformed to the recommendations of subsidiary managers and minority partners.

The subsidiary managers have been delegated much more authority over personnel decisions than over budgeting and expansion. The parent companies have refrained from participation in hiring and firing anyone below (say) the top three local executives. All lower positions are filled at the discretion of the subsidiary management in Singapore. In fact, virtually all of the positions, including most managerial posts, are filled by Singapore citizens. The American parents have responded well to Singapore's understandable desire to 'Singaporeanise' management as much as possible. The extent to which they have done so differs slightly between joint ventures and wholly-owned subsidiaries. The joint enterprises have employed expatriates relatively sparingly.[17] In a few cases the top plant management is entirely Singaporean, and in one or two others plans have been made to replace temporary expatriates with citizens within a few years. The same policy of progressive expatriate replacement has been enunciated by the wholly-owned subsidiaries, and in some instances formal timetables have been laid out. It is interesting to note, however, that each wholly-owned subsidiary expects to fill its very top post (that of managing director or general manager) with an American, European, or Australian indefinitely, although some of the parents have no hard and fast policy to this effect.

While direct explanations are lacking, reasonable conjectures can be advanced regarding the motivations underlying these policies. Parent companies of wholly-owned subsidiaries doubtless consider their interests to be better represented by a general manager with strong ties to the company, and a professional executive with experience in different countries tends to maintain a company-wide perspective. An expatriate executive is also more easily transferred from Singapore to another location when conditions warrant. The readiness of both subsidiaries and joint ventures to 'Singaporeanise' most managerial and technical positions within the first few years of production probably reflects economic more than diplomatic considerations. Expatriates are relatively

---

[17] Six joint ventures employed a dozen non-citizens in managerial and technical capacities out of a total of 897 employees at the end of 1966. Eight wholly-owned subsidiaries employed 20 to 22 non-citizens out of 1,402 employees.

expensive, and most companies seem confident that Singapore citizens can be trained to assume the same positions without undue difficulty or expense.

The same combination of tranquillity and control that the American firms have preserved on the issue of management has been sought with no less resolve in the field of labour relations. The risk of large jumps in labour cost has been reduced by a choice of production techniques to be described presently. At the same time a generally successful effort has been made to avoid heated confrontations with trade unions.

American experience with Singapore unions has depended considerably on the age of the plant. The six firms that have been producing in Singapore throughout the post-war period have been subjected to more severe pressures than the thirteen recent arrivals. Only one of the six veterans could claim to have avoided serious friction in the particularly tense political climate between 1960 and 1962. Four firms had to contend with obstructionist tactics (stoppages, slow-downs, etc.) on the part of their heavily *Barisan* workforces, and one plant was almost shut down permanently. Since then, tensions have abated, the *Barisan* unions have been de-registered, and the labour movement in general is described as more 'mature'. Union pressure, to be sure, has persisted on such issues as fringe benefits and internal promotion, but worktime losses and anti-expatriate utterances have become infrequent.

Although certain of the recent arrivals have experienced minor labour frictions, relations have been remarkably smooth. Workers in the new American-affiliated firms have not only been co-operative, but have generally refrained from unionising in the first few months of production.[18] The formula determining the length of this grace period, according to one employer, has been that 'the union comes in when the factory begins to produce well'. To judge from the experience of half a dozen recently established firms, unions request recognition some time after six months of production, and initial contracts are signed by the time that production has run about eighteen months. While no explicit policy has been announced, the grace period probably reflects informal government pressure on the unions. Such a restraining influence is certainly consistent with the recent policy statements of government

[18] The exceptions to this pattern have been three firms whose other activities have ante-dated and overshadowed their recent manufacturing ventures. In these cases the existing unions have simply absorbed the manufacturing labour force.

167

and National Trade Union Congress officials regarding the importance of productivity, employment, cost reduction, and the attraction of industrial capital.[19] Explicit mediation by the Economic Development Board recommending union restraint has also been observed (and appreciated) by at least one employer.

Within this overall context of restraint individual unions and even unorganised factory forces have nonetheless continued to press for additional benefits. Fringe benefits have been particularly popular, and have become rather standardised throughout Singapore's industrial sector. Total fringe payments (including contributions to the Central Provident Fund) have run at about 15 per cent of base wages for new firms and roughly 28 per cent for the older concerns. The overall upward pressure of wage and fringe bargaining, or unit labour costs, however, has not seemed excessive, although several of the American-affiliated firms have found costs higher than they had originally anticipated.

However gentle or pronounced the increase in wage bills may have been, the mere possibility of mounting unit labour costs has been an obvious source of concern to incoming American producers. This concern seems to provide a partial explanation for their marked tendency to retain much of the capital intensity characteristic of their American plants, although Singapore wages are much lower. The similarity in production technique between the two contexts is striking, particularly when differences in scale are allowed for. Plant layouts and basic machinery correspond to those of American plants. To be sure, a number of minor labour-saving options necessitated by high labour costs in America have been passed up in Singapore, but others have not. Only in three or four old firms, and to a lesser extent in one or two new firms, could it be said that relative labour costs have produced a significant shift away from capital-intensive techniques.

To a large extent, this selective retention of labour-saving features may be a symptom of the uncertainty and risk that American firms attach to any reliance on large foreign labour forces. Unanticipated cost increases, material losses due to inconsistent quality of product, and temporary stoppages, may be linked more with labour than with machinery. There are, of course, other possible motivations for capital intensity which must not be overlooked, such as substitutability of equipment for skilled labour inputs that are unavailable in Singapore.

[19] Excerpts from recent policy statements are reproduced in W. E. Chalmers (ed.), *Crucial Issues in Industrial Relations in Singapore* (Singapore, 1967), Appendix F.

The hypothesis is nonetheless advanced that the uncertainties associated with an unfamiliar labour force have restricted the willingness of incoming American companies to adopt labour-intensive methods.

QUANTIFYING THE AMERICAN CONTRIBUTION

The overall contribution of American manufacturing investment to Singapore's economic development is most conveniently analysed by separately examining its effects on employment, skills, value added, and foreign exchange earnings. The present section attempts a rough and partial assessment of each of these influences. It is hardly necessary to point out the limitations imposed on such an effort by the smallness of the sample and the necessity of relying on aggregate measurements as substitutes for economic events touching the lives of thousands of individuals. The value of the exercise lies in its ability, despite these limitations, to illustrate some of the patterns that are likely to govern future American investment in Singapore industry.

The country's paramount objective in welcoming foreign capital is not the one to which the American companies have made their most noteworthy contribution.

The employment directly created by the fourteen active American firms by the end of 1966 was only 2,300 persons. Even if these firms and the five under construction were soon to operate at 'full production', no more than 3,000 jobs would be created, only half of which would be provided in the plants constructed after 1960. This is indeed a very modest contribution to the additional jobs that need to be created in Singapore. Allowances for the indirect creation of extra employment by the local expenditures of these firms would not appreciably augment their job impact.

The meagre employment contribution of American-affiliated firms is hardly surprising: small workforces are a concomitant of capital-intensive techniques. If the American comparative advantage lies in labour-saving methods, it might be argued, Singapore could easily supplement American-affiliated industry with more labour-intensive factories on other sites. What is somewhat disturbing, however, is a characteristic shared by both the American-affiliated and other firms which have settled in Jurong: both groups have used large amounts of space as well as capital. Among the American concerns this characteristic has been exhibited most clearly by several of the recent arrivals, which have benefited from the generously low rents prevailing in Jurong and

169

elsewhere. By contributing to Singapore's industrial surge in the middle 1960s, these firms have acquired some of the best sites on the island.

The long-run implications of this relatively liberal alienation of land to firms using little labour are difficult to appraise, but a simple illustration may help. The relative intensity with which men and space have been employed in (say) Jurong can be crudely represented by the ratio of employees to acres on the industrial sites. This ratio can then be applied to different amounts of land to determine the levels of employment that occupancy by similar industries would imply. Thus, if industries having the same overall labour-land ratios as those currently in Jurong were somehow to occupy all the additional land that the Economic Development Board has earmarked or considered for industrial sites, and were to produce at their 'full production' levels, only some 120,000 extra jobs would be generated directly in manufacturing when this land is occupied.[20] Any subsequent growth of the manufacturing labour force, however, might prove difficult without additional industrial land.

Any simple ratio-and-gap reasoning of this sort requires some obvious qualifications. Firstly, it is highly artificial to project a fixed labour-land ratio from one context to another. Rents could adjust to space shortages, shifting the ratio in the process. In addition, as already suggested, the space intensity of Jurong and American firms could be offset by labour-intensive manufacturing activity in flatted factories and on private sites.[21] The point is simply that such adjustments may in fact prove advisable as deliberate policies.

While the total numbers employed by American firms are not impressive, the composition of the labour force being absorbed by the newer firms has corresponded to employment needs in Singapore. The

[20] These conjectures are based on land use and employment figures cited by the Economic Development Board in its 1965 and 1966 *Annual Reports* and in *The Jurong Story* (1967). By the end of 1966 the 'full production' employment in Jurong firms either in production or in the implementation phase amounted to 14,320 jobs. By the same date, 1,224 acres of Jurong industrial land had been either leased or earmarked on option. These jobs suggest a rough ratio of 11·7 jobs per acre. Applying this ratio to the 10,041 acres that the Economic Development Board has acquired, committed, or studied for industrial development yields a total employment of 117,480. Subtracting the existing employment on these sites gives an increment of under 100,000 jobs.

[21] It is encouraging to note that, at the time of writing, several prospective American investors are actively investigating the feasibility of toy factories, electronics assembly plants, and fisheries. Each of these activities has a higher employment-space ratio than the existing American-affiliated firms.

youngest working age group, for whom most of the new jobs must be provided, has been well represented in the recently erected plants, where the average and median ages have been twenty-five years or lower. In the older firms, the average age has risen into the low forties as the firm has matured. To the extent that the correspondence between the youth of firm and youth of employees continues, growing inflows of American capital will draw a high proportion of younger workers into the manufacturing sector. The employment pattern of the American-affiliated firms has also approximately matched the ethnic composition of Singapore, with Malay employees assuming a slightly higher share of the total employment than of the national population.[22]

Substantive contributions to the skills of Singapore citizens have been made by the formal training programs offered by three major corporations to subsidiary administrators and engineers. The programs combine training on the job with extended stays in the United States or Australia at company expense. The skills acquired have the additional advantage of being transferable to other types of enterprise. The number of persons already enrolled in these programs, while miniscule in relation to Singapore's overall needs, has been impressive in relation to the sizes of the individual firms involved.

These programs are unfortunately the only noteworthy investments in developing human capital that have been evident among the American-affiliated manufacturers. It has not been practical for the other firms to undertake comparable training of managers and engineers. Furthermore, none of the American-affiliated firms has made extensive outlays to train blue collar personnel. Training at this level has been confined to the four months or less of on-the-job instruction needed to raise new workers to full efficiency. The skills imparted have generally not been transferable to other branches of industry.

The smallness of the employment and training impact of the American investment contrasts with the appreciable extent of their contribution to value added in industry and to the country's foreign exchange earnings. A straightforward comparison of aggregates shows that in 1966 the nine American affiliates for which sufficient data are available generated value added of about $26 million, equal to nearly 0·8 per cent of gross domestic expenditure, whereas fourteen American affiliates employed only 0·4

---

[22] Among individual firms the only deviators from this pattern have been two joint ventures with Singapore-Chinese plant management, where only the front guards have been non-Chinese.

per cent of Singapore's workforce. The American affiliates' share of total exports of domestic goods greatly exceeded both percentages.

Readily accessible aggregates like these convey a correct impression of the ranking of the various contributions in their order of importance, but hardly suffice as measures of the amounts added to national product and to foreign exchange earnings. The task of deriving such measures is facilitated by the very great importance of foreign trade in national product. For an economy so dependent on external trade, measuring an increase in foreign exchange earnings implies measurement of increases in income, and vice versa. Because extra income leads so directly to extra imports, lasting increases in national product must be tied to improvements in the country's ability to pay for imports. The calculations that follow will therefore focus first on estimating the impact of the American-affiliated enterprises on Singapore's foreign exchange earnings, and then will specify the relationship of this estimate to the increase in national product.

The chief channels through which a foreign investment influences the host country's balance of payments can be categorised as initial effects (those occurring when the enterprise is being constructed), direct year-to-year effects, and subsequent income and price repercussions. The first group consists of the original inflows of funds and equipment, which are not repeated once the enterprise is in operation. The second includes the domestic content in new exports of final product from the host country; the replacement of imports by sales of domestic value added to domestic markets; imports of capital goods (after the initial installation of plant and equipment); and remittances of interest, dividends, fees, and royalties abroad. The final category encompasses the entire 'multiplier' process through which a part of the extra income generated by the firm's activity is ultimately spent on further imports.

Precision is hardly to be expected in the quantification of such influences, both because many of the relevant data are lacking and because measurement of any 'impact' or 'influence' implies a comparison of real and hypothetical situations. Thus the tactic adopted is to underestimate the true influence intentionally, in order to establish the simple conclusion that it must have exceeded the derived figure. Static influences relating to the activity of nine firms in 1966 are partially measured on this basis.

The major question regarding the initial capital and capital-goods imports is whether or not the former have been sufficient to cover the latter. Actual figures on the total capital inflow (including non-equity borrowing) are again lacking, but partial figures and interview responses

172

suggest that the inflow of funds has generally matched (or exceeded) the outlays on new foreign equipment. Virtually every firm seems to have financed its initial construction by issuing equity capital to the parent company. On the other hand, subsequent additions to plant and equipment have usually been covered up by borrowing in Singapore through the use of bank overdrafts. It will thus be assumed provisionally that the original combinations of financial and real capital imports have not caused a net loss of reserves by Singapore, although the evidence available is less than conclusive.

If Singapore is to achieve lasting foreign exchange gains by attracting direct foreign investments, its trade balance must be sufficiently improved by the current account activities of the new firms to offset the outflows of profits, interest, and fees, and any additional imports of equipment. The extra year-to-year exchange earnings accruing for net exports and from import replacement can be quantified fairly easily. The gains associated with the extra exports of firm i are equal to the domestic content share of export revenues, which can be represented symbolically as $(1-a_i)$ $(P_{w_i} X_i)$, where a_i is the share of each output dollar corresponding to imported inputs,[23] P_{w_i} the unit price(s) of the exported good(s), and X_i the physical volume(s) exported. If the new firms are established without any change in Singapore's tariff and quota structure, the replacement of imports by domestic sales would simply equal $(1-a_i)$ $(P_{w_i} Q_i)$, where Q_i represents the physical volume(s) sold domestically by the new firm.[24]

In many cases, however, duties have been levied in order to protect American-affiliated firms. The combination of new domestic production and protective barriers replaces previous imports in three different ways illustrated in Fig. 7.1. With protection, the value of imports replaced

---

[23] Excluded from each a_i are payments to foreigners of managerial and technical fees, royalties, interest, and dividends, which will be considered separately below. For a large country, computing the a_i's would require detailed input-output information. Singapore's heavy trade dependence, however, facilitates determining the extent to which material inputs represent import content.

[24] Two simplifying assumptions underlying the present analysis should be mentioned here. Firstly, the prices that the rest of the world receives when supplying the Singapore market (the P_w's) are assumed to be independent of conditions in Singapore. Secondly, it is assumed that, even after duties are imposed, some imports of the commodity in question continue to find a demand in Singapore. Both assumptions are convenient and broadly valid, but neither is essential to the conclusions reached.

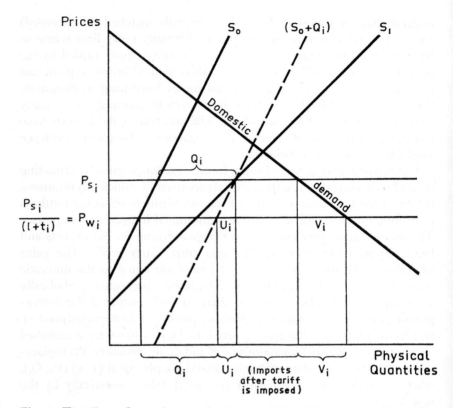

Prices

S_o (S_o+Q_i) S_1

Domestic

Q_i

P_{s_i}

$\dfrac{P_{s_i}}{(1+t_i)} = P_{w_i}$

U_i V_i

demand

Physical
Quantities

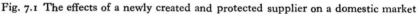

Q_i U_i (Imports V_i
after tariff
is imposed)

Fig. 7.1 The effects of a newly created and protected supplier on a domestic market

by the sales of the new firm (whose supply curve is the horizontal difference between the new domestic supply curve S_1 and the old supply
curve S_o) is

$$P_{w_i} \; Q_i \;\; = \dfrac{P_{s_i} \; Q_i}{(1+t_i)}$$

of which the share corresponding to domestic value added is

$$\dfrac{(1-a_i) \, (P_{s_i} \; Q_i)}{(1+t_i)}$$

174

where P_{s_i} is the observable Singapore price and t_i the percentage tariff rate.[25] The total displacement of imports of the commodity in question is

$$\frac{P_{s_i}}{(1+t_i)} \; [Q_i + U_i + V_i]$$

where the values of the line segments U_i and V_i depend on the elasticities of previous domestic supply (if any) and total domestic demand. Subtracting out the foreign components of the extra domestic sales then yields the direct foreign exchange gain from import replacement for each year. This net gain equals

$$\frac{(1-a_i)}{(1+t_i)} \; P_{s_i} \; (Q_i + U_i)$$

plus whatever share of V_i the domestic consumers decide to divert away from imports altogether.

There is no obvious way of measuring the elasticities that determine the values of the elasticity-related shifts (U_i and V_i) for each commodity. Fortunately, the only statement that can safely be made about U_i and V_i is the only one that needs to be made: neither magnitude could represent a negative import replacement. It is sufficient to measure the term containing Q_i, and thereby arrive at a deliberate underestimate of the true total value of import replacement. This truncated measure, combined with the corresponding export formula, shows that in 1966 domestic value added from nine American-affiliated firms replaced imports and created exports worth more than $25 million, or at least 27 per cent of their own total sales of $95 million.

From this estimate must be subtracted all remissions of dividends, interest, and fees abroad, as well as any imports of capital goods after the firm is in operation. Since it has been quite impossible to obtain data on the repatriation of funds to the United States and elsewhere, crude approximations must serve instead. A perusal of the figures on the income and fees earned by the United States on its manufacturing

[25] The difference between the Singapore and world prices has typically been slightly less than the tariff would suggest, since many firms have chosen to retain slightly lower prices than the world price plus the tariff. The use of tariff rates in some cases where true price differentials were not available implies some underestimation of the true extent of import replacement.

The present analysis would not be altered if specific tariffs (as opposed to *ad valorem*) or quotas were set up.

investments in each major area of the world indicates that annual income receipts have never reached 5 per cent of affiliate sales in the 1960s, and fees and royalties have not reached 2 per cent. Clearly, if the percentages prevailing for the Singapore affiliates have conformed at all closely to this larger American pattern, deducting the part of sales remitted abroad would not alter the fact that a substantial percentage of the current sales of American-affiliated enterprises has constituted a foreign exchange gain to the country. Neither the relatively small amounts of subsequent equipment imports nor allowance for the rise in living costs imposed by the tariffs and quotas would make a great difference to this conclusion.

There remain to be considered, however, the income and price repercussions mentioned earlier. Creating new Singapore value added sets off 'multiplier' effects, the ultimate results of which are higher overall increases in national product and reduced increases in net foreign exchange earnings. The apparent divergence between alternative measures of Singapore's gains can be resolved by observing that the chief purpose of balance of payments improvement is to enable the nation to expand its national product and imports further without suffering serious payments deficits. Any measurement of the country's static gains in net foreign exchange earnings thus quantifies the value of extra imports that Singapore can afford to purchase each year, both from incomes generated directly by the operations of these firms and through more expansionary government policies. For a country with relatively stable prices and excess productive capacity, a simple Keynesian import function can be used to convert the value of allowable extra imports into the somewhat larger increase in national income that can accompany them. Thus, if Singapore's marginal propensity to import were roughly one-half, the extra foreign exchange earnings of the United States-affiliated firms should be roughly doubled in order to estimate the extra-national product to which these earnings entitle Singapore.

Viewed in this way, the value added and foreign exchange gains are closely linked, and the contributions of the American affiliated concerns in both respects have been quite large in relation to the sizes of these firms. The American contribution, on the other hand, has thus far mirrored a basic dilemma of Singapore's industrial advance: while production and exports have expanded rapidly and impressively, relatively few of the country's unemployed have been absorbed.

8

Conclusions

When manufacturing opportunities began to open up in Singapore in the 1920s large manufacturing firms in the United States, United Kingdom, and other industrial countries were just starting to establish branches and subsidiaries abroad, so that it is not surprising to find foreign investment in Singapore manufacturing almost from its inception. By 1939 eleven foreign manufacturers from the United States, United Kingdom, and Australia had established subsidiaries in Singapore. These enterprises substantially expanded their production in the late 1940s and 1950s when another four manufacturing firms from these countries and a South African firm joined them, but the main surge of direct foreign investment into Singapore manufacturing did not come until the industrialisation impetus of the 1960s. Investment from other countries, mainly Japan, Hong Kong, and Taiwan, then also began to flow into Singapore.

The surveys on which this book is based covered 127 firms with direct capital investment from the six principal investing countries. Seven of these went out of business and one ceased to have foreign participation by 31 December 1966, so that only 119 were in production or implementing their production plans at that date (Table 8.1). Only forty-five of these firms were non-pioneer firms, but these included most of the older, well-established firms with foreign participation which were among the largest manufacturing firms in Singapore. The South African firm was the only other major non-pioneer firm with substantial direct foreign investment. The seventy-four pioneer firms surveyed included most of the pioneer firms with direct foreign investment in production or implementing. An animal feed mill with Swiss capital, a match factory with Swedish capital, a textile mill with Pakistani capital,

177

Table 8.1   Number of firms surveyed

	Pioneer firms	Non-pioneer firms	Total number of firms
Firms with capital investment from			
Australia	7	14	21
Hong Kong	31	11	42
Japan	19	1	20
Taiwan	13	3	16
United Kingdom	15	7	22
United States	8	12	20
Firms with investment from two of the above countries	11	3	14
Total number of firms surveyed	82	45	127
Firms which went out of business by 31 December 1966	7	—	7
Firms which no longer had investment from the above countries at 31 December 1966	1	—	1
Total firms in production or implementing at 31 December 1966	74	45	119

a knitting mill with Philippine capital, and a dairy product firm with New Zealand capital were the principal pioneer firms with foreign participation outside the scope of the surveys, and there were also some smaller pioneer firms with foreign participation, mainly from Malaysia. There were seventeen pioneer firms with principal shareholdings from countries other than those discussed in this book in production or implementing in 1966.[1] The surveys covered seventy-two of the eighty-eight pioneer firms with foreign participation in production or implementing in 1966, plus an additional two firms which were implementing although they were not yet included in the Economic Development

---

[1] Discrepancies between figures quoted here and official Singapore statistics are due to differences in definition of foreign investment. Census of Industrial Production figures of the number of establishments with foreign investment totalled 166 in 1965 (Singapore, *Report on the Census of Industrial Production 1965*, p. 14), but foreign investment here included portfolio investment. Pioneer firm statistics classify wholly-owned Canadian and Malaysian subsidiaries of United Kingdom firms as 'other' and 'Malaysian' respectively (Appendix tables), although they are directly controlled from the United Kingdom and have therefore been included among United Kingdom firms in this study.

Board's figures. Thus although the total number of firms covered in the surveys was not large, it represented a high proportion—119 out of an estimated 136—of manufacturing firms with direct foreign investment in Singapore.

The survey coverage for each of the principal investing countries was similar, although the percentage of firms actually interviewed varied from country to country, and the completeness of responses was naturally not the same for all firms surveyed. The diversity of responses was to some extent due to differences in company policies, but more random factors were at least as important. Many of the executives interviewed were outgoing and helpful while others were not, some were seen early in the morning and others at the end of a long, hot day. The small number of firms from each of the six countries limited the extent to which the data could be analysed; it would have been misleading to break up totals into subgroups and there was a danger of revealing information about individual firms. In spite of these limitations, however, the main characteristics of direct foreign investment in Singapore emerge from the surveys.

The Singapore case clearly illustrates the intimate connection between direct foreign investment and foreign trade, and the degree to which such investment, being product-oriented, is a direct alternative to trade.

For all except three of the firms surveyed an interest in manufacturing investment in Singapore grew out of trade with it, or through other trading activities. The majority of United Kingdom, United States, and Japanese firms which made direct investments in Singapore manufacturing were large firms with several other direct investments in manufacturing abroad, and even the other firms from these countries and the relatively small firms from Australia, Hong Kong, and Taiwan were all engaged in international trade and sometimes in other direct foreign investment in manufacturing as well. All the foreign firms studied had a markedly international outlook.[2]

For the majority of the firms surveyed the principal reason for investing in Singapore was to follow up exports which had been supplied by the parent company. Until the 1960s such firms tended to begin manufacturing in Singapore when transport costs for their imported products exceeded the extra costs of manufacturing in Singapore on a relatively

[2] This now familiar characteristic of firms which engage in direct foreign investment abroad was already recognised by E. R. Barlow and I. T. Wender, *Foreign Investment and Taxation* (Englewood Cliffs, 1955), but their conclusion that only large firms can engage in direct foreign investment and provide the bulk of such capital (pp. xxi–xxii) is not borne out by this study.

179

small scale. Their products were typically bulky or fragile and therefore had high transport costs. The pull of the local market was at least as important as the push of foreign investors in determining products in which foreign investment would take place. This was also true for manufacturing which grew from wholesaling and servicing activities for products for which Singapore was a distribution centre for Southeast Asia and even further afield. Revenue cigarette duties were the first fiscal measures to encourage local production for tariff reasons. Revenue duties also played a role in oil refinery plans in the 1950s, although political difficulties in the nearby Indonesian oil fields were important, and the world-wide trend towards petroleum refining at market sites was decisive.

Changing expectations about market prospects and the promise of protective measures lay behind the increased investment in the 1960s. Until 1963 tariffs and quotas were few since there were not many industries to protect, but the Singapore government had made it clear by administrative reorganisation and public statement that local industries would be protected, and this understanding was greatly encouraged when tariffs and quotas were imposed as soon as plants came into production. The much discussed plans for the Malaysian common market, accentuated by political union in 1963, promised a protected market of some ten million people in a pattern then becoming familiar in developing countries. Foreign manufacturing firms exporting to Singapore became afraid not only of losing their existing, but also their potential, markets to competitors, in their own countries and in other countries, who might be willing to take the plunge into manufacturing in Singapore. Even manufacturers in Singapore—and Malaysia—itself appeared to present some threat. An investment in manufacturing a product in Singapore could be expected to facilitate the export of allied goods for which manufacturing opportunities were still in the future even in the Singapore government's eyes. Thus some firms began to manufacture in Singapore to forestall their competitors while others were drawn there by their presence.[3]

A few of the firms surveyed began to manufacture in Singapore mainly to assure markets for their raw materials, but for many of those which

[3] This pattern of investment has now also been observed in a number of countries, and particularly in relation to United States investment in Central and South America. See L. Gordon and E. L. Grommers, *United States Manufacturing Investment in Brazil: The Impact of Brazilian Government Policies 1946–1960* (Boston, 1962), and D. T. Brash, *American Investment in Australian Industry* (Canberra, 1966).

were principally attracted by market possibilities the prospects of using raw materials, semi-fabricated products, and in some cases even capital equipment produced by parent or associated companies was an important consideration. Keeping up demand for crude oil on which royalty payments and hence political quiescence in the Middle East depend were considerations which petroleum companies bore in mind in addition to actual refining and distribution profits. A market for semi-fabricated products was particularly important for metal, engineering and electrical products manufacturers. The securing of markets for capital goods was mainly sought by Japan, the late comer to the international market for these products; Japanese manufacturers frequently thought they had to use special measures to overcome prejudices which, however, on the evidence of local and foreign manufacturing firms in Singapore, no longer exist.

Plywood, feather products, and some food manufacturing firms came to Singapore in the wake of import contacts because it was a collection centre for raw materials. Peeler logs for plywood were some 10 to 15 per cent cheaper than in Taiwan and Hong Kong in the early 1960s, and tropical timber peeler logs were even more expensive in the United States. Transport costs were particularly important because of the wood waste in plywood manufacture, and this more than offset the extra cost of relatively small-scale producton in Singapore. For Taiwan firms the Singapore location had an additional advantage in conferring Commonwealth tariff preference on goods shipped from there to countries in the British Commonwealth.

Commonwealth tariff preference also played a role in bringing to Singapore some other export-oriented firms, particularly those Hong Kong and Taiwan firms whose further expansion in garment and other textile exports was curtailed by import quotas in developed countries on Hong Kong and Taiwan products. Although this was an advantage to Singapore where such companies were largely responsible for the setting up of a garment and textile industry, in terms of the international allocation of resources it almost certainly represented a social loss.

Political motivations lay behind some of the decisions to invest in Singapore. To Hong Kong entrepreneurs particularly, but also to other 'overseas Chinese' from countries such as Indonesia, the Philippines, and Malaysia, Singapore represented a politically secure and culturally familiar haven in which they could expect to be free from racial discrimination. In such cases a member of the family which controlled the investing firm frequently moved to Singapore with the capital, changing its nationality as well as his own. Considerations of political security outweighed the disadvantages of relatively high labour costs for Hong Kong garment and other textile industry investors.

There were other political motives in Singapore investment. The Japanese and Australian governments encouraged firms to invest in Southeast Asia in general and in Singapore in particular to strengthen their countries' external trade and export links. Such investment was seen both as a means of aiding developing countries and of benefiting themselves in the long run through increased trade opportunities. They also sought to underline their political interest in the area. Although the Australian government did not provide any material incentives to manufacturers investing in Singapore beyond an insurance scheme against risks arising from political upheaval which evoked little interest, it had influenced several manufacturers who might not otherwise have done so to invest in Singapore. The Japanese government's support for investment in Singapore was backed by cheap loans for capital equipment exports to affiliated firms. The majority of Japanese firms investing in Singapore took advantage of this facility, but the government's general encouragement to investment abroad nevertheless seemed even more important than this specific incentive.

The investing countries' role in international trade, and to a lesser extent their geographical situation, determined their share in Singapore's industrial investment. The United Kingdom's predominantly free trade policy during its suzerainty of Singapore meant that its firms did not accumulate special trading advantages, although the agency firms came to dominate Singapore's trade. It shared the early leadership of foreign manufacturing investment in Singapore with the United States whose manufacturing firms were pre-eminent in direct foreign investment abroad in the 1920s and 1930s, and continued to hold a leading position on a world scale after World War II. Australia's relatively large share in Singapore's industry was due to its geographical proximity, even though this was not always reflected in commensurately low freight rates between the two countries. The entry of Japanese firms into Singapore manufacturing in the 1960s was part of Japan's catching up process in international trade and investment. Hong Kong, and to a lesser degree Taiwan firms, demonstrated the extent to which, given trade barriers or a danger of impediments to trade, even relatively small producers tend to participate in direct foreign investment.

The number of firms covered was not large enough to permit a detailed analysis of country investment by industry, but some general conclusions emerge. Broadly investment followed established comparative advantages in international trade so that the United Kingdom,

182

United States, Japanese, and Australian investment tended to be in industries which were capital-intensive and technologically complex or those in which international brand-names predominated,[4] while Taiwan and Hong Kong investment tended to be in relatively labour-intensive industries such as garments and other textiles, electrical and electronic assembly, and food. There was some overlap, for example in electrical and electronic products which are at various levels both technologically complex and labour-intensive, and evidence of 'technological' catching up by Taiwan and Hong Kong in chemical and pharmaceutical products under licence from the original producers in the United States or United Kingdom.[5]

The most striking conclusion of the surveys was that the foreign investors, almost without exception, stated that taxation concessions and pioneer status did not play a significant role, and for the most part played no role at all, in bringing them to Singapore. The majority of the firms which could qualify took advantage of the tax concessions available, although a few preferred not to do so because they wished to be free from government 'red tape'. But taking advantage of pioneer status or other concessions did not mean that they were important in bringing these firms to Singapore. Most firms claimed that they would have established their manufacturing operations without them. However, since concessions were available, they would have been foolish not to take advantage of them. Some benefited substantially from the tax holiday, but even they said that they would have come to Singapore without it. Some manufacturers thought that a firm could miss out on possible advantages in tariff protection, quotas against competing imports, or preference in government contracts if it did not have pioneer status, although there was no evidence that this was so. Most of the

[4] Appendix Table I gives a useful indication of the industry distribution by the newer investors—Japan, Hong Kong, and Taiwan—because the bulk of their investment was in pioneer firms, but not of the older investors.

[5] The pattern of foreign investment in Singapore by industry and by product suggests that while trade is a dominant factor, the arguments that direct foreign investment tends to consist of new, standardised and technologically complex products put by R. Vernon in 'International Investment and International Trade in the Product Cycle', *Quarterly Journal of Economics*, Vol. 80, May 1966, pp. 190–207, and W. Gruber, D. Mehta, and R. Vernon, 'The R and D Factor in International Trade and International Investment of United States Industries', *Journal of Political Economy*, Vol. 75, February 1967, pp. 20–34, are special cases applicable particularly to United States direct foreign investment in developed countries but not to all direct foreign investment in developing countries.

larger firms which had made substantial investments did not expect to make profits for several years, and on these grounds thought the tax holiday period unnecessary, provided reasonable depreciation allowances enabled them to write off their investment in five to seven years. Some of the firms had made profits within the tax holiday period and benefited from the income tax concessions, but most of these stated that they did not regard it as unreasonable to pay tax provided double tax agreements with their home country were operating[6] and taxes were within ranges to which they were accustomed at home. They were not averse to paying taxes if they were making a profit; conditions in which profits could be made rather than opportunities for taxation concessions had brought large and small investors from all six countries to Singapore.[7]

Disregard for taxation concessions seems to be due to a number of factors among which the complexity of the profit motive is the most important. Taxation concessions have been designed on the assumption that firms' short-run profit expectations are paramount for each individual foreign investment planned, and that such expectations are formulated precisely enough to enable the firms to consider the effect of taxation concessions in making their decision to invest. But the profit concepts held by firms investing in Singapore were a great deal more intricate than this reasoning suggests. Most of the firms were more interested in long-run than in short-run profits, and although this was particularly important for large firms with other international investments, it was also a very pertinent consideration for the small firms. Most of the large, multinational firms considered their overall international position more important than the operation of any one affiliated firm. Some large firms were prepared to operate 'loss leader' or 'swing' firms in Singapore, filling out orders for the parent organisations, and even small garment firms were ready to use their Singapore enterprises to produce uneconomically small runs. Many firms, moreover, including those that wished to see their Singapore affiliate profitable as soon as possible, were not able to calculate their expected profits with sufficient accuracy to be able to include taxation concessions in their investment calculations with a

[6] Singapore has a double tax agreement with the United Kingdom, Japan, Norway, Malaysia, Sweden, and Denmark, and it is negotiating such agreements with the United States, Australia, Germany, Holland, Switzerland, France, and Italy.

[7] Note, however, that Professor Davies and Professor Lindert were very cautious in interpreting these results (see above, pp. 54–8 and 159), and argued that tax incentives may have been more important than the views of the United Kingdom and United States investors they interviewed implied.

great degree of precision. For small firms new to foreign investment its risks were generally greater than those of investment at home, and in Singapore they were exaggerated by political changes in the 1960s. Large firms familiar with the risks and problems of foreign investment were able to make such calculations more precisely,[8] but their profit expectations were more generally geared to the long run.

The manufacturers' view that taxation concessions are unnecessary is probably the most important argument against them, but there are others. Taxation concessions encourage investors to overstate the amounts of investment and there is some evidence that this has occurred in Singapore.[9] This is perhaps a not too harmful form of tax evasion although it encourages unduly high profit expectations. Tax holidays and accelerated depreciation allowances could lead to excess investment and to a choice of excessively capital-intensive techniques, but there was no evidence that this was so in Singapore where other factors clearly dominated in the selection of plant and equipment. Some countries offering taxation concessions have had the experience of firms coming in with assembly operations to take advantage of tax holiday periods at the conclusion of which they moved to another tax haven, but again there was no evidence of this in Singapore.

More potent arguments against taxation concessons lie in the different impact such concessions have on domestic and foreign investors. Whether domestic investors reinvest their saved taxes in their business or other enterprises, whether they save them through banks, or whether they spend them on consumption goods or services, the taxation savings

[8] Such firms, continually engaged in making new foreign investments, were particularly adept at choosing low tax countries as bases for their investment. This accounts for United Kingdom investment via Canada, and, more recently, United States investment via the Netherlands.

[9] Appendix Table V shows that total additions to fixed assets by pioneer firms by 31 December 1966 was $326 million, $258 million being contributed by firms with foreign participation. Table 1.4 shows that between 1959 when pioneer status first became available and the end of 1966 all Singapore private manufacturing firms with ten or more workers had a capital expenditure of $277 million. There are some discrepancies in coverage. Economic Development Board data include installation costs, while Census figures may be understated by one year's depreciation because they may be book values rather than costs. Census figures notoriously underestimate such data in all countries, and Singapore's Census coverage was poor until 1963. Nevertheless, since pioneer firms in production accounted for less than 10 per cent of the manufacturing establishments covered by the Census in 1966, the figures suggest some exaggeration of fixed capital investment by pioneer firms.

flow back into the economy unless they are hoarded or invested abroad. The taxes saved by foreign investors, however, only flow back into the economy if they are reinvested. If they are remitted abroad they will, under normal double taxation agreements, not accrue to the government in Singapore, but to the government of the country of the investing firm. This represents a transfer of revenue from Singapore to another country; in the case of the United Kingdom, United States, Australia, and Japan it means a transfer of revenue from a developing to a developed country. Developed countries sometimes allow their nationals to benefit from such taxation saving at the discretion of their taxation authorities, but this allowance is not automatic and it is not even general, except in Japan where clauses allowing taxation saving are included in double tax agreements.[10] Singapore has become aware of this transfer of revenue and has accordingly made tax concessions on foreign loans of $200,000 or more subject to a taxation saving allowance by the lending country.

It is sometimes argued that since most firms do not make profits in their first few years of production, the advantages of tax holidays are more apparent than real, and that their impact consists largely of creating a good atmosphere for foreign investment. This is probably so in the case of large, capital-intensive industries, but the findings of the surveys in this book suggest that the benefits of tax holidays represented quite substantial gains to some of the firms, particularly those engaged largely in finishing, and that a significant proportion of these profits were repatriated abroad rather than reinvested in the firms. Although most of the firms studied had not been in operation long enough to indicate the magnitude of the revenue losses to Singapore resulting from taxation holidays, the evidence certainly suggests that they were not inconsiderable.

[10] This point was discussed at some length at the seminar on foreign investment in Singapore held at the Economic Research Centre of the University of Singapore in July 1967. See H. Hughes, 'Foreign Investment in Manufacturing Industries in Developing Countries: Economic Benefits and Costs', in You Poh Seng (ed.), Seminar on Foreign Investment in Manufacturing Industries: Proceedings and Discussion (Conferences and Seminars, Series No. 1, Economic Research Centre, University of Singapore, 1969) (mimeographed). Professor C. S. Shoup has drawn my attention to the fact that unless a firm remits profits earned under tax concessions within the tax holiday period, it will lose the 'tax saving' and this may tend to encourage firms not to reinvest in the developing country and hence be against such a country's interest. But a simple accounting export and re-import entry of the profit on which taxes are 'saved' in this manner would overcome this problem, so that on the tongues of developed countries' Treasury officials the argument sounds distinctly disingenuous.

There is a far stronger argument for special encouragement for local entrepreneurs than for foreign investors although in the short run the Singapore manufacturers bring less momentum to manufacturing than foreign ones. Local manufacturers are often totally inexperienced in manufacturing and therefore take much greater risks than foreign manufacturing firms, particularly if the latter have opened up the market by exports. To the local firm the investment commitment generally represents a much larger share of total resources than it does to the foreign investor. The local manufacturer takes greater risks with smaller resources and frequently does require special incentives to turn to manufacturing, particularly on a large scale. If taxation concessions are used, then the foreign investor must be entitled to them to avoid the inequity of discrimination against him. However, in view of the different incidence of taxation concessions on domestic and foreign investors, it would probably be wiser to seek an alternative means of encouraging local entrepreneurs than to grant taxation holidays to both local and foreign investors.

Perhaps the most potent argument against dropping income taxation concessions in Singapore is that since all the other Southeast Asian countries have them, and are still in the process of extending them,[11] Singapore cannot afford to be without them because it might then on a superficial view appear not to welcome foreign investment as much as surrounding countries. Although the present result of taxation and similar concessions seems to be to cancel out their effectiveness in attracting foreign investors among neighbouring countries, this is certainly a pertinent point, particularly for the next few years when Singapore faces the difficulties of the evacuation of the British armed forces.

In a longer perspective a gradual withdrawal of taxation concessions, even unilaterally, may not be unwise. The taxation revenue forgone by the Singapore government has an opportunity cost: it could be used to improve the infrastructure for industry, for employment creation, and for social service expenditures which would all boost the market for local manufactures and so stimulate foreign—and local—investment in manufacturing. It seemed clear from the attractions foreign investors did consider important in bringing them to Singapore that in the long run such expenditures are likely to bring more foreign investment than if equivalent sums are given away to firms in tax concessions.

[11] Indonesia is the most recent member of the taxation concession club (Law No. 1 of the Year 1967 Concerning Foreign Capital Investment), and Malaysia extended its concessions in February 1968 (*Straits Times* (Singapore), 1 March 1968).

The main factors which foreign investors claimed attracted them to Singapore were the government's welcoming attitude expressed in positive assistance mainly through the Economic Development Board and other government departments and instrumentalities, and the efficiency of the public services and utilities. Industrial estates were an added bonus. While Jurong may have been developed somewhat prematurely for light industries which could probably have been established with lower private and social cost closer to existing housing settlements, and although the government has probably been somewhat too prodigal in its rent and land sale policy, the industrial estates concept and the speed and vigour with which Jurong was created and administered impressed many industrialists who stated that they believed that in going to Jurong they were acquiring a stake in the island's industrial development.

There were additional, less obvious, but no less important factors. The executives of foreign firms on reconnaissance trips in Southeast Asia did not have to spend days, or even months, in preliminary investigations, and once their minds were made up they were able to negotiate agreements, almost entirely through one government organisation—the Economic Development Board—quickly and efficiently. The firms interviewed remarked on the administration's courtesy, on the ability of individual public servants who had quickly mastered the work required of them, and above all on the freedom from corruption. The Singapore characteristic which impressed foreign investors most was the absence of 'tea money'.

Behind these striking features of good government lay a sound and sophisticated system of public finance. Year after year the government of independent Singapore budgeted for, and achieved, a revenue surplus which it was able to channel into development funds.[12] Its currency management (in conjunction with the Malay states until 1967) kept currency stable in international terms, and the supply of money kept pace with the growth of the economy.[13]

Taxation concessions were initially recommended to developing countries to offset the disadvantages they had in attracting capital in competition with developed countries. They were adopted because when businessmen were asked whether they wanted taxation concessions they

[12] United Nations, *Yearbook of National Accounts Statistics 1966* (New York, 1967), p. 502.
[13] G. W. Betz, 'A Note on the Money Supply in Singapore 1957–1966', *Malayan Economic Review*, Vol. 12, October 1967, pp. 116–21.

not unnaturally replied in the affirmative, but they did not reply that taxation concessions would bring them to developing countries.[14] It now appears that they were adopted and extended with more enthusiasm than common sense and that many governments, although not Singapore, came to regard them as a substitute rather than as a complement to other government action to attract foreign investors. The flow of foreign investment into developing countries has now become quite well established, and the existence of markets in these countries, particularly if they are protected, seems a sufficient incentive to attract foreign investors in manufacturing. Developing countries could now begin to look ahead to dismantling such legislation, and if Singapore regards unilateral action in this regard as too risky in its position in Southeast Asia, it can perhaps take the lead in this direction in international councils.

BENEFITS AND COSTS OF FOREIGN INVESTMENT

Paid-up capital from the six countries studied represented an investment inflow of at least $147 to $152 million (Table 8.2) in Singapore industry. The United Kingdom was by far the largest investor, followed by the United States, Japan, Australia, and then Hong Kong and Taiwan. The total amount of capital invested was modest in comparison with total capital formation in Singapore which was $454·1 million in 1966 alone (Table 1.17), and even in comparison with capital expenditure on fixed investment in manufacturing establishments with ten or more workers which totalled $277 million between 1959 and 1966 (Table 1.4). It was, nevertheless, a significant contribution, and it led to further investment of local capital in manufacturing.

Foreign investment drew local capital into manufacturing through various joint venture forms of ownership and through public companies floated in Singapore (or Malaysia). There were marked differences among the investors from the various countries studied in this respect. United Kingdom and United States firms showed a strong preference for control of their Singapore operations either by complete and outright ownership, or by majority holdings in the Singapore companies. This generally represented the policy of parent firms with a number of foreign

[14] Barlow and Wender noted this fact as early as 1955 (*Foreign Investment and Taxation*, p. 124), and discussion of the effects of taxation incentives by the lending country in the early 1950s was equally inconclusive in evaluating companies' demands for such concessions. See particularly R. Blough, 'Taxation Adjustments for the Long Run: United States Taxation and Foreign Investment', *Journal of Finance*, Vol. 11, May 1956, pp. 180–94.

Table 8.2   Estimated Australian, Hong Kong, Japanese, Taiwan, United Kingdom, and United States paid-up capital in firms manufacturing in Singapore at 31 December 1966

Firms with capital investment from	Paid-up capital $ million
Australia	18
Hong Kong	12·5[a]
Japan	24·2[b]
Taiwan	6·1
United Kingdom	60·9
United States	25 to 30
Total	146·7 to 151·7

[a] These are minimum estimates which do not include investment in non-pioneer firms not in Jurong.

[b] Nineteen pioneer firms only. This excludes one non-pioneer firm.

operations which preferred direct control because it made planning on an international scale simpler. Some Hong Kong family firms also preferred outright ownership, but the majority of Hong Kong firms in Singapore had significant Singapore participation, and this was also true of all the Taiwan firms. Some of the Australian and Japanese firms were owned outright by the parent firms, but there was also a great deal of Singapore participation. Several Hong Kong and Taiwan firms had additional ownership from other foreign countries, and Japanese manufacturing firms tended to combine with Japanese trading firms which had handled the export of their products to Singapore before they began manufacturing there, as well as with Singapore investors.

Some of the variations in ownership patterns were simply due to the fact that Hong Kong, Taiwan, and Australian firms were relatively small and unaccustomed to foreign operations so that they found the presence of a Singapore partner who could contribute some of the capital and distribute the finished products reassuring. The United Kingdom and United States firms had often built up their own distribution channels and were much more accustomed to establishing manufacturing operations abroad. Interviews with manufacturers also revealed that in countries which were themselves venues for foreign investment there was a strong feeling of resentment against foreign investors who refused to allow the local entrepreneurs to share in their enterprises.[15] This led

[15] W. G. Friedmann and G. Kalmanoff (eds.), *Joint International Business Ventures* (New York and London, 1961), came to similar conclusions with

manufacturers from these countries to a more liberal attitude towards Singapore participation in their investment even when they thought that sharing control might entail difficulties.

In joint venture partnerships the Singapore partners were generally Singapore trading firms which had been the foreign manufacturers' distributors when the product had been imported into Singapore, and some of these were Singapore agency firms. There did not seem much ground for the British, American, and even Japanese firms' fears that local Singapore partners, being accustomed to wholesaling and retailing and hence to a rapid turnover of capital, would be unwilling to plough back profits into a manufacturing enterprise for the sake of long-term prospects. Some local partners did express the opinion that the foreign firm wanted to plough back too much capital and in some cases fears that it wished to make a loss so that it could buy out the local partner cheaply, but most of these problems arose out of mutual misunderstandings. To the local partner the equity investment in a joint venture usually represented a much greater share of his total resources than that of the foreign firm, and he had frequently borrowed to raise the capital required, which meant that he needed profits more urgently than the foreign investor. Where local shareholding took the form of portfolio shares the characteristics of Singapore shareholders are not known, but it is significant that share issues by international companies in Singapore are readily filled and frequently oversubscribed.

There was also some investment by the Economic Development Board, representing public investment, in enterprises from the countries studied. The foreign firms' desire for the Economic Development Board's participation was largely due to a wish to have government backing for an enterprise. The actual capital contribution was not important.

The foreign investors in Singapore thus contributed to a shift in local investment from trading activities to manufacturing, and, to a somewhat lesser extent, contributed to the creation of a share market which in turn built up the capital market, directly by giving large savers investment opportunities, and indirectly by giving financial intermediaries such as insurance companies opportunities to invest funds which they collected from small savers. A further stimulus to capital formation came through the demands of the foreign firms on local banks' overdraft facilities. The surveys revealed that once established the foreign firms

---

regard to Italian and Japanese firms' tendencies to form joint ventures; see their pp. 24–6, 76–80.

tended to finance further development by reinvesting profits and by borrowing on overdraft from local banks. The banks operating in Singapore have responded to overdraft demands by large firms with international reputations, and this has facilitated changes in attitudes. Banks which had been used to lending for short periods for commercial purposes became accustomed to the relatively long-term overdrafts required by manufacturers. The proportion of commercial banks' loans and advances to manufacturing industries rose from 13 per cent at the end of 1963 to 18 per cent at the end of 1966.[16]

The firms with investment from the six countries studied contributed at least a third of the value added and more than a fifth of employment in manufacturing establishments employing ten or more workers in Singapore in 1966. Table 8.3, which summarises the contribution of the firms with capital investment from the six principal investing countries, underestimates the value added contribution for all firms except those with Australian capital investment, and also underestimates the employment

Table 8.3 Estimated minimum value added in production and employment in Singapore manufacturing firms with Australian, Hong Kong, Japanese, Taiwan, United Kingdom, and United States capital investment, 1966

Firms with capital investment from	Value added in production $'000	Employment
Australia	24·3	2,121
Hong Kong	7·7[a]	2,362[a]
Japan	18·9[b]	2,646
Taiwan	4·0[c]	1,204[c]
United Kingdom	40·0[d]	2,000[e]
United States	26·0[f]	2,300
Total	120·9	12,633

[a] Only pioneer firms in which Hong Kong was the principal shareholder. Employment figure considerably underestimates the position.

[b] Only pioneer firms in which Japan was the principal shareholder.

[c] Only pioneer firms in which Taiwan was the principal shareholder.

[d] Thirteen firms only.

[e] Actual employment was 'slightly over two thousand persons', see above, Chapter 2, p. 59.

[f] Nine firms only.

Sources: Value added figures for Australia, United Kingdom, and United States and employment for these countries and Japan from survey data. Hong Kong, Taiwan, and Japanese figures have been taken from Appendix Tables VII and VIII to avoid double counting.

[16] Economic Development Board, *Annual Report '66*, p. 10.

contribution of all except the Australian firms. No allowance has been made for firms jointly owned by two of the six countries, but such double counting would be greatly exceeded by non-pioneer Hong Kong and Taiwan firms, and some United States firms not counted at all. The United Kingdom, United States, Australia, and Japan were the principal contributors to value added, but Hong Kong made the most important contribution in employment if employment in non-pioneer firms is taken into account.

The main contributions of foreign investment to the development of manufacturing in Singapore were not, however, the addition to capital resources as such, or even the contribution to value added and employment, but the bringing of new technology, management, and other business techniques to Singapore.

The 119 firms surveyed in this book represented less than 10 per cent of the 1,146 manufacturing establishments with ten or more workers in 1966 (Table 1.4), but they included most of the very large firms with more than 1,000 workers, most of the technologically complex firms, and almost all the firms in new industries which although neither large-scale nor technologically complex had been created only in the 1960s.

Foreign investment from the six countries studied had led in the establishment of petroleum refining, glass manufacture, cement production, electrical and electronic industries, motor vehicle assembly, chemicals, metal processing, and rubber tyre manufacture. It had also helped to diversify production into relatively simple industries which had not yet been established in Singapore. Garment, textile, and various food processing industries were the most important new industries of this type introduced by foreign investors.

The foreign manufacturers who came to Singapore made their choice of production techniques quite deliberately. The most important influence in their decision was the size of the market. At first this was the Singapore or proposed Malaysian market, and from 1965 the market they hoped to win for exports. Compared with the plants of their parent firms Singapore units were relatively small, and this frequently meant that they did not bring the most advanced techniques in use in the investing country because such techniques were subject to very great economies of scale. There was very little replacement of capital by labour in comparison with techniques used in investing countries. Taiwan and Hong Kong entrepreneurs found labour costs higher than at home, and investors from the other four countries tended to resist substitution of labour for capital for a variety of reasons. There were unknown factors and difficulties in employing labour in a foreign country.

193

The influence of Singapore's strong trade unions, particularly in the early 1960s, underlined this trend. The cost of fringe benefits discouraged the employment of a large permanent workforce. Firms minimised labour costs by employing relatively few workers but working a great deal of overtime. There were problems in employing inexperienced labour, difficulties in imposing factory discipline, and quite frequently language difficulties in teaching skills quickly, all of which tended to make the substitution of labour for capital uneconomic. In any case foreign investors generally chose techniques in use in their own countries principally because labour cost was a low proportion of total cost for many manufactured products, and, where it was a high proportion, appropriate levels of skill to substitute men for machines were not available. Labour-intensive methods usually resulted in higher raw material costs and more poorly finished products rather than in more mechanised methods. Singapore markets were sophisticated and quality was particularly important in exports. The techniques used, moreover, were those with which the foreign firms were familiar.

The investment in fixed capital (including land, buildings, and equipment) indicated by figures for firms with Australian, Japanese, Hong Kong, and Taiwan capital investment was therefore quite considerable, although an estimate of total investment could not be made (Table 8.4).

Table 8.4   Estimated investment in fixed assets by Singapore manufacturing firms with Australian, Hong Kong, Japanese, Taiwan, United Kingdom, and United States capital investment, 1960–6

Firms with capital investment from	Investment in fixed assets $ million
Australia	13·6
Hong Kong	19·2[a]
Japan	60·9[b]
Taiwan	13·3[c]
United Kingdom	[d]
United States	[e]

[a] Only pioneer firms in which Hong Kong was the principal foreign shareholder.

[b] This figure is some $10 million below the figure quoted for pioneer firms in which Japan was the principal foreign shareholder (Appendix Table V).

[c] Only pioneer firms in which Taiwan was the principal foreign shareholder.

[d] Only figures available are for pioneer firms classified under the United Kingdom and these are a small proportion of total pioneer firms in which the United Kingdom is the principal shareholder.

[e] Only pioneer firm data available and these are inadequate.

Sources: Survey data for Australia and Japan, and Appendix Table V.

The techniques introduced by foreign firms were not particularly innovatory, but they were on the whole well suited to Singapore conditions. It is extremely doubtful whether the same transference of up-to-date technology could have been accomplished without the foreign investors.

The foreign firms also made a direct contribution through the employment of experienced managers, technical staff, and technicians from their parent firms. The majority of chief executives in firms with investment from the six countries studied had been seconded to the position by the parent foreign firm, and most firms also had technical staff from their parent foreign firm. Managers and technical staff undertook most of the training of skilled and semi-skilled workers, and of other managerial staff. A few firms sent Singapore citizens for training to their parent firms, but with few exceptions this was confined to technical and managerial staff. Blue collar workers were trained on the job as a firm came into production.

There appear to have been few differences in the approach to training local personnel among the investors from the various countries. Firms with Japanese capital investment tended to employ a higher number of Japanese nationals than firms with investment from the other countries, a total of 179 compared with 51 expatriates employed by firms with Australian capital investment, for example. The Japanese firms were clearly newcomers, they had language difficulties in Singapore, their plants were technically complex, and they tended to control the operations of their subsidiaries more closely than parent firms from the other investing countries.

The Japanese firms also had the most formalised selection and training procedures for blue collar workers, but there is no evidence that their training was quicker or more effective than that which followed less formal procedures practised by firms with capital participation from the other five countries. Language difficulties tended to offset the attention they paid to their training programs. Taiwan and Hong Kong firms overcame language problems by employing a predominantly Chinese workforce, while the other foreign investors had the advantage of speaking English which is usually understood by the younger, educated workers.

The composition of the workforce of firms with foreign investment appeared to be representative of the Singapore manufacturing workforce as a whole, with a predominance of young workers among the newer firms. Some of the older firms had experienced serious difficulties with trade unions in the 1950s and early 1960s but these were well in the past by 1966. The firms with foreign affiliation were paying wages which

195

were prevalent in Singapore, and some appeared to be paying higher than average wages and to be providing better than average fringe benefits. Many of the firms were aware that their foreign affiliation placed them in the public eye in labour relations, and were accordingly concerned to be, and to appear to be, good employers.

Most of the firms with foreign investment in Singapore were not able to make meaningful comparisons of productivity in Singapore with productivity in their parent firms. Taiwan and Hong Kong manufacturers thought that productivity in Singapore was low, and tended to blame this on poor application by the workers. Other factors were, however, clearly evident. All Singapore firms tended to have shorter production runs than their parent firms because their markets were smaller and this lowered productivity even in labour-intensive industries, but particularly in capital-intensive industries. Most of the firms interviewed had not been in production for long, and even those which had been in production before the 1960s were still expanding. Almost all therefore suffered from excess capacity due to planning for expanding markets, and had a relatively new labour force which was only just trained for the job and scarcely accustomed to factory discipline. Most of the well-established firms on the other hand claimed that productivity was up to levels achieved in their parent plants. In terms of value added per worker the firms surveyed performed better than the average of all Singapore manufacturing firms with ten or more workers, but this was to be expected since they were among the largest, most capital-intensive, and technically complex firms.

Although it has frequently been claimed that direct foreign investment limits export expansion, and although there is some evidence of this in other countries,[17] on balance this was not the case in Singapore. On the contrary, foreign investors helped Singapore to find export markets.

[17] Evidence on this point varies and depends greatly on a country's general situation. I. Brecher and S. S. Reisman, *Canada-United States Economic Relations* ([Ottawa], 1957), wrote that 'the effects of market allocation are particularly difficult to isolate' in foreign-owned firms (p. 145); A. E. Safarian, 'The Exports of American-Owned Enterprises in Canada', *American Economic Review*, Vol. 54, May 1964, pp. 450–1, found that foreign-owned firms in Canada had a better export record than Canadian-owned firms. H. W. Arndt and D. R. Sherk, 'Export Franchises of Australian Companies with Overseas Affiliations', *Economic Record*, Vol. 35, August 1959, pp. 239–42, found definite limitations on the ability of foreign-owned firms to export in Australia, and this was confirmed in interviews conducted for the survey for Chapter 3 above, but Brash, *American Investment*, p. 240, showed that American firms are playing an increasing role in Australia's exports.

Some of the foreign investors limited the ability of their Singapore-affiliated firms to export, but they were a minority. In other cases a company's international policy had the same result although no formal agreement to this effect was signed, but the number of such companies was again small. On the other hand the entry of a number of export-oriented companies into Singapore manufacturing brought an emphasis on exports from the beginning of their activities in the early 1960s. Singapore's entrepôt trade, unlike that of Hong Kong, was attuned to the export of raw materials rather than of manufactured products, and to the import rather than the export of manufactured products. In the early 1960s re-exporting of manufactured products was limited to a narrow range of goods and to the geographical area immediately around Singapore. The Singapore traders, particularly the agency houses, were conservative in their business methods and slow to find export markets for new manufactured products in new areas. The export-oriented foreign investors brought their export markets with them, but the other foreign manufacturers were content, by and large, with the Singapore and Malaysian market, and with the prospects of the common market for Malaysia. When these hopes collapsed and as Malaysia began to protect its industries, the firms with foreign capital in Singapore were forced to turn outwards to fill their production capacity, and their parent firms were frequently helpful. In some cases they even allocated to them a share of existing foreign markets from the parent company or other affiliated firms. However, in so far as the foreign investors entered various Southeast Asian, East African, and Middle Eastern countries to which Singapore has built up exports, such market sharing is limited, for once parent companies are persuaded to build competing affiliated companies in other countries, export opportunities diminish.

In 1966 31 per cent of the sales of all pioneer firms with foreign investment were exports, and the proportion exported rose to 40 per cent for Japanese firms, 54 per cent for United States firms, 56 per cent for Taiwan firms, and 59 per cent for Hong Kong firms.[18] For nine pioneer and non-pioneer United States firms the proportion exported was 57 per cent, and pioneer firm figures in this case appear to be representative of each country's total performance. The proportion of sales exported in 1966 by all manufacturing establishments with ten or more workers was 44 per cent if rubber processing is included, and 31 per cent without rubber processing, so that pioneer and probably other firms with

[18] See Appendix Table X.

197

foreign investment performed about the same as all firms.[19] The government hopes that the favourable tax treatment for income on exports will increase the firms' export sales, and delay, if not put off indefinitely, plans to begin manufacturing in some of the neighbouring countries. Income tax reductions on exports are open to many of the same objections as other tax concessions, particularly those relating to the difference in incidence between foreign and local investors, but Singapore's export needs are urgent and immediate, marginal pricing from a small domestic market is very difficult without special assistance, and delays in the establishment of competing firms in other Southeast Asian countries could be crucial in the next few years. It will take some time for export channels to be built up. Both foreign and local firms appear to be relying on the government excessively in the search for new markets, but until this problem is overcome, no alternative direct export incentives appear to be available.

The spread of foreign investment in Singapore among six major and several other foreign investors provides a natural defence against economic or political pressure which any one of the investing countries could impose inadvertently through its own economic difficulties or deliberately. The spread has arisen mainly out of Singapore's free trade experience, but it has been fostered by the government's welcome to all comers backed by a political policy of non-alignment. Foreign firms have been accused of pressure which led to the tightening up of working conditions and remuneration in 1968, but although they undoubtedly supported the government's new legislation, so did the local employers. Nor can the new legislation really be said to aim at 'peeling the skin, removing the muscles, breaking the bone and sucking the marrow of the working class'.[20]

In addition to direct control by parent firms, some indirect and often inadvertent pressures are exerted on company policies by parent firms through expatriate managers.[21] A great deal therefore depends on the degree to which local executives replace expatriates. Singapore's foreign

[19] Singapore Department of Statistics data. The figures of total sales abroad are probably slightly underestimated because some of the sales to wholesalers in Singapore probably also found their way abroad and figures are only for firms with ten or more workers.

[20] Statement by the Industrial Workers' Union which probably gains in imagery in translation from the Chinese. *Sunday Times* (Singapore), 26 May 1968.

[21] Brecher and Reisman, op. cit., p. 134.

investment experience is too recent for any judgment on the degree to which expatriates are being replaced. The government's policy of granting working permits to expatriate managers and technical staff has on the whole been reasonable and more generous than in some neighbouring countries, although a few firms complained of bureaucratic delays in the granting of permits. Only a handful of the predominantly foreign firms have yet been handed over to local management entirely but the older firms do have a number of local citizens among top managers. Replacing expatriates by local managers does take time if it is to be done satisfactorily, and most of the firms studied, particularly the Japanese, Hong Kong, and Taiwan firms where the numbers of expatriate managers and technicians appear to be the highest, have not had time to train local executives and technical staff and give them sufficient experience to take over management satisfactorily.

There is some evidence that the firms with foreign investment have benefited from protection not only by being able to produce at a profit in a market in which they could not otherwise compete because their scale of production was too small, but also to a certain extent by exploiting, at least initially, before competitors entered the industry, a monopoly situation, both through high prices and through relatively poor quality products. Local firms have of course had such advantages though perhaps to a lesser degree because the foreign firms' technological advantage sometimes prevented other, local, firms from entering.[22] The social costs of protection for foreign firms are higher if their monopoly profits are remitted abroad than for local firms whose monopoly profits flow back into the economy, but Singapore's separation from Malaysia and the collapse of common market hopes put an abrupt end to extreme protectionist policies and to foreign investors' hopes of monopoly and oligopoly profits in this situation. Since 1966 protection has been sparingly applied, and the social costs may be outweighed by the social benefits of the extra employment provided by protected industries. Even in a market as small as Singapore's, moderate protection can be justified in terms of employment creation for well selected 'infants'. Protection can also provide opportunities for the establishment of industries which go on to export, but which would not be established at all without such initial assistance.

The Economic Development Board has attempted to control prices in industries protected by quotas and tariffs. There is little evidence of

[22] E. T. Penrose, 'Foreign Investment and the Growth of the Firm', *Economic Journal*, Vol. 66, June 1956, pp. 220–35, discusses the foreign firms' advantages in growth and profit accumulation in relation to local firms.

199

such controls, but the abrupt change in protectionist policies probably eliminated the need for them. Considering the 1966 rise in the price of rice the relatively slight rise in the consumer price index between 1960 and 1966 (Table 1.16) suggests that such import substitution as has been achieved has come without many price increases.

Perhaps the greatest costs of foreign investment have arisen out of unduly high entry by large foreign firms which are accustomed to competing on an international basis, and whose interest in Singapore manufacturing was determined by defensive as much as by profit motives. Such firms tend to bring with them an oligopolistic structure of administered prices. These enable them to produce at inefficiently low levels of production and yet make a profit if imports are restricted either by tariffs or quotas, or if all the major international competitors in a particular field have become committed to manufacturing in Singapore, so that no major competitor is left to threaten with low-priced imports.[23]

The limitations of Singapore's domestic market and the narrow range of tariffs and quotas have tended to restrict the opportunities for oligopolistic behaviour in comparison with other countries, but there is some evidence of it in petroleum refining, paint manufacture, cosmetic preparations, pharmaceuticals, and, potentially, in electronic and electrical products and in motor cycle and motor vehicle assembly. Such an oligopolistic structure not only tends to raise prices in the short run, but it is usually a barrier to expansion into forward and backward linked industries in the long run. The production of semi-fabricated metal and electrical and electronic components and of chemical raw materials which feed these industries are generally more technologically complex and capital intensive than the assembly stage first set up in Singapore. Economies of scale are even more important, so that large production runs are essential to economic production, but with a number of assembly firms in the field none has a large enough component demand for economic production. Firms competing in the sale of final products are reluctant to become dependent on a rival end-product producer for component or raw material supplies. This reinforces the tendency to continue the purchase of such products from parent firms which operate large plants in the investing country. The step towards backward linkages can thus be delayed beyond the point where one semi-finished product or raw material plant would be economic for Singapore because

[23] This point and its consequences were argued in some detail in Hughes, 'Foreign Investment in Manufacturing Industries'.

the fragmented structure of the final assembly industry imposes a need for several backward linked firms. For petroleum refineries, the step towards petrochemicals may similarly be delayed because the output of each refinery is too small, whereas if combined in one plant further processing might be justified.

Alternative policies are difficult to evolve and they have their dangers, but they may lead to better results than the free play of economic forces. In this case this does not lead to pure competition but to non-price competition among differentiated products which may well result in a negative consumer's surplus.

Because of the competition among large international companies to enter new and particularly tariff protected markets, the Singapore government can negotiate with individual companies for concessions in return for a measure of monopoly (if necessary with a time limited tariff protection for an 'infant' period). Local capital participation and the guarantee of further processing either in forward or backward linked industries could be bargaining points. Such a policy is admittedly not without peril, but particularly in Singapore where the Economic Development Board has shown ability in sophisticated economic thinking and effective administration, the dangers appear to be less than those of unrestricted oligopoly.

Another alternative would be to set up statutory corporations to run such enterprises on the government's behalf. The National Iron and Steelworks and public utilities have demonstrated that statutory corporations can be efficiently run in Singapore, but it is doubtful whether sufficient executive and technical manpower resources would be available for a substantial extension of such enterprises. Moreover, foreign and local investors could be very sensitive to such a policy.[24]

Industries operating on an economic scale are more likely to become exporters than a number of small producers because, while competition even among small numbers of firms can be a useful regulator of prices, for most modern industrial products the base price floor is set by the scale of production so that competition operates within technologically imposed limits. Export considerations will undoubtedly continue to be of prime importance in Singapore's policy making because it has to import the bulk of its raw materials, and foreign investment imposes an additional balance of payments liability in the long run.

[24] E. L. Wheelwright, *Industrialization in Malaysia* (Melbourne, 1965), pp. 111–13, advocated this policy for Singapore and Malaysia.

Singapore pioneer firms with foreign participation imported 91 per cent of their raw materials, and the proportion rose to 95 per cent for Hong Kong and United States firms which were, however, also the leading exporters, and to 94 per cent for the United Kingdom. Locally-owned pioneer firms imported only 61 per cent of the value of their raw materials, and the average for all pioneer firms was 86 per cent.[25]

The high import ratio for pioneer firms with foreign participation reflects the degree to which they are dependent on chemicals, refined metals, and semi-fabricated products. Many of these products can eventually be produced in Singapore when the market is sufficiently large and provided it is not too fragmented. Some like crude petroleum and other basic materials will have to continue to be imported. This, however, is no drawback to industrial development if economic industries are being created. Japan and Hong Kong have shown remarkable industrial development on the basis of imported raw materials.

Nor is the total foreign investment in manufacturing likely to prove an unduly high burden on the balance of payments. Most of the firms surveyed had not been in operation long enough to show profit returns which would be a reliable indicator of long-run trends.[26] The published rates of return on United Kingdom investment in Singapore were about 30 per cent in 1960, falling to 15 per cent in 1966, although the rates for manufacturing firms in the 1966 survey were found to be 9 per cent. Fifteen to 20 per cent was the average return for well-established firms with Australian capital investment in 1966. This does not include royalty, licence, and similar payments, but these appeared to be important only for Japanese firms. Assuming a return of 10 to 20 per cent on a paid-up capital of some $150 million from the six countries studied in 1966, this would mean a net liability of $15 million to $30 million annually if none was reinvested locally. It is more likely that some proportion of this sum will be ploughed back into Singapore investment. Together with new investment from abroad, this will initially reduce the balance of payments burden, although the capital servicing liability will increase in the long run. Total manufacturing export sales were already $672 million (including rubber processing) in 1966[27] and the repatriation of profits is therefore likely to be easily manageable in the foreseeable future.

[25] See Appendix Table VI.

[26] Firms were deliberately not pressed about profitability to ensure a full response to the rest of the questions asked.

[27] Singapore Department of Statistics data for firms with ten or more workers.

202

SINGAPORE'S DEVELOPMENT STRATEGY

Singapore's main emphasis in economic development since independence has been on the establishment of an industrial sector, and it is by its performance in industry that its achievements must to some extent at least be judged.

There is no doubt that Singapore's industrial growth between 1959 and 1966 was considerable. Value added in establishments with ten or more workers rose from 9 per cent of gross domestic expenditure in 1960 to 14 per cent in 1966. Capital expenditure in these establishments rose from 8 per cent of gross capital formation in 1960 to 17 per cent in 1966. Whereas in 1961 it represented 9 per cent of private capital formation, in 1966 it accounted for 26 per cent of private capital formation, and private capital formation was increasing faster than public capital formation in the mid-1960s.[28] Since some 27,500 workers were added to the manufacturing workforce in establishments with five or more workers between 1960 and 1966,[29] the proportion of manufacturing employment in the total workforce has probably grown. An accurate assessment of the increased share of manufacturing labour in the workforce is not possible. The proportion recorded as employed in manufacturing rose from 15·6 to 19·2 per cent between 1957 and 1966, but both these percentages include unemployed as well as employed workers, and total unemployment doubled in this period.[30]

[28] Calculated from Tables 1.4 and 1.17. The share of private capital formation in 1966 is rather high because the Census of Industrial Production figures then included manufacturing establishments in the public sector, but their share in total industrial capital formation was swamped in 1966 by private capital formation in industry. Stocks have not been included in capital formation calculations because the rapid growth of industry has made for wide fluctuations.

[29] See above, p. 42.

[30] See Table 1.7. It seems even more dubious to take the figure of 104,400 employed and unemployed in manufacturing in the 1966 Household Survey, subtract the 56,334 employed in manufacturing establishments with ten or more workers in 1966 (Table 1.4), and conclude that 48,100 workers were employed in manufacturing establishments with fewer than ten workers. This residue not only includes unemployed once engaged in establishments with ten or more workers, but a larger number of workers who regard themselves as manufacturing workers but may in fact not be thus classifiable. See *Singapore Sample Household Survey, 1966. Report No. 1. Tables Relating to Population and Housing* (Singapore, 1967), pp. 132–4. Cf. H. Oshima, 'Growth and Unemployment in Singapore', *Malayan Economic Review*, Vol. 12, October 1967, p. 45.

Table 8.5   Value added in Singapore manufacturing establishments
with ten or more workers, 1959 and 1966

	1959		1966	
	Value added $'000	Per cent of total	Value added $'000	Per cent of total
Food manufacturing industries	16,615	10·6	35,913	8·3
Beverage industries	20,055	12·8	30,974	7·2
Tobacco manufacture	4,384	2·8	26,649	6·2
Manufacture of textiles			1,985	0·5
Manufacture of footwear, other wearing apparel and made-up textile goods, except rubber footwear[a]	3,703[a]	2·4[a]		
			10,890	2·5
Manufacture of wood and cork, except manufacture of furniture	9,199	5·9	24,292	5·6
Manufacture of furniture and fixtures	1,619	1·0	6,709	1·6
Manufacture of paper and paper products	1,496	1·0	4,671	1·1
Printing, publishing and allied industries	22,451	14·3	37,757	8·8
Manufacture of leather and leather products, except footwear	a	a	1,790	0·5
Manufacture of rubber products including rubber footwear but excluding rubber processing	2,606	1·7	11,019	2·6
Manufacture of chemicals and chemical products	9,378	6·0	20,654	4·8
Manufacture of products of petroleum and coal	b	b	61,746	14·3
Manufacture of non-metallic mineral products except products of petroleum and coal	9,521	6·1	28,047	6·5
Basic metal industries	1,885	1·2	17,025	3·9
Manufacture of metal products, except machinery and transport equipment	8,301	5·3	27,669	6·4
Manufacture of machinery, except electrical machinery	7,943	5·1	11,618	2·7

Table 8.5 *(continued)*

	1959		1966	
	Value added $'ooo	Per cent of total	Value added $'ooo	Per cent of total
Manufacture of electrical machinery, apparatus, appliances and supplies	11,598	7·4	13,408	3·1
Manufacture of transport equipment	10,453	6·7	32,198	7·5
Miscellaneous manufacturing industries	1,573	1·0	10,030	2·3
Rubber processing	14,072	9·0	16,120	3·7
Total manufacturing including rubber processing	156,853	100	431,163	100

[a] In 1959, manufacture of all leather products included with manufacture of textiles, footwear except rubber footwear and made-up textile goods.

[b] In 1959, included with chemicals and chemical products.

Note: Figures exclude manufacturing activities of the public sector. In 1959 the coverage for establishments with ten to thirty-nine workers was incomplete.

Sources: Singapore, *Report on the Census of Industrial Production 1959*, and Singapore Department of Statistics data.

Singapore's industrialisation program will have to be intensified if it is to absorb more workers in manufacturing. Paradoxically the difficulties of increasing employment opportunities have been exaggerated in the short run by Singapore's success in raising labour productivity. Value added has grown faster than employment in manufacturing in the 1960s. Not all the difference in rates of growth of value added and employment reflects labour productivity, for investment in fixed capital has grown even faster than value added, but because of the lag in effective capital utilisation in production it is too early to judge changes in capital productivity. In the long run increasing labour and capital productivity will of course accelerate Singapore's industrial expansion.

From 1959 to 1966 Singapore succeeded equally importantly in introducing a large number of new industries and in considerably diversifying its industrial base (Table 8.5). These new industries still consisted largely of assembling and finishing plants which relied on imports of raw and industrially produced materials and semi-finished products. Future industrial growth will require not only a further broadening of the industrial base, but also the development of backward linked industries producing semi-fabricated parts and raw materials. This is likely to prove more difficult than the initial steps towards industrialisation, for such industries are generally more technologically complex than assembly and finishing operations. It is therefore likely that Singapore will continue to require injections of foreign capital to bring the sophisticated techniques required, although some of these developments can be carried out by the foreign firms with established manufacturing operations in Singapore which will be able to finance such expansion out of accumulated profits.

Local Singapore entrepreneurs who have been acquiring industrial experience in the 1960s, alone and as partners in joint ventures, should also be able to play an increasing role in Singapore's industrial growth. The Economic Development Board's energies were inevitably heavily engaged in drawing foreign investors to Singapore in the past, but Singapore entrepreneurs need rather more assistance both in becoming established and in overcoming difficulties once they are in production than the large firms which are typical foreign investors. In future the Board may be able to devote more of its energies to the needs of the local manufacturers. Because of Singapore's recent history and its concentration on entrepôt trade until the 1950s, it has no long-established, traditional, small-scale industrial sector which has grown out of handicraft industries. It has begun to industrialise at a stage of technological development in which labour-intensiveness cannot be expected to give its small-scale industries advantages by which they could overcome the competition of large-scale, capital-intensive, industrial establishments. The Economic Development Board's Projects and Technical Services Divisions have already demonstrated that they can do much to help local entrepreneurs, and the proposed industrial development bank could become important in financing such enterprises and helping them with commercial problems. While the variety and balance of foreign investment in Singapore suggests that the state has little to fear from political or economic pressure from abroad on these grounds, foreign investors have already a substantial share in Singapore manufacturing, and this is likely to grow faster than the industrial sector as a whole because of the quasi-rent elements in the earnings of foreign firms arising out of their superior technology, and their advantage in being able to exploit backward and forward linkages. It may be wise to take steps to redress the balance.

The problem of markets will have to be faced in the exploitation of forward and backward linkages and the further broadening of industrial production. Since economies of scale are as a rule even more important for producer goods than for consumer goods industries and for industries which produce industrial inputs, an expansion into these industries can only be made, even if excessive entry is not a problem, if industrial production expands considerably in Singapore. The political separation between Singapore and Malaysia need not last forever, and although the prospects for a common market are at present very poor, some form of economic association is likely in the future. A common market would ease both countries' immediate market problems, but for long-term development Singapore's present economic isolation may have advantages because it has forced its government to abandon highly protectionist policies and look outwards for markets. Here the difficulties are very great indeed.

Much of Singapore's industrial export at present goes to developing countries which are themselves seeking to industrialise and many of which are large enough and have enough primary resources to do so behind protectionist barriers. This emphasises Singapore's need to expand in relatively sophisticated products not yet produced by these countries, and to embark, before it has had much experience in industry, on a program of upgrading its production technically as Japan and to some extent Hong Kong are doing. This Singapore is currently planning to do.

The problems of exporting to developed countries with potentially much larger and richer markets are even more serious because of the protectionist policies they pursue in a much wider range of products. The imposition by the United States of quotas on imports of cotton textiles from Singapore in April 1966 closed ten garment factories employing over 1,000 workers. Other firms had to curtail production throwing another 2,500 people out of work.[31] During 1967 Singapore endeavoured to negotiate an agreement with Australia which would have enabled it to finish semi-fabricated products imported from Australia, and then export half of the total back to Australia duty free, selling the rest in Singapore and other countries. The negotiations failed, although such agreements are operating between Japan and the Republic of Korea to the mutual advantage of both countries. Tariff preference to Singapore in developed countries would be of some assistance,[32] but the real need is for those countries which are continually exhorting developing countries to help themselves by obeying economic principles to act on their own advice at home. Until they do so Singapore will have to struggle to find export markets as best it can.

[31] Economic Development Board, *Annual Report '66*, pp. 8–9.
[32] H. G. Johnson, *Economic Policies Toward Less Developed Countries* (Washington, 1967), Chapter 6, 'Trade Preferences for Manufactured Goods', pp. 163–211, has put the case for such preferences.

For Singapore the importance of industrialisation lies in the lack of alternative strategies. However much attention the government pays to entrepôt trade, the long-term prospects are not hopeful because the countries for which Singapore carried out entrepôt functions in the past now wish to undertake them themselves. The relative importance of entrepôt trade to Singapore is therefore likely to decline, and because productivity is growing in this sector, the share of employment in entrepôt trade may decline even faster.

The government is encouraging deep sea fishing for food supply and as a raw material for industry, and there are perhaps slightly better agricultural opportunities than the smallness of the island would suggest. Singapore is almost self-sufficient in pork, chickens, and some vegetables, and more could be achieved in horticulture partly by closer attention to farming methods, but partly too by a gradual encroachment on the area under rubber and coconuts which covers more than half of Singapore's cultivated area of some 32,000 acres. Prices for rubber and coconuts have been falling in recent years, and even Singapore's rubber tyre factory uses more than 40 per cent synthetic rubber. Horticulture could supply tropical fruits, mushrooms, and similar products for canneries as well as for local consumption, but there are likely to be political and economic difficulties in converting plantation land to such uses. The process will take time, and the island's small size sets an upper limit to agricultural production.

Building and construction have played a particularly important part in sustaining the Singapore economy during the 1960s. Public capital formation was higher than private capital formation in the critical Confrontation years of 1963 and 1964, but here too there are limits in a small economy. The construction of infrastructure facilities for the economy will have high productivity only if it supplies real needs as it did in the 1960s and as it can continue to do on a modest scale for some time to come. Urban planning and renewal are socially and aesthetically important and create secondary production and employment opportunities, but a state of Singapore's size and income can afford only a limited rate of growth in this sector. Singapore has, and is using, the construction sector to offset fluctuations due to external economic factors and will have to continue to do so carefully so as to have funds and projects in reserve when a new need for priming the economy arises.

Tourism has recently received a great deal of attention. The government's 'instant Asia' promotion was so successful that there was an almost continuous shortage of hotel rooms in 1966 and 1967, but this is now being remedied. The opportunities for the tourist industry are also

208

limited by the island's size. The investment requirements for tourism are high, and particularly so in relation to direct job creation. At the end of 1967 $45 million had been committed to investment in five tourist hotels with 1,500 rooms, which were expected to create direct employment for 2,500 people.[33] This represents an investment of $18,000 per person employed, and is somewhat higher than the $17,000 required to place a worker in the manufacturing workforce in pioneer firms.[34] There is no evidence concerning the relation between secondary job creation in tourism and manufacturing, but since much of the former is in personal services it is likely to be lower paid than factory labour. Nevertheless there is no doubt that with its critical unemployment problems Singapore cannot afford to ignore any avenues for economic development, particularly those which are labour intensive and engage unskilled workers.

Perhaps the most difficult task facing the Singapore government over the next decade is the balancing of the desire to maintain a relatively high standard of living against the need to reduce unemployment.

At present Singapore is a high labour cost economy, partly because productivity is low, but partly also because real wages and earnings are the highest and conditions of work the best in Southeast Asia. Recent labour legislation should improve productivity, but it is unlikely to have a marked effect on real earnings. It is very much to Singapore's credit that it has achieved a considerable measure of industrialisation without reverting to nineteenth-century working conditions and without forgoing relatively high levels of remuneration for its workforce. The Trade Union Congress and the unions associated with it have certainly become less militant in the last few years, but this seems to stem as much from a recognition of Singapore's economic difficulties and from the fact that it cannot create a socialist state in the midst of private enterprise countries on which it is economically dependent, as from government pressure. Nor does it follow that they will become so ineffectual in this situation that they will cease to be an important countervailing power to employers and the government as some critics aver.

[33] Dr Goh Keng Swee, Finance Minister, Budget address to the Legislative Assembly, 5 December 1967 (*Parliamentary Debates*, Singapore, Vol. 26, 1967).

[34] Calculated from total capital outlay in fixed assets for all pioneer firms at 31 December 1966 and estimated employment at full production. Economic Development Board, *Annual Report '66*, pp. 64–5. The figure is probably somewhat high because all pioneer investment figures appear to be high, but the tourist investment figure is probably similarly inflated.

Since it is doubtful that low labour costs are a substantial attraction to foreign investors or an important advantage in an international industrial environment in which labour cost is not a very important component of total cost in many industries, and in a world in which trade barriers are all pervasive, the pursuit of particularly low labour cost does not seem to be very fruitful, and the Singapore government is well aware of this.

With Singapore family structure still heavily weighted towards the family group which usually includes several wage earners, it is also by no means clear that Singapore workers would prefer to make marked sacrifices in their living standards for fuller employment. The government's aim of wage stability, increased productivity, and the spreading of employment opportunities, seems a sensible compromise between preserving existing living standards and achieving a high level of employment. It has the mark of wisdom which has enabled Singapore to overcome its economic difficulties year by year since independence with quite remarkable success.

Pioneer Firm Statistics

Firms with foreign partners have been grouped according to principal foreign shareholder at 31 December 1966 to avoid double counting. Where two or more foreign countries have an equal capital share, classification has necessarily been somewhat arbitrary.

The total number of firms varies from table to table with the quality of information available. One foreign-affiliated firm has never submitted any returns to the Economic Development Board, and other firms, in early stages of development, have not been able to provide full returns.

These tables are based on data supplied to the Economic Development Board, but the coverage of firms is not always the same as that in the Economic Development Board's *Annual Reports*.

Table I   Paid-up capital and percentage paid-up capital investment in

		Aust.	H.K.	Japan	Malaysia
I	Food and beverages				
	Capital investment	1,710	2,768	1,380	2,736
	Percentage	5	8	4	7
II	Textiles, garments, and leather				
	Capital investment	—	3,871	2,000	448
	Percentage	—	23	12	3
III	Wood and paper products				
	Capital investment	—	100	882	—
	Percentage	—	1	9	—
IV	Rubber and rubber products				
	Capital investment	—	100	5,500	4,650
	Percentage	—	1	50	42
V	Chemicals and chemical products				
	Capital investment	—	1,950	550	1,000
	Percentage	—	14	4	7
VI	Petroleum and petroleum products				
	Capital investment	—	—	—	—
	Percentage	—	—	—	—
VII	Non-metallic mineral products				
	Capital investment	—	—	2,400	400
	Percentage	—	—	36	6
VIII	Metals and engineering				
	Capital investment	859	—	10,741	1,161
	Percentage	2	—	23	3
IX	Electrical products				
	Capital investment	100	552	425	158
	Percentage	2	10	8	3
X	Miscellaneous				
	Capital investment	—	25	350	115
	Percentage	—	—	4	1
All	industry groups				
	Capital investment	2,669	9,366	24,228	10,668
	Percentage	1	5	13	6

pioneer firms at 31 December 1966, by country and industry group[a] ($'000)

Taiwan	U.K.	U.S.	Others	Local	All firms with foreign participation	Firms totally Singapore-owned	Total pioneer firms
—	—	895	4,410	17,313	31,212	5,286	36,498
—	—	2	12	47	86	14	100
632	—	100	180	8,401	15,632	1,499	17,131
4	—	1	1	49	91	9	100
1,042	—	—	—	3,393	5,417	4,421	9,838
11	—	—	—	34	55	45	100
—	—	—	270	280	10,800	150	10,950
—	—	—	2	3	99	1	100
2,575	600	80	—	2,608	9,363	4,945	14,308
18	4	1	—	18	65	35	100
—	3,800	12,000	15,000	—	30,800	5,500	36,300
—	10	33	41	—	85	15	100
—	200	—	—	1,750	4,750	2,003	6,753
—	3	—	—	26	70	30	100
—	2,300	—	1,815	13,531	30,407	15,399	45,806
—	5	—	4	30	66	34	100
528	58	—	160	1,216	3,197	2,230	5,427
10	1	—	3	22	59	41	100
126	80	480	862	3,349	5,387	2,427	7,814
2	1	6	11	43	69	31	100
4,903	7,038	13,555	22,697	51,841	146,965	43,860	190,825
3	4	7	12	27	77	23	100

[a] Figures refer to actual investments from the countries concerned and cover 133 firms: 72 firms with foreign participation and 38 local firms in production, and 15 firms with foreign participation and 8 local firms in implementing stage.

Table II   Pioneer firms by country and year of
pioneer certificate granted

	1961	1962	1963	1965	1966
Australia			3	4	
Hong Kong		2	6	3	5
Japan		1	15	2	1
Malaysia		1	6	1	4
Taiwan			6	5	
United Kingdom	1		3	2	1
United States			5		2
Other	1		7	2	1
Unclassifiable		2[a]	24[b]	1[a]	
Totally Singapore-owned	2	2	26	10	7
Total pioneer firms	4	8	101	30	21

[a] These firms have ceased production.

[b] Twelve firms have surrendered pioneer certificates; three firms have ceased production; nine firms became inactive before production start.

Note: Firms with foreign participation are grouped according to principal foreign shareholder at 31 December 1966.

Table III   Number of pioneer firms with foreign participants,
by size of foreign share in 1966, and by country[a]

Foreign share percentage	Australia	H.K.	Japan	Malaysia	Taiwan	U.K.	U.S.	Others	Total firms with foreign participation
100	1	8	1	5	—	3	3	4	25
Over 51	3	4	7	3	5	1	—	3	26
51	—	—	1	—	—	—	1	—	2
50	2	—	—	1	1	1	—	1	6
49	—	—	—	—	—	—	—	—	—
Under 49	1	4	10	3	5	2	1	2	28
Total	7	16	19	12	11	7	5	10	87

[a] These figures cover 72 firms with foreign participation in production during 1966 and 15 implementing firms with foreign participation.

Note: Firms with foreign participation are grouped according to principal foreign shareholder at 31 December 1966.

214

Table IV   Number of pioneer firms, by amount of paid-up capital and by country, 1966[a]

	Total foreign paid-up capital in firm, $ million						
	1·0 or less	1·1 to 2·0	2·1 to 4·0	4·1 to 6·0	6·1 to 10·0	10·1 or more	No. of firms
Australia	6	1	—	—	—	—	7
Hong Kong	13	2	1	—	—	—	16
Japan	12	3	2	1	1	—	19
Malaysia	11	—	—	1	—	—	12
Taiwan	10	1	—	—	—	—	11
United Kingdom	4	2	1	—	—	—	7
United States	3	1	—	—	1	—	5
Other	7	1	1	—	—	1	10
Firms with foreign participation	66	11	5	2	2	1	87
	Total paid-up capital						
Firms totally Singapore-owned	37	6	1	1	—	1	46

[a] These figures cover 133 firms: 72 firms with foreign participation and 38 local firms in production, and 15 firms with foreign participation and 8 local firms in implementing stage.

Note: Firms with foreign participation are grouped according to principal foreign shareholder at 31 December 1966 but all foreign capital in the firm is included.

Table V   Investment by pioneer firms in fixed assets by country at 31 December 1966[a]

	Machinery[b] $'000	Percentage of total fixed assets	Total fixed assets $'000
Australia	2,945	61	4,844
Hong Kong	12,155	63	19,243
Japan	47,527	65	72,626
Malaysia	7,736	58	13,283
Taiwan	7,474	62	12,071
United Kingdom	18,668	68	27,385
United States	48,962	92	53,135
Other	47,535	86	55,130
Firms with foreign participation	193,002	75	257,717
Firms totally Singapore-owned	47,248	69	68,198
Total pioneer firms	240,250	74	325,915

[a] These figures include 72 firms with foreign participation, 38 local firms in production during 1966, and 23 implementing firms which submitted figures on investment.

[b] Includes cost of installation. The total cost of installation was $7,335,000.

Note: Firms with foreign participation are grouped according to principal foreign shareholder at 31 December 1966.

215

Table VI   Value of local and imported raw materials used
by pioneer firms, by country, in 1966[a]

	Total $'000	Local $'000	Imported $'000	Percentage imported
Australia	11,206	1,899	9,307	83
Hong Kong	46,918	2,329	44,589	95
Japan	32,232	3,672	28,560	89
Malaysia	18,172	1,021	17,151	94
Taiwan	9,545	774	8,771	92
United Kingdom	25,671	1,443	24,228	94
United States	48,119	2,662	45,457	94
Other	112,632	14,252	98,380	87
Firms with foreign participation	304,495	28,052	276,443	91
Firms totally Singapore-owned	56,654	22,199	34,455	61
Total pioneer firms	361,149	50,251	310,898	86

[a] Figures cover 68 of the 72 firms with foreign participation and 35 of 38 local firms in production. The seven firms excluded did not give data on raw materials used. One each came from Hong Kong, Japan, Malaysia, other categories, and three were local firms.

Note: Firms with foreign participation are grouped according to principal foreign shareholder at 31 December 1966.

Table VII   Total number of employees in pioneer firms,
by country and type of employee, at 31 December 1966[a]

	Managers and supervisors	Clerks and sales	Technical staff	Skilled and semi-skilled workmen	Unskilled workmen	Others	Total
Australia	32	70	16	37	54	10	219
Hong Kong	86	75	89	1,214	719	179	2,362
Japan	187	189	121	1,117	877	115	2,606
Malaysia	27	52	34	132	333	15	593
Taiwan	45	105	87	280	670	17	1,204
United Kingdom	39	44	41	126	52	54	356
United States	28	24	45	267	62	2	428
Other	40	54	32	206	116	8	456
Firms with foreign participation	484	613	465	3,379	2,883	400	8,224
Firms totally Singapore-owned	189	290	116	918	1,125	285	2,923
Total pioneer firms	673	903	581	4,297	4,008	685	11,147

[a] These figures cover 124 firms: 72 firms with foreign participation, 38 local firms in production, 12 firms with foreign participation, and 2 local firms in implementing stage.

Note: Firms with foreign participation are grouped according to principal foreign shareholder at 31 December 1966.

Table VIII   Value added by pioneer firms in production
during 1966, by country[a]

	Value added $'000	Percentage of firms with foreign participation	Percentage of total pioneer firms
Australia	1,605	1·9	1·3
Hong Kong	7,696	9·1	6·4
Japan	22,548	26·6	18·9
Malaysia	1,404	1·7	1·2
Taiwan	4,026	4·7	3·4
United Kingdom	6,815	8·0	5·7
United States	10,678	12·6	8·9
Other	30,045	35·4	25·2
Firms with foreign participation	84,817	100·0	71·0
Firms totally Singapore-owned	34,582	—	29·0
Total pioneer firms	119,399	—	100·0

[a] These figures cover 72 firms with foreign participation and 38 local firms in production in 1966.

Note: Firms with foreign participation are grouped according to principal foreign shareholder at 31 December 1966.

217

Table IX Total sales during 1966 by pioneer firms, by industry group and country[a]
$'000

	Aust.	H.K.	Japan	Malaysia	Taiwan	U.K.	U.S.	Other firms with foreign participation	Total firms with foreign participation	Firms totally Singapore-owned	Total	% sales by firms with foreign participation
I Food and beverages	10,169	40,310	—	13,141	—	—	2,379	18,174	84,173	5,867	90,040	93
II Textiles, garments, and leather	—	18,921	1,332	37	2,364	—	—	n.a.	22,654	876	23,530	96
III Wood and paper products	—	—	7,069	—	4,713	—	—	—	11,782	6,063	17,845	66
IV Rubber and rubber products	—	—	10,500	135	—	—	—	—	10,635	—	10,635	100
V Chemicals and chemical products	—	59	143	—	5,539	138	151	—	6,030	1,876	7,906	76
VI Petroleum and petroleum products	—	—	—	—	—	45,089	54,725	124,923	224,737	46,710	271,447	83
VII Non-metallic mineral products	—	—	8,448	6,328	—	—	—	—	14,776	849	15,625	95
VIII Metals and engineering	3,640	—	27,283	823	—	2,601	—	7,023	41,370	26,554	67,924	61
IX Electrical products	970	552	2,399	—	2,528	693	—	—	7,142	4,120	11,262	63
X Miscellaneous	—	—	735	90	1,111	373	2,658	—	4,967	2,319	7,286	68
All industry groups	14,779	59,842	57,909	20,554	16,255	48,894	59,913	150,120	428,266	95,234	523,500	82

[a] Figures cover 69 of 72 firms with foreign participation and 34 of 38 local firms in production. Seven firms, one each in Hong Kong, Japan, and 'other', and four local firms, did not give figures of sales.

Note: Firms with foreign participation are grouped according to principal foreign shareholder at 31 December 1966.

Table X   Gross value of sales by pioneer firms during 1966,
by market area and country[a]

	Singapore sales $'000	Exports			Total sales $'000	Export percentage of total sales
		Malaysia $'000	Rest of world $'000	Total exports $'000		
Australia	10,951	2,649	1,179	3,828	14,779	26
Hong Kong	24,548	9,817	25,477	35,294	59,842	59
Japan	32,447	5,567	19,895	25,462	57,909	44
Malaysia	15,686	3,927	941	4,868	20,554	24
Taiwan	7,108	476	8,671	9,147	16,255	56
United Kingdom	38,741	2,850	7,303	10,153	48,894	21
United States	27,770	2,267	29,876	32,143	59,913	54
Other	137,449	12,602	69	12,671	150,120	8
Firms with foreign participation	294,700	40,155	93,411	133,566	428,266	31
Firms totally Singapore-owned	43,590	10,901	40,743	51,644	95,234	54
Total pioneer firms	338,290	51,056	134,154	185,210	523,500	35

[a] Figures cover 69 of 72 firms with foreign participation and 34 of 38 local firms in production. Seven firms, one each in Hong Kong, Japan, and 'other', and four local firms, did not give figures of sales.

Note: Firms with foreign participation are grouped according to principal foreign shareholder at 31 December 1966.

Index

Subjects and references which occur only in the Historical Background section, pp. 1–14 of Chapter 1, have not been indexed

221

Index

Text set in 11 point Monotype Imprint, one point leaded
and printed on 80 gms Esparto paper
by Cathay Press, Hong Kong.